SOUTH SIDE VENUS

SOUTH SIDE VENUS

THE LEGACY OF
MARGARET BURROUGHS

MARY ANN CAIN
FOREWORD BY HAKI MADHUBUTI

NORTHWESTERN UNIVERSITY PRESS
EVANSTON, ILLINOIS

Northwestern University Press
www.nupress.northwestern.edu

Printed in the United States of America

10   9   8   7   6   5   4   3   2   1

Library of Congress Cataloging-in-Publication Data
Names: Cain, Mary Ann, author. | Madhubuti, Haki R., 1942– writer of foreword.
Title: South side Venus : the legacy of Margaret Burroughs / Mary Ann Cain ;
    foreword by Haki Madhubuti.
Description: Evanston, Illinois : Northwestern University Press, 2018. | Includes
    bibliographical references and index.
Identifiers: LCCN 2018020944| ISBN 9780810137950 (pbk. : alk. paper) | ISBN
    9780810137967 (ebook)
Subjects: LCSH: Burroughs, Margaret Taylor, 1917–2010. | African American
    poets–Illinois–Chicago–Biography. | African American artists–Illinois–Chicago–
    Biography. | Arts administrators–Illinois–Chicago–Biography.
Classification: LCC NX512.B88 C53 2018 | DDC 700.92–dc23
LC record available at https://lccn.loc.gov/2018020944

For George, now and always.

And for the ancestors.

CONTENTS

FOREWORD

Haki Madhubuti

> how did we arrive?
> mothers as artists and seers
> as earth toilers, sun consumers
> workers at midnight and dawn
> nurtured us with apples, bananas, open hearts, seeds,
> cultural language, illustrations, and institutions.
> lovingly cut the umbilical cord,
> not the commitment or sacred findings.

The very large question that this well-researched and heartfelt biography by Mary Ann Cain asks is, "What role did art, history, culture, mentors, and political activists play in the life of Margaret Burroughs?" Buried in Cain's *South Side Venus* you will find answers that are conclusive, definitive, and long-term. Her subject emerges from this study as true and timely as the art she created and the institutions that she was instrumental in founding as well as guiding: the National Negro Museum and Historical Foundation, the South Side Community Art Center, the National Conference of Artists, the Lake Meadows Art Fair, and Chicago's internationally respected DuSable Museum of African American History, the first of its kind in the United States.

It was a Saturday morning in the summer of 1962 when a twenty-year-old soldier from Fort Sheridan, Illinois, found himself at the home of Margaret and Charles Burroughs, which also served as the newly established Ebony Museum of Negro History. The young man was in search of answers to a multitude of questions raised by his short life and voracious reading–questions that interfered with his life, particularly his sleep, rendering him ill-tempered during his workdays and increasing his anger about the plight of his people.

That young man was me, Don L. Lee. I had read about the museum in the *Chicago Defender*, and the first Saturday I had off, I knocked on the door of this Bronzeville mansion at 3806 S. Michigan Avenue on the South Side of Chicago. A white man answered the door, and at once I felt that I was at the wrong address. But he greeted me warmly as I asked for Margaret Burroughs, who was listed as the museum's founder. This was Eugene Pieter Feldman, a Jewish white man and another one of the founders, who had been unwelcome in his home state of Alabama and, like hundreds of thousands of black people before him, had migrated to Chicago. Feldman, a historian, writer, and long-distance activist, immediately escorted me to the kitchen, where I was introduced to Margaret Burroughs. She was working on a linoleum cut, or linocut—a form of art that was new to me—but what struck me immediately was her natural hairstyle, which she proudly wore in 1962, years before the "Black Is Beautiful" movement started, marking her as one of the originators and proponents of "the natural."

Mary Ann Cain shares this bit of history and leaves out very little in her exploration of Margaret Burroughs. The many *firsts* of this remarkable woman are highlighted, as they should be; however, we are also privy to the interiors, the loneliness, and, in many ways, the complications and confrontations that color the transformative journey spanning the ninety-plus years of her illustrious life.

The clearest betrayal of a worthy ancestor is to forget his or her name. A greater slap in the face of any of our significant long-distance runners is to offer insecure, unprepared acknowledgment of their contributions to civilization in the times in which they lived. Mary Ann Cain spent special time with Dr. Burroughs toward the end of her life; thereby, she is able to render a portrait of this multitalented, committed artist and activist that would be lacking if such interactions—intimacies and visual perceptions—did not occur. She writes:

> Margaret Burroughs learned early on that art and language
> were her passports for crossing. But her crossings were not so
> much in search of acceptance as they were to issue invitations
> to join the revolutionary vision of true democracy—all humans
> created equal, of equal worth, full participants in the shaping of
> their worlds. How Burroughs learned to make those crossings,
> how she used art and writing to accomplish them, and how she

learned how to pass on that knowledge are what is at stake. Those crossings are on the verge of being lost to generations who know only technology and the navigation of cyberspace alone in the brave new world of entrepreneurs writ large. . . . She was raised with the notion that she had something to say and something to give. Art was her first and most lasting means of making it up and passing it on.

How Taylor understood her legacy—through making a contribution by struggling to make something happen—is what is important to examine, not simply the end results of those struggles. Her story is unique in that it was not about a single achievement—not just as an artist, a museum founder, a teacher, or an activist. It was unique in its success at being and staying connected to a larger experience. Her art was the means by which she made and maintained these connections by crossing otherwise uncrossable lines.

In *South Side Venus*, Dr. Burroughs emerges as a part of the air we breathe, the green juice of life, from warm smiles of deep memory. Her life's work stands firm alongside the unforgettable first-class artists and activists of her day in what is now the age of Twitter, Facebook, and Instagram; she represented what the social media do not have time for—the complicated yesterdays, todays, and ill-defined tomorrows. We are dealing with people whose enslaved ancestors were branded like cattle and who are now more occupied with building their personal "brands" on the internet than with seeking an understanding of the politics, history, culture, and economics of their people. Margaret Taylor Goss Burroughs blossomed in the twentieth century, a century that was not kind—one that was forcibly unjust, deliberately and legally unaccommodating to black people. Her legacy, according to this fine book, is that she defined her times even while the times tried to define *her*.

Art, *visual* art, informed her life to the point that there was no life without art. It was clear to me, and Cain confirms this impression, that all artists are decision-makers, which makes them to some degree the freest people in any culture. No one told Dr. Burroughs what to create. She decided on the medium (printmaking, drawing, painting, sculpture, poetry, or prose) and subject matter of her art. Cain's book reveals that at a very young age, Burroughs became a "decision-maker" rather than, like most people, making choices within the parameters of other people's decisions. This was critical to her own maturation and ultimate station in life.

In concert with all of her accomplishments, especially during the early years, Margaret Burroughs endured ostracism, government harassment, the negative fallout from Chicago's Red Scare, and a critical whitelash due to her choice of friends, mentors, and acquaintances. One of her most important and pivotal influences was the multitalented, internationally acclaimed vocalist, actor, and activist Paul Robeson. Other defining influences were Harriet Tubman, Sojourner Truth, Carter G. Woodson, W. E. B. Du Bois, Shirley Graham Du Bois, Alain Locke, Ida B. Wells, Richard Wright, Katherine Dunham, St. Clair Drake, Vivian Harsh, and Charlemae Rollins. Yet few influenced her more than Robeson, whom she openly supported during the worst of the McCarthy years, when all liberals were viewed as communists.

> you with the brushes, canvas, paint, tools, and ideas
> with African hair, mind, and memory
> instigated an uprising to change the conversation
> quickening our run toward saneness, smiles, and fear
> outpacing a leadership that moves
> like a roach with Alzheimer's.

As an artist, teacher, and mentor to literally thousands of young people, including me, Burroughs always led with her heart and resources. Slow to criticize the young, she was our example, and with encouraging words she would always say, "Go see for yourself," as well as "I'll stand my ground, you stand yours." Cain succeeds in capturing the artist's humility and generosity, creating a biographical portrait that echoes the essence of a woman who wholeheartedly believed that what we achieve is not about "me" but about *us*. Cain gives us insight into Burroughs's personal life, especially her marriages to Bernard Goss and Charles Burroughs, and her children, Gayle and Paul. Equally important is Cain's further recognition that Burroughs remained mindful of the "little people," among whom she always claimed membership.

Dr. Burroughs possessed what I would call the integrity of doubt and doing. One should never have all the answers, but most certainly one should have many. Consequently, she surrounded herself with the best of the best, many of whom would become lifelong friends: Gwendolyn

Brooks, Timuel Black, Ishmael Flory, Charles White, Elizabeth Catlett, Gordon Parks, George Neal, and many others. Her commitment to Africa, African Americans, and world history early in life gave her the impetus to teach and build institutions that enlightened even the least of us.

Being defined early in her life as a "race woman" never distracted her from her lifelong pursuit of using her art in the bonding of the "races." This too is partially the legacy of Dr. Burroughs. Her view of the world was one of infinite possibilities in creating a climate of togetherness. Cain highlights Burroughs's community-oriented vision and notably explains that her phrase "lived up from the roots" was not to be interpreted so as to leave anyone out. As noted by the author, Burroughs's yearlong sabbatical in Mexico was a "watershed moment in her life." Mexico and its artists confirmed that in order to be oneself, one must have a knowledge of one's history and culture, and that black identity and social justice institutions are critical to an informed people.

I took the model from Margaret Burroughs's DuSable Museum and Dudley Randall's Broadside Press in 1967 to start the Third World Press with $400 and a used mimeograph machine in my basement apartment in the Englewood community of Chicago. I exist, in part, because they existed, but it was Margaret and Charles Burroughs who lit the fire in my young, impressionable mind and soul. And yes, it was also Malcolm X, Hoyt W. Fuller, Barbara Ann Sizemore, and the great Gwendolyn Brooks who sealed my future. Mary Ann Cain, in this wonderful biography, connects them all and much more. In writing about the life and legacy of such an important historical figure, Cain also gives us an unacknowledged history of Chicago—a Chicago that Margaret Taylor Goss Burroughs helped to create.

I and millions of blacks were told that the best way to hide something was to put it in a book. The secret is now out, and books are no longer tangential to our existence. Books represent water, light, soil, and fire. It is absolutely necessary that we add *South Side Venus: The Legacy of Margaret Burroughs* to our reading lists and libraries.

> yesterday and today, we, on jet powered roller skates
> still eat your dust
> still are wondrous of the measure
> of your gifts.

ACKNOWLEDGMENTS

The first time I visited the DuSable Museum of African American History, in 2003, I had hoped to learn more about the Bronzeville community in Chicago. Although I had grown up in the city's southwest suburbs, I had only recently discovered that this South Side neighborhood had a name as well as its own unique history. Also, thanks to early dial-up internet technology, I had just found the DuSable Museum online. Excited but also self-conscious about my ignorance, I entered the museum on a mission. My novel-in-progress at the time included characters from Bronzeville, and so I set forth on a research trip to round out my knowledge.

Back then, I never would have dreamed that not only would I meet the founder of the DuSable Museum, Dr. Margaret Taylor Goss Burroughs, but that I would write a book about her. Had it not been for the friendly security guard who inquired what I was writing about in my journal as I moved through the galleries, had he not called a staff member, registrar Theresa Christopher, to further assist me with my research (given that the museum did not have Bronzeville exhibits at that time), had she not sat with me in a quiet corner of the Harold Washington wing for half an hour and given me the names and contact information of important Bronzeville people, including Dr. Burroughs, this book would never have come into being. These were the people who first set me on my path of discovery, of Bronzeville, to be sure, but eventually of Dr. Burroughs and her immense but too often overlooked legacy.

After Dr. Burroughs passed on in 2010, my friend, teacher, and community partner in Fort Wayne, Indiana, Omowale Ketu Oladuwa, had recently begun a new community organization, the Three Rivers Institute of Afrikan Art and Culture (TRIAAC). In 2011 we decided to memorialize Dr. Burroughs, who had visited Fort Wayne twice in recent years, and whom Ketu had met in Chicago in the early 1980s, with a presentation that I would give at TRIAAC. Afterward, I felt compelled to reciprocate

Dr. Burroughs's generosity and kindness toward me. I decided to write a book focusing on her life and its legacy. I had no idea how much further her legacy would extend to me until I began to research this project.

This book came into being in large part because those who knew Margaret Burroughs wanted it to happen. At every turn I met with openness, assistance, hospitality, and commitment. I received rides, names and contact information, corrections and clarifications, but also a sense of enthusiasm and eagerness to see this project come together. It has truly been an honor and a privilege to meet those who knew Dr. Burroughs and what she stood for, but also what she has left behind. Among those I was fortunate enough to interview, I want to thank Theresa Christopher, former registrar at the DuSable Museum, for setting me on this path; Eric Toller, eldest grandson of Dr. Burroughs, who deeply understands his grandmother's contributions and their value; Dr. Haki Madhubuti, founder and publisher of Third World Press, emeritus professor at Chicago State University, and University Distinguished Professor at DePaul University, for his initial, unquestioning support of this project as well as his ongoing encouragement; Timuel Black, Chicago's oral historian par excellence; the attorney and emeritus South Side Community Art Center board member Lawrence Kennon; Clarice Davis Durham, teacher, friend, and fellow activist to Dr. Burroughs; Art Center board member and former president Diane Dinkins Carr; artist and former Art Center director Doug Williams; artist Debra Hand; prison minister and Operation PUSH organizer Reverend Queen Mother Helen Sinclair; Daniel Texidor Parker, emeritus professor at Olive Harvey College, professor at Chicago State University, and collector of African and African American art; Bennett Johnson of Third World Press, a fellow traveler with Margaret and Charles Burroughs; and Omowale Ketu Oladuwa, community artivist, writer, drummer, and instructor, whose gracious sharing of his immense knowledge of African and African American history and culture set me on a path to write this book.

Another friend of Dr. Burroughs who provided valuable time, resources, and encouragement is Dr. Gloria Latimore Peace, producer of the Chicago cable series H3O and a former professor at Northeastern University. Arcilla Stahl of the South Side Community Art Center opened up archives, answered questions, and overall made sure I received whatever assistance needed; and George Stahl counseled me on how to push for greater access to key resources. Rose Perkins, assistant to Dr. Madhubuti at Third World Press, provided timely, gracious, and precise assistance throughout this project.

I also deeply appreciate the assistance of museum curators, archivists, librarians, and administrators, including Masequa Myers, executive director of the South Side Community Art Center; Leslie Guy, former chief curator, Skyla Hearn, archivist and special collections librarian, Kate Swisher, registrar and collections manager, Troy Ratliff, chief operating officer, and Perri Irmer, CEO, at the DuSable Museum; Liz Wolf, exhibitions and collections coordinator at the Mary and Leigh Block Museum of Art, Evanston; and Allison Hausladen, cataloger and reference librarian at the Ryerson and Burnham Libraries of the Art Institute of Chicago. Closer to home, Sue Skekloff, research librarian at Purdue University Fort Wayne, provided much research guidance, as did Carrie Brooks, former student and current faculty at Purdue University Fort Wayne, who also read and reacted to parts of the manuscript.

I want to further thank the excellent staff at Northwestern University Press for their warm reception, professionalism, and honesty, including former acquisitions editor Mike Levine, who first encouraged this project; editor in chief Gianna Mosser, who steered me toward sound writing and revisions; former acquisitions assistant Maggie Grossman, for keeping it all on track; and Anne Gendler, managing editor and director of editorial, design, and production, for trustworthy advice and timely assistance. A very special thanks to Jill Lisette Petty, acquisitions editor, for her savvy guidance, reassurance during the early editorial transition, and mutual fandom of Margaret Burroughs.

The Indiana Arts Commission and Indiana University provided important grants to fund my travels for research. I am also indebted to the university's vice chancellor of academic affairs, Carl Drummond, as well as my department chair, Hardin Aasand, and Dean Eric Link for allowing me release time to complete this project at Purdue University Fort Wayne. Writers Jeff Johnson and Lynn Sweet deserve thanks for helping me with contact information. My friend Susan Hunter, a Clayton State University emeritus professor and department chair, has taken me all over Atlanta in search of relevant materials and exhibits.

My sister, Linda Cain, fed me important Chicago-based information throughout the writing of this book. My brother, Tom Cain, took mental walks down memory lane with me to help contextualize some of these materials. My mother, Ruth Seaman Cain, deserves credit as a South Sider who raised me right, along with my father, the late Lester Ray Cain.

Last, but by no means least, I wish to thank my husband, life partner, and beloved, poet George Kalamaras, for helping me light the creative torch and think through the snarls and obstacles, offering support and encouragement at all the right moments. What a joy it has been to share the writers' life with you and our beloved beagles, past and present, Barney and Bootsie, reminders that our animal selves matter in everything we do. Together we have conjured a household conducive to creativity, study, critical thinking, political analysis, and, of course, playfulness. I love you now and always.

SOUTH SIDE VENUS

PROLOGUE

Perhaps one of the most important legacies that Dr. Margaret Taylor Goss Burroughs has left is to ask us to consider our own. I first met Dr. Burroughs in 2003, when she was already eighty-six years old. She had a firm grasp on her own legacy by that point—most notably the DuSable Museum of African American History, which she and her second husband, Charles Burroughs, began in 1961 in their living room at 3806 S. Michigan Avenue at the behest of her DuSable High School students. She was still serving as a Chicago Park District commissioner, advocating activities that broadened the parks' offerings beyond the typical sports-centric agendas to include the connective tissue of the arts. Her own production and growth as a printmaker, painter, and sculptor were still very much in evidence as she continued to take classes and create and distribute copies of her linoleum prints to anyone she deemed worthy of such a prize. She was still conducting workshops, giving talks, and raising funds, not only for the DuSable Museum and the South Side Community Art Center (another institution she had helped found) but also for her "boys" in Stateville, Joliet, and other prisons and correctional facilities across the state to whom she taught classes in art and poetry. And a few years later, just as she turned ninety, to further drive home the point that she was far from resting on her laurels, she took up roller skating.[1] Few people have taken the meaning of legacy so much to heart as Margaret Burroughs. She intended to be an example of what was possible; she wanted people to pay attention and learn. She had arrived at a point in her life when she knew what she had to pass on and that she had the responsibility to do so.

Those who knew her—as a contemporary, teacher, mentor, friend, elder, and organizer—called her a Renaissance woman. While she left her most visible mark as an institution builder and artist, her accomplishments go much further and deeper than the fragments of written and visual accounts suggest. Her interests were wide-ranging; she was gifted in multiple media in the fine arts (printmaking, drawing, painting, and sculpture)

3

and as a poet and writer, but she was also interested in theater, dance, and music, not to mention journalism, educational research, and curriculum development. She was someone with vision, yes, but she was a visionary who executed her visions. Some called her a builder. She helped build two arts institutions, but her building extended beyond brick-and-mortar sites and into organizing people and groups. For instance, she began the National Conference of Negro Artists in 1959 and headed its leadership until a few years before her passing. With the help of her close friend and travel agent, Eleanor Chatman, she spent decades organizing tours of countries that spoke to her sense of African legacy, those of the African diaspora. But she also aimed to visit every country in the world, a goal she had not fallen all that short of by her life's end in 2010. She was constantly organizing people, connecting one person with another. As her longtime friend, Clarice Davis Durham, commented, Margaret was always inviting people to come to her house and sit in the legendary meeting place in her kitchen. She was not much for chitchat; she always had a goal, and one of them was organizing people to accomplish tasks that she deemed important.[2]

Indeed, Burroughs's legacy is so vast and deep that it is a challenge to attempt to map it out. Her accolades were many, including the Legends and Legacy award given by the School of the Art Institute of Chicago just weeks before her passing. And so it would seem that her position in history rests secure, her legacy firmly established.

Yet on some level I can't help but think she also worried a little about that legacy being passed on. One day as we finished lunch at Pearl's Place, just down the block from her South Michigan home, I caught a look from her. Beneath her mauve beret, in between bites of Mary's seafood gumbo, Creole-style home cooking reminiscent of her childhood in St. Rose, Louisiana, she gave me a look that questioned even as it seemed to calculate. *You're a writer*, it seemed to say. *Why not write about me?* This was perhaps my second meeting with her of only a handful; I had yet to discover just how many people had already written about her. She had yet to publish her autobiography. But she was as far from an egotist as they come. As her eldest grandson, Eric Toller, noted, she was completely selfless when it came to promoting herself.[3]

And yet that look. The concern that everything she knew and stood for might be lost. It wasn't about her. It was never about her. It was always about her "little people," of which she counted herself one. It was about getting through. About passing on the torch of justice and equality through artistic expression. Margaret Burroughs was uniquely gifted in her ability to do just that.

Just ask the poet hawking his latest collection across from the Art Institute on Michigan Avenue.

"How'd you get interested in poetry?" I asked, flipping through his pages. Just for kicks, I added, "Do you know Dr. Margaret Burroughs?"

Big smile. He knew he had me now. "I owe it all to her," he said. "She got me started. Dr. B is the best." I handed him a ten-dollar bill; he handed me his verse.

Later that night there was the djembe drummer just up the street on the Michigan Avenue bridge. Same story. *She's everywhere*, I think. Who doesn't know her? She's cast her net much farther than I could ever imagine.

But that look. She knew on some level how fragile even the largest net can be.

What Margaret Burroughs surely knew was at risk of being lost is an enormous body of knowledge, not just of artifacts, ideas, and lives, but also ways of doing and being that she herself embodied. She came of age in a time and place when African Americans, the ones who kicked away southern dirt and crammed into Illinois Central trains, came north to Chicago in two waves, during one world war and just before and after another. Unlike the earlier "old settlers," these migrants were penned into ghettos by housing covenants and street corner violence, starting with the 1919 race riots three years before five-year-old Margaret Taylor made the long trek northward from St. Rose Parish, Louisiana, which lay just upriver from King Oliver and his legacy, Louis Armstrong. But even as blacks were being railroaded into exclusive contact with each other in northern cities, a cross-cultural, cross-class, and cross-racial current was offering young people a window on themselves and their circumstances that linked them to the struggles of others in history and around the world. Not only was there the cross-pollination of national and international figures such as Paul Robeson, Burroughs's lifelong role model, traveling from one urban center to another. There was also that of working-class Jews and other ethnic whites and Latinos who for various reasons found purpose in crossing the lines of color, class, and ethnicity and who were teaching young people how to make those moves themselves.

Margaret Burroughs learned early on that art and language were her passports for crossing. But her crossings were not so much in search of acceptance as they were to issue invitations to join the revolutionary vision of true democracy—all humans created equal, of equal worth, full participants in the shaping of their worlds. How Burroughs learned to make those crossings, how she used art and writing to accomplish them, and how she learned how to pass on that knowledge are what is at stake. Those crossings are on the verge of being lost to generations who know only technology and the navigation of cyberspace alone in the brave new world of entrepreneurs writ large. It's not that Burroughs was not herself an entrepreneur; if anyone could lay claim to that title, she could. Instead, she situated her entrepreneurship as not simply a survival-of-the-fittest contest but as bringing people on board with a shared vision of the past, present, and future in which African Americans and, later, Africans, were given their due with respect to their contributions to humanity. She saw her own lot improved when all of her people were seen in their true light.

To Margaret Burroughs, it was a given that legacy mattered. She had benefited so much from those who had come before—from her parents, Octavia Pierre and Christopher Alexander Taylor, who had risked passage to a cold North and labored at domestic and stockyards work to ensure that their three daughters would have a better life; from teachers such as Mary L. Ryan, a white Catholic at Carter Grammar School who guided and supported young Margaret's interest in the visual arts despite the lack of available role models; from Kathleen Blackshear, who paid anonymously for Margaret's tuition and art supplies when she was about to be forced out of the School of the Art Institute for lack of funds and poor performance due to work hours; and from historical ancestors such as Harriet Tubman, Ida B. Wells, and Sojourner Truth, all of whom became subjects of Burroughs's printmaking so that their legacies would continue on through hers. She was always surrounded by people who similarly valued legacy, and in her later years this was demonstrated to her over and over through the many awards, recognitions, and acknowledgments she received. She came from a world and an era in which it was practically unthinkable *not* to think of legacy.

Her passing in November 2010 may just mark the end of that era once and for all. One visibly missing link in the legacy chain is at DuSable

High School, where the current art teachers did not even know that Margaret Burroughs had taught there, for nearly twenty-five years no less.[4] Furthermore, her efforts to incorporate African American history into the curriculum are now being displaced by a testing culture that places more emphasis on learning "metrics" than on the imperatives of identity and continuous connection between the generations, past, present, and future. Fewer students now learn this history, their history, than before. But the problem may not simply be that fewer and fewer people care about the legacy of African Americans—a debatable proposition in and of itself. Instead, it is the very idea of legacy that can be said to be at risk. We live in an information age, one in which information, facts, and data are transmitted not from person to person but from computer network to network. Who provides the information matters less than what it yields. No one has to rely upon sustaining relationships when one can simply go online and find whatever is needed, with no direct human connection required. In the age of the ahistorical entrepreneur, legacy begins to look like yet another relic of a past in which blacks were not the only ones who were constrained by geography, time, and technology. Who needs to pass on a legacy when so much is readily retrieved, independent of human relationships?

Some might argue that legacy, or at least Burroughs's notion of it, belongs to a particular time and place—Bronzeville, Chicago's own Renaissance of the 1930s and 1940s. There was unity of purpose—to uplift the race—and there was also a pressure-cooker atmosphere where blacks had no choice but to live among themselves. Such close proximity might be said to have created a make-or-break environment. It forced Bronzeville to look inward, to muster its own resources, while the rest of Chicago and the nation turned its back.

And now that unity of purpose has diffused, just as the black population has scattered, leaving the poorest, most vulnerable residents behind in the old neighborhoods. Some might read this ironically: the very things Burroughs's generation agitated for—good housing, schools, jobs, a sense of race pride, opportunity beyond the Black Belt—have caused this decline in unity by virtue of black people's success. The generational links are frayed or gone, the passing of the torch harder to maintain. This inevitably raises the question: Is legacy, as Margaret Burroughs knew it and practiced it, a relic of an irretrievable past? Was it simply a product of a certain historical moment, never to be reproduced? Does it matter now, decades later, to have had an African American family in the White House, one whose own roots run deep in Bronzeville (on Michelle Obama's side) and in community and organizing (Barack's coming of age politically on the South Side)?

The elders to whom I have spoken would all, I am sure, insist that legacy as they have known it still matters, is still necessary. But is passing on such legacies now possible? In writing this book, I confirmed at least for myself that it is not only possible but urgently required. I hope for readers that they will make their own discoveries as well.

ONE

EARLY CROSSINGS

Had I not seen it with my own eyes, I might not have believed it. Everywhere she went that day, Margaret Burroughs, or Dr. B, as she was known, was stopped on the street, greeted, and thanked profusely. People, her people, "the little people" as she affectionately called those with whom she identified, those who lingered on the streets of Bronzeville that hot, humid, quintessential Chicago August afternoon, knew this eighty-eight-year-old elder by sight. We could scarcely walk a block or two without someone rushing up to say hello, someone whose life she had touched. For all its purported problems, the South Side clearly cherished its homegrown treasure.

We had begun our afternoon walk at 3806 S. Michigan Avenue. Once the home of Margaret and Charles Burroughs and their children, Gayle and Paul, this historic building represents decades of Bronzeville art, artists, and sociability. It was also a haven for those who suffered from bigotry and hatred, a place to repair, rejoice, and relax. The first home of the DuSable Museum of African American History, Burroughs called it her home for decades, but it was a home that, like her life, had more gatherings, conversations, activities, and planning sessions than anyone can ever account for. The house at 3806 S. Michigan Avenue was the old Griffith mansion, later the Quinn Club, a railroad workers' boarding house, and it would eventually become the Ebony Museum, predecessor to the DuSable Museum that twenty years later would move eighteen blocks south to Washington Park.

But today, 3806 was simply her home. Burroughs ushered me into the dim, regal foyer paneled with rich mahogany, a worn but still vibrant ruby carpet underfoot, while she gathered her things. A Siamese cat sauntered over from the living room, closely pursued by two children, a preteen girl and a much younger boy, swishing red-and-white pompoms. The Siamese cat seemed undisturbed, more curious about the newcomer. When I reached down, he graciously allowed me to scratch his silky head.

"That's Humphrey Bogart," said Dr. B, adjusting her hat. "You must be a good person. He doesn't like everybody."

For a moment, I wondered just how good a person would ask an eighty-eight-year-old to walk her around the neighborhood to snap photos of local landmarks on such a sultry day. All Dr. Burroughs knew was that I was writing a novel that used Bronzeville as a backdrop. True, we had had other meetings prior to this; I had brought her to northeast Indiana as a visiting artist for the university and community center a year or so earlier. But when I asked her if she'd walk me around Bronzeville, she never questioned my motives or hesitated in her response.

On this, my first visit to her home, Dr. B made sure I saw the rooms where it all began. These would be the only rooms, aside from the vestibule, that I would see, at least in person.

The young sister-and-brother pair mugged for my camera and then disappeared upstairs. I pondered who these children might be. I also wondered to what use this sprawling Victorian mansion had been and was currently being put. For Margaret Burroughs was a practical woman who was loath to waste anything.

I knew this firsthand from her visits to Fort Wayne, Indiana, where she insisted on trips to the local thrift stores to enrich her and others' wardrobes. Always colorful and well-coordinated, Dr. B's clothes were enviably stylish; she could rake through racks of thrift shop goods and zoom in on a find so quickly that I could barely work one rack before she was ready to move on to the next store. One of her closest friends, Eleanor Chatman, recounted a story about a similar trip she took with Dr. B. Burroughs had found a desirable item of clothing, a skirt, for the modest sum of four dollars. But she had refused to buy it, claiming she could get the same item at a store on another side of town for only three. Call her what you may, Dr. B was thrifty but not cheap. That dollar she saved almost certainly went toward buying art supplies for her "boys" at Stateville Penitentiary in Joliet. Indeed, Margaret Burroughs was known and loved by many as the most generous of women.

When I inquired about the parents of the boy and girl I had seen, Dr. B told me that they were boarders. She had always lived with many others around her, first in St. Rose, Louisiana, among extended family and community. Upon her arrival in Chicago, she continued to live in close quarters with family, ten or so to a flat. Far from evoking the haunting images of Richard Wright's *Twelve Million Voices*, Dr. B's recollections of such living arrangements are of warmth and sharing. Her entire life had been in shared residences of one form or another. When she and her new roommate, the artist Elizabeth Catlett (whom Dr. B would later introduce to her first husband and Dr. B's high school chum, Charles White), shared an apartment, their flat was a frequent destination for artists and aficionados when they flung open their door and made room on the walls and floors for their fellow artists' latest endeavors. Even after Margaret's first marriage to Bernard Goss, their place, as noted by the art critic Willard Motley, was perhaps modest in décor but rich in art and the people with whom they shared it. And of course, the Burroughses' kitchen table salons were renowned and revered among Bronzeville residents and beyond for the lively conversations, hospitality, and the art that hung everywhere in their home. Even before she and Charles took up the former Quincy Club owner on his offer to sell them the mansion that dwarfed the carriage house to its rear where Margaret and Charles had been living, 3806 S. Michigan Avenue had housed many railroad porters away from home on their train runs.

At the time of this, my first visit, however, I did not imagine my host as anything other than very practical and sensible. After all, she had lost Charlie over ten years ago, and to live alone, pay heating bills, and keep up such a sprawling residence would be an enormous challenge for anyone, let alone an eighty-eight-year-old widow. Taking on boarders seemed entirely logical. Only years later did I understand how this assumed practicality—to pay bills and have help with maintenance—was my own projection. For Dr. B, sharing her residence was familiar and welcome. According to her eldest grandson, Eric Toller, she was not interested in collecting rent. On the contrary—she saw herself as having the room, and seeing the need, she took people in. She did not wish to profit from other people's vulnerabilities.

The living room, dark and cool in this August heat, beckoned. The Siamese cat, Humphrey Bogart, cried in that eerie caterwaul that only Siamese produce. The house was thick with cat smells; many cats had taken up residence in the now-abandoned basement. My eyes, initially captured by worn but still regal ruby carpeting and burled oak moldings and panels from the original mansion, were startled by shocks of bright colors and simple, modern forms from murals decorating the walls. I dutifully took out my camera and snapped a couple of shots, trying to comprehend this dim, somewhat cluttered parlor as the beginnings of a proud museum.

I did not know at that time that many, if not most, institutions dedicated to African American history had similarly homespun beginnings. The fact that Margaret and Charles took on the responsibility and also the sacrifice to open their family home to busloads of schoolchildren, as well as the stray arts devotee, was difficult for me to comprehend as I stood before a mural of three young women. All of them were wearing "naturals," just as Dr. B so famously had done a decade before Black Power made Afros a sort of racial union card, and all three were absorbed in a large, hardcover book they held aloft. Before them stood a globe tilted to show the bronze continents of the Americas cupping the blue waters of the Atlantic, mirroring a similar continental "hand" to the east with Europe and Africa. Above the three women were dark shapes of human forms lined up behind a Middle Passage boat. In the middle was the bust of an African man, a Western sculptor's interpretation perhaps of an African face, drawing upon traditional tribal masks. To the right of this mural was another. Painted vines and house plants framed a colorful interior scene, with a clock almost out of Dalí, not melting but tilted on a stair, half its numbers scattered from its face, along with toys and other educational items. In the window of this scene, a red-and-green car waited, as if to say to the young visitors, "Learning is your vehicle to this world and beyond."

The scale and subject matter of these murals claim a much more public space than in the typical family dwelling. Not only would one expect murals to be a rare decoration in Bronzeville, or for that matter, most single-family homes, but certainly two that depict reading, history, and the joys of travel are exceptional for any place and time. These were far from merely decorative accoutrements; they served a clear educational purpose, so much in keeping with what Dr. B's art aimed to do. I would later learn of just how many busloads of people from all walks of life, from neighbors and fellow artists to Charlie's beloved Russian circus performers, would sit at the picnic table in the downstairs kitchen and talk art, literature, politics, and, given Dr. B's ever-present agenda of coordinating and organizing people, about the next civic project or action. Long after the Supreme Court decision in 1947 to overturn the last housing covenants that had barred blacks from living beyond Bronzeville, the Burroughses' kitchen table was still *the* place to come.

Dr. B seemed satisfied by my photographic documentation of the murals. She regarded such documentation as essential, to the point, I dare say, of obsession. She looked to institution building for creating repositories of such documents. Her own home continued to serve as such a place even after the DuSable Museum moved to Washington Park and the South Side Community Art Center continued to sponsor artists, writers, and performing artists decades after its founding during the Great Depression. Very few such artifacts escaped her notice or interest.

As Dr. B made her way down the grand staircase leading to the street, her hand firmly on the iron rail, I could not help but notice the steady confidence in her movements. When she reached for my elbow as we crossed the first of many streets that afternoon, I did not know for certain if that was to steady herself or to steady me, the obvious outsider. Later that afternoon she would make the same gesture as I prepared to board a northbound bus back to the Loop in the center of downtown, but it quickly dissolved into a friendly, heartfelt hug.

"Let's go," she said. As if she knew she was bringing me home to a place that until now I had never understood as my own.

By all accounts, Margaret Taylor Goss Burroughs fit Horace Cayton and St. Clair Drake's definition of a "race woman" in their groundbreaking study *Black Metropolis*. Everything that Burroughs stood for, from her teen years to her final time as a celebrated elder, was focused on uplift of the race, both African Americans and Africans, including the diaspora. At the same time, her coming from the rural South during the first wave of the Great Migration positioned her as someone who was less influenced by the reformist attitudes of the old settlers of Chicago, that is, those African Americans already living in the city, and more by what Davarian L. Baldwin notes as the "New Negro" identity of the urban North. Consumer culture, not the morals-driven values of the old settlers, helped define a new racial identity that Margaret Burroughs would embrace in pursuit of her art. While Burroughs was, for most of her life, critical of consumerism per se, she saw art as an extension of a more highly conscious mode of uplift, as articulated by historian Carter G. Woodson. Throughout her life, Burroughs would turn to history as a necessary element in shaping black identity, and Woodson was one of those whose work she, along with scores of others involved in uplift, turned to for guidance and inspiration. As Baldwin wrote, "Woodson moved from a racial uplift to black radical analysis to conclude that black workers and entrepreneurs were making progress in the city because of their ancestral legacy from African and southern cultures, and any regression was the responsibility of the U.S. nation-state."[1]

This more critical attitude toward "racial uplift" would at times set Burroughs at odds with those, both black and white, who regarded migrants from the South, especially the rural South, as lacking in skill, culture, and morals. The lure of urban life, with its shiny new consumer culture and leisure time, or the Stroll, as Baldwin noted, offered a much more complex and fluid means by which to identify as black. Respectability was no longer a simple choice between moral, physical, and other restraints versus undisciplined, pleasure-seeking pursuits. Instead, new settlers such as Burroughs were open to the "'popular arts' in ways that complicated old settler prescriptions about appropriate labor versus leisure."[2] Such tensions cut across class and race lines within and beyond the South Side and would provide much grist for Burroughs's creative and critical consciousness.

Burroughs's art was a tool toward this end, and she stated this explicitly throughout her life. While her childhood friend and fellow poetry group member, Gwendolyn Brooks, at various moments in her writing made a "marked departure from the note of social protest," according to another Bronzeville poet and critic, Margaret Walker, Burroughs never saw art as about anything else.[3] She was not about to try to unravel what so many white modernists had already dismantled so successfully, namely the connection between politics and personal life, the political vision and the artist's vision. While some have argued that Brooks gained more range in her period of experimenting with the more "personal" as well as technical aspects of her poetry, even as she maintained a certain measure of social critique, Burroughs never deviated from her mission as a race woman.[4] This is hardly to claim that Burroughs's art was mere propaganda, or that it lacked intimacy or vision. It is simply to acknowledge that Burroughs declared very early in life that she saw she had a choice as an artist—to follow the trends of abstract expressionism (which she does so masterfully in her painting *Still Life* of 1943) and, as she acerbically commented, make a lot of money, or to stay with more representational, figurative art, including aspects of social realism that flowered in the Depression under the auspices of the Federal Art Project. What would benefit her people the most? Her choice was clear. She followed quite proudly and deliberately in the footsteps of Paul Robeson, whose choices she understood to be similarly guided by reaching out to the masses rather than catering to an often racist arts elite. Of course, Robeson's choices were hardly that stark in reality and were always more complicated and even strategic, as were Burroughs's. But Burroughs very clearly found it impossible to divorce art from politics. They were simply different dimensions of the same messy human enterprise.

Burroughs came of age during a period in which many black Chicagoans, especially women, also regarded their public work as similarly intertwined with social activism. As Anne Meis Knupfer commented, three strands of activism—"pan-African intellectuality; promotion of the expressive arts, including literature, drama, dance, and art; and social protest" were "all interwoven" and crucial to the overall movement toward black identity and social justice. This backdrop was certainly instrumental to Burroughs's development, particularly because she would spend her entire adult life pursuing and interweaving all three strands as an artist, a teacher, and a community organizer. "Clearly, a pan-African intellectual activism framed the perspectives and activities of Chicago's black teachers, librarians, clubwomen, and social protest groups. The creative arts also drew upon a pan-African identity. At the same time, the arts were a powerful form of social protest against the discriminatory social and economic conditions that besieged the black Southside communities." While Burroughs would later in life draw back from direct action protests, she would nonetheless insist that her cultural work supported others' actions and interventions.[5]

While much modernist art and literature scoured the presumably private recesses of the individual psyche, Burroughs's embrace of the personal and political as inextricably tied would create a legacy for another generation of black artists in the 1960s and 1970s, namely the Black Arts Movement (BAM) and, in Chicago, the Organization of Black American Culture (OBAC, pronounced "oh-bah-see") and AfriCOBRA. These artists followed in the wake of those contemporaries of Burroughs who had, during the McCarthy witch hunts, shed their political stripes and racial pride for the sake of survival and/or personal gain. This new generation of artists would, like Burroughs, resist the false dichotomies that placed the personal and the political, the individual and the collective, the private and the public, into separate and opposing spheres. While it can be argued that modernism was an important corrective to what sometimes amounted to a predictable, monotone vision of social realism and naturalism, Burroughs's work never gave in to the idea that such a dichotomy was true.[6] The tensions were there, but never as merely opposing worlds competing and conflicting for dominance.

To be a race woman, then, did not require Burroughs to operate in strictly political terms. As Knupfer notes, black women's activism should not be "polarized" into separate and competing categories of politics, and into categories of political versus cultural or intellectual work. Burroughs did not have to choose between what Baldwin called "a solidly industrial logic and a seemingly deviant consumer culture" or between bodily restraint versus bodily release. As Baldwin observed, many "intermediary" institutions of mass appeal, most of which were organized by women, played a powerful shaping role in the lives of young people such as Margaret Taylor.[7] Nor did it require her to take a back seat to male leaders, to do the caretaking work of her gender and leave the spotlights, few as they were, to the men. Burroughs was fortunate to come of age at a time and a place in the Black Belt, as Bronzeville was known at the time, when even a working-class young African American girl who simply liked to draw could hope to be an artist. As Baldwin noted, the high arts of Burroughs's formative years were very much integrated with the Stroll's consumer marketplace.[8] Instead of having to choose between art and popular culture, or intellectual life and street life, that girl could easily find conversation with slightly older peers at venues such as the Washington Park intellectual and political forum, George Neal's Art Crafts Guild, and later, the South Side Community Art Center. These peers were ready, willing, and able to discuss, in freewheeling fashion, their views on current events, politics, intellectual ideas, and art in the most radical and open ways imaginable. Being female, black, and working class did not keep Margaret Burroughs away from her life's purpose as an artist. If anything, these characteristics propelled her more deeply into it.

How Margaret Taylor became an artist, let alone one of acclaim, is a story of unlikely odds defied. Her parents, Octavia Pierre and Christopher Alexander Taylor, worked hard but had little, even before the

Great Depression gutted their already limited resources. They'd left St. Rose Parish in Louisiana in 1922 when Margaret, one of three daughters, was only five years old. They didn't know it then, but they were part of the first wave of the Great Migration, a journey north made by millions of African Americans in the twentieth century to escape the Jim Crow South. As Isabel Wilkerson so beautifully chronicles in her Pulitzer Prize–winning book, *The Warmth of Other Suns*, the southern blacks who came north forever changed the character of dozens of northern cities as well as the country as a whole.

> Perhaps it is not a question of whether the migrants brought
> good or ill to the cities they fled to . . . but a question of how
> they summoned the courage to leave in the first place or how
> they found the will to press beyond the forces against them
> and the faith in a country that had rejected them for so long.
> By their actions, they did not dream the American dream,
> they willed it into being by a definition of their own choosing.
> They did not ask to be accepted but declared themselves the
> Americans that perhaps few others recognized but that they had
> always been deep within their hearts.[9]

Burroughs's parents and, later, Burroughs herself pushed hard to claim the promised freedom and opportunity of the North even as they faced continued oppression and violence upon arrival. In Chicago, that violence had displayed itself only three years earlier in the 1919 race riots and would define race relations in Chicago, especially the South Side, for decades to come. The rising tensions between blacks and whites following the first wave of migration had come to a head that summer in 1919 over the use of public beaches. Prior to the first wave, blacks who lived in Chicago enjoyed relatively free mobility in housing. African Americans lived side by side with white neighbors with very little conflict. The old settlers were at times as distressed by the huge wave of southern migrants as their white counterparts, if for no other reason than the newcomers undermined their own efforts to be seen as part of the urban North.[10] But with the flood of newcomers from the South, housing grew scarce, labor unions contested the cheap "scab" labor provided by the descendants of slaves, and the city overall grew overwhelmed by yet another group of migrants, many of whom were in desperate need of social services. With

these tensions as a backdrop, conflict erupted one July afternoon, when
an African American boy drowned after receiving a blow to the head
from a rock thrown by a taunting white man aiming to drive blacks away
from the Twenty-Ninth Street beach. For a week, whites attacked blacks
and vice versa, and fires raged, deaths piled high, and the resulting dev-
astation was a misery shared by all, but felt especially by black migrants,
whom the whites clearly intended to put in their place as a result of this
violence.

Taylor's family recalled only too well the South's version of such violence. Burroughs remembered what was a precipitating event for the family's eventual migration, namely, the death of a family member at the
hands of the Klan.

> My parents never talked about it, but one night the night riders
> came to the house in the middle of the night, with shotguns and
> flaming torches and calling out for Uncle Ike's father. Papa told
> them that he wasn't there, and that made them plenty angry,
> but they finally went off to look elsewhere. Uncle Ike's father
> never came back after that. Then, just before the letter arrived,
> I heard Papa say that someone found something terrible outside
> town, sprawled out in a field, and Papa went down to look at it.
> He said it was Uncle Ike's dad, sure enough—he could tell by a
> scar. Uncle Ike and Papa wrapped up the body and had a quick
> burial, and none of us girls was allowed to see.[11]

Like many migrant families, the Taylors moved north in the wake of
other family members, in this case one of Margaret's uncles, who had
obtained employment and housing.[12] They no doubt had heard of the
1919 violence and thus were well aware of the hazards that they would
be facing with a move north. But as for many migrants, the oppression of
the South was so great that a move north was their only hope for resistance and change. As Wilkerson chronicled, the opportunities for decent
jobs and education in the North far outweighed the risks there.

Burroughs recalled how limited the educational opportunities were in
St. Rose. School was interrupted for six months out of the year so that
sharecropper families could pick cotton and cut sugarcane. The school
itself was borrowed from the Baptist church, as African Americans could
not hold title to their own school. Classes were held in a back room. Bur-

roughs speculated, "Had I stayed down there I would have been going to inferior schools. I probably would have married early. I probably would have had about fifteen children and never had any accomplishments or achievements."[13]

Southern violence no doubt shaped Margaret Taylor's perceptions from the start. While her memories of St. Rose were, as she admitted, sketchy, she did understand that dangers lurked about her. The natural world was yet another danger, perhaps one that also provided a metaphor for the ceaseless threat of violence onto which her imagination could take hold. She recalled the pervasive threat of floods from the Mississippi:

> I think the main thing I recall about that town—really it was a
> village—was the floods. It was right on the Mississippi River and
> when the river would rise everybody would be so upset and
> excited and frightened. The children, we were really frightened
> because the water would come right up to the edge of the levee
> and flap on over sometimes. We had to leave our houses and go
> into the big church, the Baptist church, to be safe.[14]

Despite its terrors, the Mississippi also provided passage to a place of Margaret's ancestral roots, namely the town of Ama on the opposite shore. There resided her maternal grandmother, "Mae-Mae, a full-blooded Creole who spoke only French. Her father came from Martinique, a fact of which one of my uncles has always been very proud. Mae-Mae entertained us with stories of our ancestors and the trials they endured as slaves on the vast Southern plantations."[15] Burroughs would retain strong memories of such stories, as well as the rich mix of languages and cultures that influenced her from a very early age. She recalled her father being especially adept with words and the blending of languages—"French, Spanish, Creole and even some Native American tongues" that he could employ at will. Her parents' propensity for inviting people from different backgrounds and cultures to the dinner table, along with her father's ease in translating what was being said, would eventually lead to her own version of the kitchen table cross-cultural exchange in Chicago:

> Over a home-cooked meal, my sisters and I all enjoyed the
> music of these different languages and accents, and the rapport
> my father would have with people of different cultures as he

translated for us what they were saying. Those were fun times, meeting and learning about people of different cultures, and it certainly had a significant impact on me. I look back now, and it seems that the Chicago Salon that would come later was actually my family's St. Rose dinner table from memory; displaced good times transferred across state, class, and cultural lines.[16]

Stories became a way of transforming the terrors of everyday life into something exciting and meaningful. The river's threats and its joys were deftly interwoven by the town's only riverboat operator, John, who regaled his passengers with stories of "colorful towns where people dressed and spoke and behaved differently. He would impress us and scare us and tantalize us with tales of daring feats and eccentric people, and it made us wonder what it would be like to be there, beyond the boundaries of St. Rose and Ama."[17] Thus from a young age, Margaret learned that such crossings, both literal and metaphorical, could, despite their dangers, produce great gifts, gifts that she carried with her throughout her life, sharing with others what she had learned about such crossings and providing opportunities for them to learn how to make such crossings themselves.

As part of the legacy of her migrant forebears' courage to will their dreams into being, young Margaret Taylor got the idea that she had a responsibility to do better, to not only survive but, building upon her parents' sacrifices, to thrive. Burroughs remembered her Catholic mother teaching school to local children in St. Rose, including herself and her sisters, in the back room of the Baptist church. Her mother, with only an eighth-grade education, was typical of rural southern black teachers of the time. But it was clear to Taylor from the beginning that her family valued education, and not simply vocational or technical skills as a means to employment, although making a living was always a consideration. Instead, as Burroughs recalled, education was a way of identifying and drawing upon a child's natural abilities and talents: in short, a means of helping individuals understand themselves, both as individuals and in relation to others. For Taylor, as for the African ancestors she would come to draw inspiration from in later years, having a purpose was key to a successful life. This purpose was necessarily rooted in the individual's unique makeup, but it also applied to the collective needs of those around her. From an early age, Taylor was schooled by principles that were less about the industrial labor values of efficiency, restraint, and hard work, and more about relationships and collective well-being.

Octavia Taylor clearly took this broader view of education to heart when observing young Margaret's behavior. As Burroughs recalled, her mother noticed how her youngest daughter, "the quietest, most mature one," had a keen interest in drawing.

> I remember that I was the one that was always drawing things.
> My mother did not discourage me. In fact, she encouraged me.
> Sometimes I would be drawing, and if there were dishes to be
> washed, well, my sisters had to wash them because my mother
> didn't want me disturbed from my drawing. My sisters got
> very upset about that, saying that Mother was favoring me,
> you know, for letting me do this.[18]

As Burroughs and her fellow DuSable High School teacher, Timuel Black, would comment in their later years, their task as teachers was to identify and promote the natural abilities and talents of their students. In contrast to the more utilitarian aspects of vocational training, both Burroughs and Black recalled trading comments about their students and claimed this as a strength of DuSable High School at the time, namely, how teachers knew students as individuals, and students were secure in the knowledge that teachers knew them all and worked together in their best interest.[19] So Octavia's keen eye and quick response to her daughter's absorption in what might otherwise be seen as a frivolous and unproductive activity was clearly a cornerstone of her daughter's legacy. Art was valued by Octavia as much as any activity that a child would find interest in because it brought out the best in the child. As the "quietest, most mature" of the three daughters, Margaret was, in a sense, privileged over her sisters by Octavia to pursue a deeply absorbing interest. Later in life, when Burroughs started the Ebony Museum in her home at 3806 S. Michigan, her sister, Marion Hummons, would be at her side, volunteering as membership director of the nascent museum as well as a secretary to her sister, tasks for which Burroughs herself had little patience or interest.[20] While Margaret's sisters may have felt some initial jealousy about their mother's "favoring," the spirit of Octavia's intention was passed on to Margaret and her sisters, who understood it as a way of relating to all children as individuals in need of such attention, guidance, and support.

The modernist concept of art for art's sake did not appear to be part of Taylor's early experiences with art. Instead, art was never divorced from purpose, even a certain utility. It was something in and of itself, but it was also a skill that others could draw upon and reward:

> When I was eight or nine, I began to develop some conscious-
> ness about art. I used to make paper dolls, and other kids would
> pay me three cents to draw the doll. I would give them a tracing
> of the dress, and then they would use that as a model. I was the
> doll maker.[21]

She was raised with the notion that she had something to say and something to give. Art was her first and most lasting means of making it up and passing it on.

How Taylor understood her legacy—through making a contribution by struggling to make something happen—is what is important to examine, not simply the end results of those struggles. Her story is unique in that it was not about a single achievement—not just as an artist, a museum founder, a teacher, or an activist. It was unique in its success at being and staying connected to a larger experience. Her art was the means by which she made and maintained these connections by crossing otherwise uncrossable lines.

From a very early age, Taylor understood art as a means to connect with others. Like many southern migrants, her family shared a small living space with as many as ten people at a time. When they first arrived in Chicago, they lived with her uncle near Twelfth Street and Michigan Avenue, close to the Illinois Central train tracks that had brought them north, as many blacks did at the time.[22] Burroughs remembered how she and her two sisters found audience with extended family as well as visitors. Immersed in the constant attention of others, she found her early abilities with line, form, and color quickly recognized and encouraged. While Margaret drew and recited, her sister Dorothy sang and Marion danced the Charleston to the weekend crowd at her uncle's "whiskey flat." Guests showered them with quarters, nickels, and dimes for their performances. Margaret and her sisters used the money to go to shows.[23] From these experiences, Taylor learned that such performances would gain her favor as well as income. At the same time, she recognized how creativity brought people together.

Fortunately for Taylor, her artistic inclinations were recognized and fostered beyond home and family, at school. Burroughs recalled one teacher in particular, a white woman, who supported and nurtured her students' emerging talents. Mary L. Ryan at the Carter School at Fifty-Eighth Street and Michigan was the first teacher to single Taylor out for her artistic bent. As Burroughs recalled, "Miss Mary L. Ryan, a Catholic lady, a maiden lady . . . recognized my talent early. She was very encouraging. She had taught people like Charles Sebree and William Sanford."[24] However, Mary Ryan went beyond encouraging Taylor to pursue her art. She actively pursued a mentoring relationship with her student beyond their time together in the classroom, one that went above and beyond simply modeling a path toward her goals. As Burroughs remembered, Ryan was her first role model: "I found myself just looking at how she dressed and how she acted, how she talked . . . she was the first role model I had outside my parents."[25] Later on, their relationship matured into one focused on helping Taylor find a pathway to her art and a career:

> This woman, Mary Ryan, realized that I had few opportunities,
> so she would have me come back to see her from time to time.
> I would make watercolors and bring them to show her. She
> would frame them and would hold raffles to sell them, and then
> would give me the money. With the money, I could buy books
> and pay for carfare and have lunch money.[26]

Ryan not only demonstrated to Taylor that her art was worthy of display and purchase, but she also impressed upon her that she could meet her practical needs for school by using what she'd learned as an artist to earn money. Even after Taylor graduated, Ryan urged her to come by and visit her. Burroughs commented:

> I went to see her every day at my old grammar school and
> would help her in the classes, whether it was washing out the
> sinks and the brushes or cleaning the studio. A lot of times she
> just let me sit there and paint. Then she would coach me, and
> when I took the examination, I passed it.[27]

Clearly Ryan left Taylor with the impression that one could set high
goals by helping to steer her former student toward a college education,
which at the time was obviously a rare opportunity for young, black,
working-class girls. Ryan did not allow Taylor to give in to other people's
limited expectations of her. For instance, Burroughs described one of her
uncles as discouraging her from taking art classes, urging her instead to
take up something more "practical." But Ryan helped Taylor resist such
assumptions by instilling in her a strong work ethic, one that demonstrated that all work, no matter how menial, was important and worthy,
especially if it led to one's higher goals. Later on, when Burroughs began
what would become the DuSable Museum in her living room, no task
was too small or menial for anyone. She instilled the same work ethic
in all of the museum's volunteers, some of whom went on to become
paid staff and curators when the museum found a permanent home in
Washington Park.[28] Furthermore, Ryan demonstrated the power of relationships. As a teacher, she took an interest in Taylor's life and future, and
not only in her ability as an artist. Ryan knew well how limited the opportunities for careers were for African American women, and she stepped
in to guide Taylor and other students through the mystifying process of
grasping what opportunities there were. Burroughs noted:

> I had no other opportunities to go to college, because my people
> were working people, with very little money. I did get a scholar-
> ship to Howard University, but the scholarship just paid tuition,
> and I had no money for room and board, so I wasn't able to
> accept it. . . . However, Miss Ryan, my old teacher, said that
> after graduation I should report to her every day, just as if I was
> going to school, and she would coach me to get into the local
> teachers' college. . . . The teachers' college was called Normal
> College, and it was a three-year school. After three years you
> got a certificate, and some people could go right into teaching,
> but at that time there were long waiting lists. There were five
> hundred students there, out of whom there were ten Blacks.
> Most of the white girls were able to go on to the University
> of Chicago and get their degrees. Most of the black students
> couldn't, so they started a course which they called "cadet
> teaching," which meant that you went out and taught under a
> master teacher for a semester, and that gave you an additional

certificate. You could specialize in art or whatever your field of interest was. Luckily, I was assigned to the school where my former elementary teacher, Miss Ryan, was, and I was able to work under her again.[29]

Taylor's early educational experiences were not always so positive. At times, familiar racist attitudes toward blacks seemed to have migrated along with them up from the South. Burroughs remembered being chastised by a white teacher for learning her alphabet ahead of the scheduled lesson. Taylor was crowned with a dunce cap, which she never forgot.[30] Throughout her childhood, her family changed residences several times, moving farther south in the city, closer to racial boundary lines. As Lorraine Hansberry, a slightly younger contemporary of Burroughs, also experienced and wrote about, Burroughs remembered when her family moved to Sixtieth Street, a "transitional area [where] racial taunts were hurled, bricks were thrown through windows, and finally [our] front porch was firebombed."[31] She also remembered having to face threats of whites throwing stones as blacks integrated into Englewood High School: "Black kids had to gang together to get to school. . . . We had to go in bunches for self-protection."[32] Amazingly, the Taylors remained in the neighborhood, and Margaret graduated from Englewood High School, along with other talented peers such as the artist Charles White.

She further noted, "After I became a teacher I understood what was happening. Many of these people, their main role was to try to discourage you and try to break your spirit. Fortunately, that did not discourage me, because I kept right on, you see."[33] Still, to Taylor and her family, the gains of moving north outweighed even these drawbacks. They took opportunities wherever they were presented.

Many young people, then and now, spend their time between home and school. For many Bronzeville children of Taylor's generation, jobs were a third way they spent their time. Fortunately for Taylor, the South Side supported many other venues for social, cultural, and political education beyond home and school. As Ian Rocksborough-Smith notes, from the late nineteenth century, black Chicago had already cultivated a rich tradition of promoting African American identity through institutions, events, and social groups dedicated to fostering historical education.

From at least the 1890s, broad cross sections of middling public school teachers, librarians, clergy, community historians, business people, fraternal order members, and clubwomen led Emancipation jubilees and black history exhibits at industrial expositions in Chicago, as had occurred in black communities across the country since the end of the Civil War.[34]

By the time Taylor came of age in the 1930s, these efforts, now under the weight of the Great Depression, expanded into a "cultural renaissance" equal to that of Harlem in the 1920s. According to Rocksborough-Smith:

A cultural and literary renaissance flourished from the 1930s through to the 1950s and is frequently understudied in comparison to its more acclaimed and earlier counterpart in Harlem. As a movement organized primarily by African American clubwomen, the Chicago literary and cultural renaissance was manifested through public lectures, plays, literary readings, discussions, public exhibitions, and programs in libraries, churches, schools, union halls, and community centers such as the George Cleveland Hall Branch Library, DuSable (originally Wendell Phillips) and Dunbar High Schools, the Parkway Community House (initially known as the outreach ministry of the Congregational Church of the Good Shepherd), and the South Side Community Arts Center.

The cultural renaissance in Chicago underscored the city's prolific role in showcasing African American urban cultural production throughout the mid-twentieth century and arguably beyond the city's usual status as a "second" to New York.[35]

Theresa Christopher, a DuSable Museum registrar and longtime co-worker of Burroughs, also emphasized the importance of public institutions such as the George Cleveland Hall Branch Library, with its renowned librarians Vivian Harsh and Charlemae Rollins, on Taylor's and other young people's development. These public institutions provided space, resources, and even mentoring to young people like Taylor who were seeking places to meet, talk, and exchange words, images, and ideas.[36] Both public and private institutions fostered a spirit of community awareness, resolve, and resistance to the status quo for African Americans, who by the 1930s had grown weary of strategies employed by those active in the Harlem Renaissance, namely to educate, and by doing so, win whites' approval and acceptance. One consequence of the Great Depression was the disappearance of white patrons' funding of black cultural education efforts; without such funding, those efforts simply could not continue, as was the case with the Harlem Renaissance. The Great Depression saw blacks shift their goals from cultivating influential white benefactors in hopes of persuading the general white population of black people's humanity, to an inward gaze of developing identity, self-reliance, and self-defense in the face of white indifference and, at times, outright hatred and violence.[37]

It was against this backdrop that the Washington Park Forum gained traction with young people and emerging adults such as Taylor. Lawrence Kennon, who was later in life strongly influenced by the somewhat older Burroughs, remembered the forum as including weekend lectures delivered from soapboxes in the park. Speakers near and far delivered their lectures. Kennon recalled how Paul Robeson, one of the speakers and a huge influence on Burroughs throughout her life, had a voice that carried far, literally and figuratively, on those soapboxes.[38] The organizers were "like older brothers and sisters."[39] This influenced Taylor and others like her to embrace progressive politics and activism. Art thus became an integral part of social justice movements. The forum attracted a rich cross-section of racial, political, class, and ethnic participants, mirroring the kinds of social intermingling and identity crossings that Taylor experienced at Englewood High School. Timuel Black attributed these kinds of diversified experiences and relationships to the success not only of the forum but of the South Side, or Bronzeville, as it had come to be known by 1930. The influence and subsequent legacy of the forum and many other groups were directly tied to the unusual degree of cross-cultural intermingling. And art, as Burroughs understood very early on, was a means of transporting people across otherwise uncrossable boundaries.

Another group that significantly shaped Taylor's perspectives was the Art Crafts Guild, a group of young artists that Taylor helped form in 1932. Their principal teacher, George Neal, was an artist who, like many artists from lower-income, migrant, ethnic, and minority backgrounds, was taking classes at the School of the Art Institute of Chicago. He also taught at the South Side Settlement House (later the McKinley Center) at Thirty-Second Street and Wabash. Neal gathered aspiring teenage artists around him, and every Saturday he would share what he had learned that week.[40] Neal opened his coach house studios at Thirty-Third Street and Michigan (a mere five blocks from what would later become the first home of the DuSable Museum) to teen artists who could not otherwise afford the School of the Art Institute classes. As Neal was ejected from one "improvised studio" after another due to his inability to pay rent, his students continued to follow him.[41] Noted Burroughs, "He deserves creditable mention for having inspired and kept together our whole generation of young artists."[42]

The Art Crafts Guild was the legacy of an earlier generation of artists who had studied, and then later taught, at the Hull House Settlement, or South Side Settlement House. Morris Topchevsky was one of those teachers, an immigrant from eastern Europe and, like many of his generation, a left-wing radical in his politics. Like other Hull House artists, Topchevsky regarded art as able to improve social conditions, an attitude that Burroughs also carried quite consciously and vocally throughout her life.[43] Just as with the Washington Park Forum, Taylor and her peers experienced early on formative and generative relationships with ethnic, working-class whites. Such experiences later influenced Burroughs in the formation of the DuSable Museum, where the founding board included a white Jew from Montgomery, Alabama, named Eugene Pieter Feldman.

While studying at the Settlement House, Taylor gained positive support similar to what she had received from teachers such as Mary Ryan. She remembered her first prize for an art contest at the Settlement House. The contest was sponsored by an insurance company; in that "little exhibit," Taylor found much encouragement: "And I won my first prize. . . . It was a certificate, and I think we got ten dollars, which was like a hundred dollars back then."[44] Later on in her life, Burroughs herself would create similar opportunities for young artists, including the Lake Meadows Art Fair, as she remembered the power of such early experiences on her own work.

Out of the Settlement House, Taylor and her contemporaries, along with teacher George Neal, launched the Art Crafts Guild (ACG). One of their goals was to find places to exhibit their work, which was a major challenge not only because of their youth but also their race. William McGill, a commercial sign painter, was president of the ACG. They met from house to house, including Neal's studios. Later on, many members of the ACG helped start the South Side Community Art Center, partly in response to the racial discrimination they had faced as black artists. During this time, Burroughs remembered exhibiting at "little art fairs."[45] At the Grant Park Art Fair, she sold a watercolor that many years later came back into her possession:

> About forty years later somebody called me from Hyde Park and said, "Was your maiden name Taylor?" I said, "Yes." "Did you used to do watercolors of little brown children?" I said, "Yes." They said, "Well, there's a lady in Hyde Park and she's retired and moving away and she's breaking up housekeeping and all. And she's selling her things, and she has this little water-color. She said that she bought it from a young black girl so many years ago in Grant Park at an art fair." I found out where this caller was and I immediately went down and bought the painting.[46]

Despite these early successes, Taylor and other black artists, young and old, carried the burden of the Great Depression as a further obstacle to creating, exhibiting, and selling their work. For instance, Robert Bone and Richard Courage described the situation faced by the Chicago artist Archibald Motley upon his return from a Guggenheim Fellowship in France during the summer of 1930. Motley, who had seen significant success after attending the School of the Art Institute,

> found his homeland plunging into depression, and Chicago was especially hard hit. Fewer than a quarter of the unemployed received relief, homeless women slept in Grant and Lincoln Parks, men fought over barrels of garbage behind restaurants, and teachers fed malnourished students, even while the city withheld their paychecks.[47]

Like many artists, Motley found the market for fine art "decimated" and returned to manual labor to survive.[48] Similarly, Taylor could hardly expect to support herself solely on her artistic efforts. She and fellow ACG members worked feverishly to secure whatever private and public spaces they could to create, exhibit, and sell their work. Such efforts further politicized an already politically aware and motivated Taylor. With the onset of the Great Depression, the racial divide that these young artists had faced grew even starker against a dire economic backdrop.

As early as 1908, the School of the Art Institute of Chicago (SAIC) had already generated a legacy of documentary-style painting that would over time reach Taylor and her contemporaries. Archibald Motley was a student of George Bellows, who encouraged the "Ashcan School," with paintings depicting the everyday venues of the working and poor classes. Bellows in turn had been influenced by Robert Henri, who led a group of white SAIC students to paint whatever was in their immediate purview, including "city streets and rooftops and such plebeian entertainments as the barroom, pool hall, vaudeville theater, skating rink, boxing arena, and dance hall."[49] This shift in aesthetic away from gilding the upper classes' image had a powerful impact on Taylor quite early in her artistic career. To her, it reinforced the exhortation of Booker T. Washington to "cast down your bucket where you are" by valuing one's own neighborhood, people, and experiences and portraying them as truthfully as possible. From Henri to Bellows to Motley to George Neal, Taylor benefited from this radical shift in aesthetics at a time when her own political awakening was gaining momentum.

The noted Chicago historian and lifelong friend of Burroughs, Timuel Black, explained that Chicago's cultural renaissance of this period depended upon the richness and fluidity of its artistic, intellectual, political, and social groups. He and Burroughs both enjoyed this extracurricular education to such an extent that they continued this legacy throughout their very long, active, and accomplished lifetimes. Black was quick to point out that Burroughs's art was, at its heart, deeply political, progressive, and even radical for its time. The lines separating art, politics, and intellectualism were virtually nonexistent. Even a self-avowed non-artist such as Black still learned how to appreciate art because of his acquaintances with the likes of Burroughs and the Washington Park Forum, the Art Crafts Guild, and later, the South Side Community Art Center and the DuSable Museum.[50] Black and Taylor, along with other young, rising artists and writers such as Gwendolyn Brooks, who was also a lifelong friend of Margaret's, found common purpose in a variety of organizations within and beyond the realm of the arts. Margaret Taylor and Gwendolyn

Brooks, for example, attended meetings of the NAACP while still in high school. Burroughs recalled protesting the arrest of the Scottsboro boys:

> When I saw a group of teenagers rallying and marching for the purpose of freeing the Scottsboro Boys (nine black boys held for allegedly raping two white women), I joined in. We would march a few blocks and then Robert McGee, who later became a minister, would put down the soapbox he was carrying and jump up on it and preach against lynching. Then a few more blocks, and Robert would get back up on that soapbox. The police stopped us because we didn't have a permit, but our beautiful sponsor—a teacher, Mrs. Frances Taylor Matlock— charmed the police, and they let us go on.[51]

In an interview with Richard Courage, Burroughs further recalled how, "in one small but spirited march, [we] walked the streets of Bronzeville wearing paper shackles around [our] necks and carrying handmade signs denouncing the scourge of lynching and the frame-up of the Scottsboro defendants."[52] Using art for dramatic effect to make a political statement was clearly something Burroughs embraced from a very early age. Unlike some of her peers, Burroughs recalled not being swayed to stick to conventional teenagers' lifestyles and concerns: "I was just whetting my appetite for activism. . . . Many of my friends were still having too much fun going to high school socials, parties, and dances. Even though it was the slums we lived in, still our parents struggled to provide food and a thin roof above our heads."[53] She knew even at five years of age what injustice looked like, especially with regard to race. She would leave her first elementary school, the Doolittle School, in the afternoon only to be greeted by male prisoners literally reaching out between the bars of their jail cell at the nearby police station, imploring Taylor and her companions with proffered nickels to let their families know they were in jail. As Burroughs commented, "I think that developed early in me an attitude about the police and police brutality."[54]

Certainly, the number of such groups and their participants was a key element of Bronzeville's Renaissance at that time. But perhaps equally noteworthy was how participants moved among these diverse groups easily and with a sense of shared purpose. And as George Neal's example illustrates, such groups reached out to their younger constituents in demonstrable ways, and the younger generations returned the favor and sponsored many events for their older mentors and role models.[55] Burroughs herself was to enjoy such sponsorship throughout much of her life.

Another important resource to Burroughs and her fellow artists and activists was the creation, in 1935, of the Federal Art Project (FAP), and, in parallel development, the national Artists Union. According to Bone and Courage, "the project and the Union provided rich opportunities for collaboration across racial lines and helped create a key Bronzeville institution: the South Side Community Art Center."[56] To put the creation of the FAP into some perspective, one must understand how unfathomable it was to the average person of that time, first of all, to pay for art, and second, for the government to include artists on its payroll to produce it. From the beginning, resistance from conservative and reactionary groups was strong, suspecting as they did that the FAP and its statewide affiliates were a "giant boondoggle or government-funded cover for communist propaganda."[57] Fortunately for Taylor and for Bronzeville, in the eight years of the FAP's existence, African American artists and writers received financial support and public exposure at a crucial time, providing a rallying point around which they could continue to press for more opportunities for black artists to be seen and valued equally. For instance, the first director of the Illinois Art Project, Increase Robinson, was ousted in large part because of the Chicago Artists Union's continuous pressure to include artists in the decision-making processes of selection and project supervision, including African Americans.[58] Later, when the FAP began an initiative to sponsor neighborhood art centers, the ACG "dissolved itself into the campaign" and became a vital force in the creation and administration of the South Side Community Art Center (henceforth referred to as the Art Center). Unlike many conventional arts institutions, the Art Center would be founded with public monies, along with a Mile of Dimes street corner campaign that would provide a crucial counterbalance to the private donations of well-heeled Bronzeville patrons, giving the artists a stronger position and a more powerful voice in the mission and day-to-day operations of the Art Center than might normally be the case. Burroughs would be a lifelong participant in the Art Center, although her relationship with it fluctuated with the political winds.

In interview after interview, Burroughs was quick to credit those individuals, groups, and institutions that set her on her path as an artist-activist. In later years, she grew ever more conscious and deliberate about describing the legacies she was so fortunate to receive, as well as the legacies she herself would leave behind. Her persistent, careful work in identifying and sustaining the crossings between her own life and that of her ancestral benefactors, both during her lifetime and historically, in the United States and Africa, was a key element in her motivations as an artist and in her selection of subjects. Such crossings also fueled her sense of purpose in the founding of the two primary institutions in her life, the Art Center and the DuSable Museum. For Burroughs, as for many of her contemporaries and predecessors, knowing one's relationship to the past was essential to understanding one's purpose in life. The creation of legacies depended upon such knowledge.

Burroughs had a strong awareness and understanding of her own family's roots, going back three generations to elders who had been slaves—a remarkable legacy, given the destruction of many African Americans' sense of legacy then and now. Such a legacy is also remarkable in light of the assimilationist drive of many white, ethnic immigrant families. Her own life provides a powerful example of the effects that previous generations can have on their inheritors. But of course, for Burroughs such efforts extended beyond family ties and into the public realm. Burroughs recollected the cooperative work within her birthplace of St. Rose, Louisiana: "There is a certain strength that comes from pulling together, working together, laughing and crying together."[59] That spirit followed her and her family up the Mississippi River and infiltrated the lifeblood of Bronzeville, a legacy that carried Margaret Taylor and her generation much further than anyone could reasonably expect during the worst economic times of a century. That legacy helped build a new community up north "where its citizens could trade in their survival mentality for a sense of hope and future."[60] Such hope was an incredible gift that Margaret Taylor used to its fullest extent and never forgot to keep passing on.

TWO

A MILE OF DIMES:
CROSSING INTO INSTITUTIONS

Dr. B adjusted her pink straw bowler hat to shield herself from the brutal afternoon sun. "Ready," she declared. The vibrancy of her outfit echoed the bright, appealing colors of the murals inside her home. Sky-blue culottes grazed pale white tights at the knee and meshed with a floral short-sleeved shirt that crisply blended the pinks, blues, and whites of the other pieces. Just for fun, red sneakers complemented a straw tote with a similar lipstick-red woven into its pseudo-African pattern. Burroughs certainly knew how to draw the eye and invite a sense of play.

She paused before the park strip, gazing upon pigeons scavenging for food. "I tried green beans the other night," she said, pointing to the decimated remains. "Guess they didn't like those." She pulled out a roll from her tote, most likely a leftover from a Pearl's Place lunch, and broke it up into pieces, scattering them like snow.

All eyes, it seemed, were on us as we made our way south on Michigan Avenue toward Thirty-Ninth Street. Whether it was the heat or her age or perhaps even a deliberately measured stride, we kept a slow but steady pace—plenty of time for folks to approach. And approach they did: "Dr. Burroughs, I have never forgotten you. I became a teacher because of you." "Dr. B, I finished my master's degree. I know how much you care about education." "My sister had you at DuSable. You were always an original." "Good to see you, Dr. B. Keep on keeping on."

There was no escaping this impressive display of hero worship. Dr. B took it all in stride, literally, stopping just long enough to return the greeting and receive the warm wishes. But she displayed no interest in standing still. Or sitting. For the next two hours, we would keep on keeping on, without regard to heat, sun, or busy sidewalks. We were on a mission.

The first stop on our tour would be the South Side Community Art Center, just across the street at 3831 S. Michigan Avenue. Grand, like the Griffiths mansion that Dr. B claimed as her home, the Art Center had a broad and majestic entryway, with a wide, massive staircase and fluted columns supporting a Georgian Revival pediment, echoing a Greek or Roman temple. To the left of the staircase stood a round black column whose top third was painted in sharp black-and-white African designs and topped with a pale cap reminiscent of tribal hut roofs. The architectural mix would continue on the inside, with the original plan designed by the renowned architect L. Gustav Halberg for the Chicago grain merchant George A. Seaverns Jr.[1] But outside, the grandiose columns, curved windows stacked like a layered wedding cake, and brick and ivy walls mingled with plain commercial signage and the traces of air pollution and gentle decay that blackened the building's august facade.

I asked Dr. B to pose again before yet another institution she had founded. Then she led me inside, and we were greeted by one of the Art Center's staff, who immediately acknowledged Dr. B with a warm welcome and offers to look around inside. The exterior promise of a faded wealth and grandeur gave way to a simpler, modern interior. In 1940 the brownstone had been purchased by the Art Center. Dr. B proudly described the fund-raising campaign: "I stood on the corner of Indiana and Forty-Ninth with a can and collected dimes for a Mile of Dimes campaign. The reason this Center is still going today is because we bought the building outright. None of the other WPA [Works Progress Administration] art centers did, which is why they are no longer around."

In contrast to the somewhat faded grandeur of the exterior, this interior, remodeled before its inauguration by First Lady Eleanor Roosevelt in 1941, glowed in simple, warm, handcrafted wood finishes. Designed in New Bauhaus style by Hin Bredendieck and Nathan Lerner, the first-floor gallery provided the perfect backdrop for visual arts exhibitions. Utility and aesthetic richness blended in a quietly gracious yet elegant style. The handcrafted feel of the hand-hewn wood was wedded with the handcrafted African design outside. Clearly the designers and the building's subsequent generations of artists understood the need to work both with and against the classical and European architectural elements to create spaces for a different kind of aesthetic.

Dr. B pointed out a New Bauhaus–style bench seat in the first-floor gallery. She said she had just given a donation for its purchase. The hand-hewn wood invited viewers to sit, linger, and soak in the muses on the walls and around the floors. The space was open yet also intimate, homey yet quietly regal. Compared to the many galleries of other, more famous local institutions such as the Art Institute of Chicago and the Museum of Contemporary Art, grandeur seemed beside the point; even though the Art Center bespoke of great dignity, it did so with an eye toward inviting the community to gather and even to grow in its comfortable presence.

I wondered what my life would have been like had I grown up in the presence of such a place. Out in south suburban Chicago during the 1960s and 1970s, it seemed to me that everything of any merit lay strictly within the city limits. Even the Scottsdale branch of the Chicago Public Library that my family frequented and that I am sure contributed to my eventual career as an English professor was just over the city border at Seventy-Ninth Street and Pulaski. Instead, I grew up seeking out the secrets of the natural world, in its last remaining vestiges. The vacant lot across the street was called a "prairie." We biked to municipal parks that were open, flat, and, in the summer heat, scorchingly treeless. Girl Scouts provided summer camp in the forest preserves where I learned the names of plants, trees, and animals that sometimes made cameo appearances in our backyard or in the grassy alleys where neighborhood kids congregated to play group games.

However, midwestern winters always forced my activities inside, where, like Margaret Taylor, I turned to drawing and painting from an early age. Crayons and watercolors on whatever paper was available were my main media. But in sixth grade, spurred on by my horticulturally inclined older brother, I entered a coloring contest that won first him, and then me, free tickets to the annual garden show at the McCormick Place exhibition center, along with a set of oil paints. At the time, I knew no one who used such expensive and seemingly difficult materials, except perhaps my older cousin, Kathy. But she lived forty-five minutes away in Indiana, and besides, she was just old enough to want to keep me out of her business. Nonetheless, I unknowingly followed in the footsteps of Margaret, Bernard Goss, and a host of other Bronzeville artists when I used these precious paints on whatever surface was available.[2] I remember painting a portrait of the family dog on cardboard from a gift box that I had cut down to size. Since the oils were thick and difficult to spread, I decided that the angular features that emerged were "modern art" and so named the piece "Modern Art Heidi." It had never occurred to me to ask for money for canvas, or even special paper. Around our household, the message was to use what you were given. Special requests came with birthdays and Christmas. At the time, I thought I was being inventive.

If there had even been an art center in or near the South Stickney Sanitary District (later Burbank) where I grew up, I'm not sure my parents would have known about it or, had they known, signed me up. And even though other neighborhood kids produced similar kinds of "kid art," none of us gathered together and formed the kind of club that Margaret Taylor and her youthful cohorts did on the South Side. So the achievement of first forming a club, the Art Crafts Guild, and then joining forces to establish a community art center, attests to the powerful vision and will of not only Dr. B and her peers but also of Bronzeville as a community. Such efforts reflect how this and other African American communities sought to envision a way of life that resisted the kinds of identities that had enabled their enslavement by creating cultural expressions and institutions that envisioned something better.

After our tour of the upstairs gallery and work spaces, Dr. B steered us back down the stairs and out the doors to continue our walking tour. Later I would learn more about Dr. B's difficult relationship to her beloved Art Center, the struggles for control between the artists who founded it and the moneyed class who paid for the privilege of its benefits. But for now, I compared the sturdy, peaceful interior with the gently decaying facade and surveyed the nearby empty lots that were so far from my childhood prairies, housing the ghosts of mansions and Richard Wright's kitchenettes past. I considered the fragility of an enterprise that had always depended upon a community's support and pondered what community was now left to keep the doors open.

One of Margaret Burroughs's most significant and persistent legacies is her beloved South Side Community Art Center. But just as important a legacy is how the Art Center came into being. To truly grasp Burroughs's legacy, one must understand how she moved within a web of relationships inside and beyond her community. Her individual actions in creating the Art Center would not have amounted to much had she not already been actively engaged in the vibrant social, cultural, and political life around her. As she herself noted, she knew others of her age group who chose the more typical teen route of parties, dancing, and dating.[3]

But even as a teenager she chose a different path, in large part because alternatives were present and quite visible to the community overall, alternatives such as the Washington Park Forum that prodded her to question the conditions around her: "I started just by questioning things, not taking everything someone told me as Gospel, becoming more critical of what I was learning and of the attitudes of teachers."[4] As she was learning to question everything, prompted by the dearth of education about her race and her people in the schools ("Often I would daydream or doze off in class until a teacher happened to mention or refer to Negroes, coloreds, blacks, Afro-Americans or any specific black person—anything concerning my people"), she found others with similar questions as well as some powerful answers.[5] Many of the women around her, such as the visionary librarian Vivian Harsh, formed the clubs, schools, centers, programs, and institutions from which Taylor, in some way or another, benefited, including the development of an African American history curriculum that she would eventually pursue herself as an art teacher at DuSable High School and later when founding two major African American museums.

For years prior to its founding, the Art Center's artist-organizers had already been visibly active within Bronzeville organizations and cultural, political, and social projects, most notably with the Art Crafts Guild and Margaret Taylor's mentor, George Neal. In addition, fellow race women Pauline Kigh Reed, Susan Morris, Marie Moore, and Grace Carter Cole were interested in developing an arts center that artists such as Taylor could help cultivate for the purpose of promoting positive racial identity.[6] In 1935, the fortunes of Taylor and her fellow artists would take a drastic turn for the better. That year marked the beginning of the Federal Art Project (FAP), commissioned by the Franklin D. Roosevelt administration. National Director Holger Cahill followed the liberal, pragmatic philosophy of John Dewey, "which emphasized learning by doing and understood art as a process of human relations rather than a material object." Within this philosophical perspective, Cahill sought to bridge the gap between fine and applied art, making art something to be experienced by all.[7] Such a perspective found ample reception among Art Crafts Guild members, who were already busy producing work and cultivating an audience that engaged the daily lives of their community.

The FAP provided a unique moment in Bronzeville's development. In the past, whenever Bronzeville residents targeted a community need, they typically approached private, white-dominated sources as well as Bronze-ville business elites: "The creation of the Art Center broadly resembled the process by which the Wabash Avenue YMCA and other key institutions had been established. Blacks identified a need and approached a white-dominated institution, traditionally the Rosenwald Fund, for financial support."[8] However, this time it was the community that was approached by the FAP and its state arm, the Illinois Art Project (IAP). Instead of private monies or foundations, the FAP offered public funds through a "national model of project/community cooperation." The FAP would provide funds to employ artists and renovate a space if the community rallied to purchase a building and pay for utilities and supplies.[9] Fortunately for the Art Crafts Guild, George Neal had already been cultivating a similar vision of a community arts center, a vision that had captured the imagination of the group and stoked its creative fires. But until the FAP's proposal, the artists were struggling just to exist, unable to do much to act upon such a vision.

Concurrent with this shift away from private, usually white-sponsored funding was the *Chicago Whip*'s "Don't Spend Your Money Where You Can't Work" boycott campaign, which became a national movement, as well as a similar, perhaps more middle-of-the-road campaign by the NAACP, "Don't buy where you can't work."[10] The economy of the urban North, especially that of Chicago, lent itself to more investment by blacks in black-run businesses, commodities, and cultural productions, spurred by the momentum generated by interest in racial pride and history.[11] Margaret Taylor was no stranger to such sentiments as she became an integral part of the founding of the new Art Center, which she would later proudly proclaim was the result of the black community's rallying to meet the FAP's requirement of funds for the purchase of the Art Center's building. The attitude of supporting black life by blacks was practically inescapable in Bronzeville at this time.

Before the FAP, Bronzeville artists had to rely primarily upon limited community resources for their training, supplies, and exhibition spaces. One such resource was the South Side Settlement House, founded in 1919 by Ada McKinley. The Settlement House provided much-needed social services and cultural education to new Great Migration families such as the Taylors, including classes taught by and for a diverse group of immigrant, ethnic Europeans. One of those teachers was George Neal. In 1932, just three years prior to the FAP, Neal organized his students into a separate group, the Art Crafts Guild.[12] It was this group of young artists who played a crucial role in the founding of the Art Center.

Neal proved to be a pivotal figure in Bronzeville art history in several ways. First, he set an example, later followed by Burroughs, of forging alliances across the ethnic, racial, and political lines of fellow artists, many of whom, like the Settlement House teacher Morris Topchevsky, tacked radical in their social activism, a path Taylor would also follow. Neal would also form alliances with the Communist Party (CPUSA), a powerful force in Bronzeville during the Great Depression, with the largest African American membership in any major U.S. city at that time.[13] Neal helped these and other groups establish the Chicago Artists Union, part of a national union that developed alongside the FAP and IAP. The union, which supported a core group of well-trained and vocal organizers from the CPUSA, reached out to artists, including African Americans, to claim a central role in the decision-making processes of selection and project supervision:

> One might suppose that, under ordinary circumstances, organizing artists into a trade union is akin to training cats in close-order drill, yet the Federal Art Project created a truly extraordinary situation: thousands of artists across the country . . . were employed full-time by the government to make art. The Artists Union grew alongside the Art Project with the goals of serving as bargaining agent for its employees, increasing hiring quotas, ensuring the participation of artists in all major decisions, and making the project permanent.[14]

For artists who, by and large, had had little or no previous experience organizing *as* artists, the union provided the means by which they could claim a greater share of the decision-making power, which was unprecedented for most artists of that and previous eras. In turn, the union would cross identity lines in search of members who could support its agenda of diversity and "documentary-style" aesthetics.

These pathways of organization, along with the Art Crafts Guild's own organizational imperatives, provided Taylor with many opportunities to hone her activist skills that, from an early age, she was eager to exert. Previously Taylor had marched in the streets against lynching when, starting at age sixteen, she signed on to the NAACP Youth Council, where she

joined forces with her lifelong friend, Gwendolyn Brooks. She had also
frequented the soapbox talks at the Washington Park Forum. As she developed her artistic abilities through the South Side Settlement House
classes, along with some scattered opportunities at the School of the Art
Institute, she joined other young artists in collectively seeking studio and
exhibition space, materials, and competitions that could bring much-
needed exposure as well as revenue. As Burroughs remembered, the attitude among her peers was one of mutual support and encouragement.
Since everyone in Bronzeville faced the same racist hurdles regarding
Chicago art galleries, they chose collaboration over competition. While
they did not shrink from competing against each other for prize money,
they celebrated any victory of their peers.

Taylor and her fellow young artists learned not to wait for someone
else to pave the way. With Neal's encouragement, they began the Art
Crafts Guild and strategized more vigorously for the necessary resources
to sustain their art.[15] Neal helped them not only by opening his home
studio space to them, but also by fostering fund-raisers and exhibitions in
whatever community spaces were available: libraries, churches, schools,
homes, the YMCA, and so on. As Burroughs recounted, Neal "was responsible for the sustained interest and development in art manifested
in many of the young black artists of those Salon days."[16] In addition to
sharing lessons from his Art Institute classes, Neal also took the young
artists on sketching tours and visits to downtown galleries and the Art
Institute. He sponsored outdoor showings of their work; summers were
the only times the group could count on because, as Burroughs recalled,
"few people came to the studio in the winter because there was only one
coal stove, and it wasn't very effective."[17]

The Art Crafts Guild also promoted the distribution and purchase
of art, especially those of fellow African Americans, an effort later mir-
rored in the language of Holger Cahill's FAP. One direction recounted by
Burroughs was the shift toward convincing community members of all
economic classes that art was something they could and should purchase
for their own dwellings: "Back then many people were under the belief
that paintings were just to look at, and would never consider buying any
to grace the walls of their homes, much less fathom the effort or messages
spilled upon the canvases."[18] But to the ACG, art was not simply for the
wealthy or educated elite; instead, it was something that could reflect
back racial identity and pride, something that connected blacks to their

own unique histories, and something that contributed to a local, grass-roots economy and culture.

With public monies now offered directly to artists for their work, they suddenly found themselves in positions of greater control over their labor, including the institutions that they and their art made possible. This proved equally true for the ACG. But even before the FAP, many activities and organizations provided the education and inspiration for the ACG to successfully focus their energies and activist pursuits. The historical backdrop to the ACG's organizing efforts included political de-velopments that reached far beyond its roots, particularly the activities of radical labor and civil rights groups. On the South Side, the Communist Party had "replaced its call for a proletariat-led global revolution with a call for a 'Broad People's Front' coalition of liberals, radicals, trade union-ists, farmers, socialists, blacks and white, anti-colonialists and colonized," and at the same time it "inaugurated a campaign to promote what it called 'people's' culture."[19] This "Popular Front" political and cultural ori-entation was clearly part of Burroughs's lifelong commitment to using art to forge broad alliances among diverse groups of citizens for the purpose of democratic expression and participation.

While Burroughs never became a member of the Communist Party, her art, organizing, and vision reflected much of that group's goals. As she explained, "The history of black resistance to oppressive authority cannot be seen entirely through the lens of socialism, as it was then [in the past] and even sometimes today. Rather, it must be viewed in the context of the unique experience of African Americans."[20] Given how the CPUSA had supported the defense of the Scottsboro boys, how it was vehemently anti-lynching, and how, during the Depression, it sought out African Americans as part of its Popular Front, it is no wonder that Taylor and other politically aware artists found the CPUSA favorable to African American interests. Burroughs was quite clear in how she viewed the relationship between blacks and the CPUSA:

> What is often lost, I think, is that it was not even blacks em-bracing communism that was at work, so much as communism embracing blacks. The Communist Party realized that support from black Americans could help its cause, and blacks merely incorporated this positive support—so rare, indeed—into their developing nationalism. Communism never really took hold

among blacks any more that it did in America as a whole,
except perhaps in the area of the arts, where many writers and
artists gravitated towards any kind of progressive thinking—and
such thought was surely not to be found in U.S. governmental
dogma.[21]

Burroughs in this way embraced aspects of the CPUSA without specifically joining the party. Throughout her life, she would, like her role
model, Paul Robeson, adhere to the principles of equality and justice she
had found in the CPUSA's Popular Front as what was commonly known
as a "fellow traveler."

As Taylor was coming of age, the CPUSA stepped up its efforts to
reach out to African Americans. In turn, Bronzeville residents like Taylor
recognized a shared vision with the CPUSA. As the Depression wore
on and the WPA and FAP began to exert influence, the CPUSA and
Bronzeville found common purpose in organizing for political and social
power, along with the financial resources provided. By the time the Art
Center was proposed, Taylor and her colleagues had a clear sense of
mission as well as the organizational skills to create the necessary space,
resources, and visibility for a diverse group of artists, but primarily those
who had answered the call to provide "people's culture."

The Federal Art Project, which lasted from 1935 to 1943, was highly
significant despite its relative brevity. And it is perhaps no coincidence that
while its state arm, the Illinois Art Project, was establishing itself, artists
in Chicago were organizing to form their own union. Whether Taylor
was directly aware of the Chicago Artists Union, she was most certainly
influenced by one of its founders, George Neal. She may not have been
aware of the union's power to influence the IAP's leadership, but she likely
was aware of a shift in the IAP's interest toward the social realism that the
ACG was producing and which she so passionately embraced her entire
life. That shift further empowered the ACG to apply for the kinds of employment crucial to the careers of writers such as Richard Wright, whose
South Side Writers Group at one point found a home in the Art Center.

In its initial days, the IAP was directed by Increase Robinson, a painter
and gallery owner who directly challenged Holger Cahill's broad popu-
list ethic for art and community education. She put strict limits on subject
matter—"no nudes, no dives, no pictures intended as social propaganda"—
she avoided hiring union artists, and she neglected children's classes and

community art centers. Had the union not filed charges against her in 1938 with Cahill, and had she and her elitism not been replaced by George Thorp, the Art Center might never have come into existence, and Taylor might never have found the home base she needed to develop her burgeoning artistic and organizational skills.[22]

Empowered by this victory with the IAP, the Chicago Artists Union was able to successfully gain its members employment as well as connections. While Taylor may or may not have been a union member herself, she clearly benefited from the IAP's shift away from a more conservative stance and toward the "documentary-style" art rising up around her. She benefited from the IAP's outreach to Bronzeville when, in 1938, shortly after Robinson's ouster, George Thorp reached out to the North Side gallery owner and IAP staff member Peter Pollack for ideas on how to start a community arts center on the South Side.

As a socially visible, artistically trained group, the Art Crafts Guild could not help but capture Pollack's attention. As Burroughs recalled, in 1938 Pollack and the IAP director George Thorp "called together a small group of 'leading' black citizens including a few young artists like myself to talk about this proposed Art Center. Our first meetings were held at the south-side Settlement House at 32nd Street and Wabash Avenue."[23] Part of the reason Pollack may have sought out ACG members is because they frequented his gallery, which was the only one in the city to exhibit works by blacks. In addition, the South Side Settlement House had been providing sponsorship to young artists: "A public-spirited businessman, Golden B. Darby, was at that time Chairman of the Board of the South Side Settlement House. He had recently inspired that institution to present a contest for the young black artists of the community. His insurance firm provided cash awards and certificates."[24] Taylor herself was awarded a blue ribbon and certificate, thus distinguishing herself among her fellow artists as well as bringing her to the attention of influential figures like Pollack.

A slightly different perspective on the Art Center's beginnings is represented in a separate account by James Graff, which was also featured in the 1991 fiftieth anniversary program, along with Burroughs's account. Graff's account begins prior to Pollack's approaching the "'leading' black citizens" noted by Burroughs. Here Graff noted how Pollack (inaccurately named as director of the IAP) approached Metz Lochard, editor of the *Chicago Defender*, about "arranging for Chicago businesses to display some of the fine but largely unrecognized work of local black artists." Lochard brought Pollack "unannounced" one Sunday to the society maven Pauline Kigh Reed. Graff characterizes this meeting as the origin of the Art Center idea: "She suggested to Pollack that they go beyond merely displaying works in businesses and establish instead a community art center of the kind that was springing up in other cities under the encouragement of the WPA. This one would be for black artists."[25] While this version of whose idea the Art Center sprang from is markedly different from Burroughs's account, it is perhaps, as Bill Mullen points out, no surprise that different, even somewhat competing, narratives exist: "The dozens of poor painters and cultural workers who saw the Art Center as a chance, in Burroughs' words, 'to stop shining shoes all week and just paint on Sundays' found themselves pushed to the margins by the numerous black socialites who had come to attach themselves to this sudden institutionalization of black culture."[26]

Mullen goes on to discuss the ongoing tensions between artists and society people as part of a larger, internal struggle within the South Side over political aims and affiliations. Burroughs herself did not dismiss this struggle within the Art Center, although in her fiftieth anniversary account as well as other sources, she is quick to credit women such as Reed and Frances Matlock (a teacher who had also led Margaret Taylor into the streets to protest with the NAACP Youth Leadership Council) for their assistance and resources in founding the Art Center. But no matter how the idea for an art center began, it is clear from Art Center organizational meeting minutes that various artists, including Taylor, were involved in the planning stages from the very beginning in 1938.

These planning meetings, and later board meetings, proved yet another invaluable learning opportunity for Margaret Taylor, later Goss (upon her 1939 marriage to the artist Bernard Goss, who was also part of these meetings). She characterized her role as "the 'Jane Higgins' and the 'go-for.'" "I kept my eyes wide open and learned much from such cultural leaders as K. Marie Moore, Pauline Kigh Reed, Katherine Dickerson and others. I served for many years in the post of Recording Secretary, then as President and finally as the Chairman of the Board in 1952."[27] Even as Taylor Goss apprenticed herself to "civic-minded" women of Bronzeville, she also maintained her radical roots, roots which the Art Center depended upon for its founding as well as its continuity in the decades ahead.

Fund-raising is often an activity that many artists shun, but Taylor Goss embraced that role immediately as plans for the Art Center took shape. With numerous skilled female fund-raisers around her, Taylor Goss quickly learned how to solicit funds as well as public support for her and her fellow artists' projects. In 1939, after months of meetings, the Art Center Committee began a "Mile of Dimes" campaign. Burroughs recalled, "I was twenty-one years old and I stood on the corner of Thirty-Ninth and South Parkway (now Martin Luther King Drive), collecting dimes in a can. I believe I collected almost $100 in dimes."[28] Her eagerness and enthusiasm for the project translated into an attitude that no task was too small or mundane if it helped reach the goal. The mentorship of George Neal also proved to be invaluable for this project. Burroughs noted how Neal taught his young protégés to roll up their sleeves and transform his coach house into a working studio and school.[29] She also learned from Art Center organizers such as Ralph Scull, "a prominent dermatologist," how to develop a membership campaign that to this day helps sustain the Art Center. Later, the Artists Committee of the South Side Community Art Center continued the manual labor, teaching, and lobbying of the board: "We were at the Center during all of our spare hours. We were deeply dedicated—teaching classes, scrubbing floors, painting walls and standing firm on issues brought to the board of directors and officers. At times, we were kicked out of the Center, but we regrouped, planned new strategies, bound up our wounds, and limped back into battle with reinforcements."[30] Persistence, hard work, and determination were lessons learned with a cohort of like-minded artists.

But perhaps one of the biggest fund-raising lessons that Taylor Goss learned was during 1938's first annual Artists and Models ball. Here socialites, "race men and women," professionals, businesspeople, and artists worked diligently and at times at fever pitch to host an event that for many years was "the" place to be, no matter what one's race. This event marked perhaps another singular moment in Taylor Goss's development, as she learned the value of and methods for reaching across the class and social divides within Bronzeville to bring a creative, community-centered vision into being. But even as she embraced these crossings and continued them throughout her life, she also maintained a critical dialogue about the shortcomings and blind spots of the "bourgeoisie." For instance, the excitement of the Artists and Models ball propelled so many from across the Bronzeville spectrum to join forces that the event in some ways took on a life of its own. For many, the fund-raising aspect of the Art Center declined in importance compared to the "see and be seen" aspects of attendance at the ball. Had it not been for the efforts of artists such as Taylor Goss, along with teachers and community organizers such as Frances Matlock, as well as socialite women such as Pauline Kigh Reed, the ball might not have enjoyed the widespread success that it did for many years.

Another important contributing artist was Elizabeth Catlett. A young Catlett arrived in Chicago from New Orleans during the summer of 1940 to study at the Art Center and see a major Picasso exhibition at the Art Institute. Befriended by Taylor Goss, Catlett returned to Chicago the following year while on break from teaching in New Orleans.[31] Taylor Goss offered her a room in her coach house apartment, and Catlett was subsequently swept up in the activities around the new Art Center. She immersed herself in planning a Queen of the Ball costume for the November 1941 ball, for which she won first place, and which drew rave reviews from the *Chicago Defender*: "Her outfit was 'Mexico' itself even to detail of accessories."[32] Catlett seems to have taken Chicago by storm even before her move north. In 1940 at the American Negro Exposition, part of the seventy-fifth anniversary of the Emancipation Proclamation, she took first prize in sculpture for her *Negro Mother and Child*.[33] And upon her return in 1941, she stole the heart of one of Burroughs's longtime friends, Charles White, to whom Burroughs had introduced her. Catlett was just one of many artists whose talents and magnetism drew crowds to the ball and to the Art Center in general. Charles White, her soon-to-be husband, also commanded much attention with the unveiling of his first mural at the 1938 Artists and Models ball, part of what later became a three-part series of Chicago work.[34]

Of course, the Art Center committee artists alone could not generate the necessary buzz to bring artists, performers, and ticket buyers from across the country to crowd the Savoy Ballroom. Marva Trotter Louis, wife of the heavyweight boxing champion and black icon Joe Louis, co-produced the 1942 ball, along with Helen Page Taylor, bringing many ticket buyers through the ballroom doors.[35] The *Chicago Defender*, newspaper of the Great Migration, enthusiastically promoted the annual event to its audiences throughout the country, drawing trainloads of travelers seeking to join the prestige and glamour. Businesses near the Savoy Ballroom on Forty-Seventh Street offered their store windows to display artists' work.[36] Frances Matlock, Pauline Kigh Reed, Katherine Marie Moore, and other socially prominent Bronzeville women did their fair share to stir the fund-raiser's pot.

The colorful, exotic, and varied performances and attractions of the Artists and Models balls generated enormous excitement and interest. Burroughs credited herself with directing one such performance, characteristically reflecting her border-crossing instincts. Called "Cavalcade of the United Nations," it captured the attention of a *Chicago Defender* news columnist who wrote, "The show was original, daring, aesthetic and artistic."[37] In 1943, the last year before the FAP ceased its funding, the teacher and actress Brunetta Mouzon produced a show themed "Below the Border," "complete with Latin-American songs, dances and costumes."[38] In other years, the illustrious Chicago dancer Katherine Dunham pitched in.

Burroughs's recollections of these days are lively. She noted how her friend Elizabeth Catlett's first-prize-winning costume was "made from our window drapes." Another year, the dancer Lester Goodman captured her imagination when he "painted himself all over in gold and shook up the whole audience." She went on to remember how "those who saw here [*sic*] will never forget Valerie, a half-black and half-German young lady from Vienna. She was six feet tall and was the featured dancer. Those really were the days and nights!"[39]

The international themes in the early days of the ball and of the Art Center itself were no coincidence. Taylor Goss and her fellow artists embraced the activities of the National Negro Congress (NNC), whose new president in 1939 was a civil rights activist, labor leader, and Communist Party leader in Illinois, Ishmael Flory. He was also "a neighbor and friend" to Margaret and Bernard Goss. Flory engaged with many other left-leaning groups that the Gosses and the artists' committee would later host at the Art Center, including the NNC, Union Workers, Artists Union, and the International Workers Order.[40] The international and interracial thrust of many of the activities promoted by Flory and the CPUSA was eagerly embraced by Taylor Goss and carried throughout her life. At the same time, a pan-African consciousness had already been developing in black urban centers like Chicago since the turn of the century, fostered in large part by women activists on the South Side.[41]

The organizational work of founding the Art Center provided Taylor Goss with a crucial focus for applying many of the political, cultural, and international perspectives she had adopted previously in a very tangible way. Throughout her life she never wavered in her assertion that the Art Center and other such ventures were valuable assets to the community: "The S.S.C.A.C. was a worthwhile contribution made to all the people of the community, indeed all the people of Chicago. The Art Center provided an affordable opportunity for self-expression and development for anyone who wanted to participate in its programs."[42] More conflictive moments during the formation of the Art Center may also be said to have contributed further not only to her organizational acumen but also to a deepening of her progressive political stances, in particular with clashes, then and in the future, with the board's more conservative outlook on the artists' role and the role of the Art Center in the community: "They were with the Center when it was riding high, but when the going got rough and the tinsel and glamour was gone, leaving only hard work to keep the Center afloat, the majority of our fine bourgeois blacks found any excuse to put the Art Center down."[43] As grateful and even complimentary as she often was toward the board, Taylor Goss never lost her critical understanding of the class differences that accompanied the formation and operations of the Art Center.

As a result of these fund-raising campaigns, membership drives, and galas, the Art Center committee raised about $8,000, enough to purchase the Georgian-style 1893 house of grain merchant George A. Seaverns Jr.[44] Taylor Goss surely learned yet another lesson in persistence when at first no sound building was to be found in Bronzeville, which was host to slum landlords, kitchenette apartments, and general disrepair and decay in the midst of great poverty. Even the final selection at 3831 S. Michigan Avenue had been chopped into kitchenettes. The renovation of this mansion would prove no small task. But with FAP funding, a cutting-edge New Bauhaus design by Hin Bredendieck and Nathan Lerner, and much dedicated effort by the artists and community members, the Art Center opened its doors in December 1940 for its first, informal inauguration.[45]

Taylor Goss and the artists' committee would taste "the first fruit of their labor" with a showing of forty-two oils and watercolors by a variety of African American visual artists, including Charles White, Archibald John Motley Jr., Eldzier Cortor, Henry Avery, William Carter, Charles Davis, Joseph Kersey, Ramon Gabriel, and Bernard Goss. The *Chicago Defender* reported hundreds in attendance.[46] Concurrent with this sweet taste of success was the July 4, 1940, opening of the American Negro Exposition at the South Side's Chicago Coliseum. As Bill Mullen explains,

"Planned to commemorate the seventy-fifth Anniversary of the Emancipation Proclamation, the eight-week exposition, funded in part by a $75,000 grant from the Illinois State Legislature, showcased the achievements of black writers, journalists, musicians, and visual artists."[47] Alain Locke, a Howard University professor and author of the highly influential treatise "The New Negro," chaired the exposition's art committee and wrote an introduction that, like "The New Negro," aimed to "update prevailing African-American imperatives."[48] The exposition brought a national spotlight to the former Art Crafts Guild members, along with numerous other black artists, many from Chicago, a spotlight that launched many national and international careers throughout the years, including Taylor Goss's. For instance, in February 1941, three months before the official inauguration of the Art Center by First Lady Eleanor Roosevelt, Alonzo Aden of the Art Gallery at Howard University, who had also curated the art exposition at the American Negro Exposition, opened a partial rendering of that show at the Howard University Gallery of Art, including work by Taylor Goss.[49] Furthermore, the assistance of New York's Harmon Foundation, a primary funding agency for visual arts during the Harlem Renaissance, made the exposition's visual arts exhibit a "blockbuster" that "offered a unique opportunity to place black visual arts on the nation's cultural map" as well as strengthen links among artists across the country.[50]

This meteoric rise in the national spotlight must have been thrilling to a barely adult Taylor Goss, and it undoubtedly cemented her notion of how rewarding such hard work could be, literally and figuratively. While the exposition ultimately suffered in its goals, as directed by the Associated Negro Press founder Claude Barnett (for whom Burroughs would steadily write and draw a modest income), in the long term it did provide a sense of a future vision as well as more immediate, tangible support to young Chicago artists like Taylor Goss, as well as raising the profile of the visual arts among the commercially driven popular arts in black Chicago. As Adam Green notes, cross-currents of black independence and self-reliance, along with corporate whitewashing of black history and uncertain alliances with state sponsorship, hindered the attendance and thus the financial success of the exposition. Yet at the same time, "as a premonition of the broad infrastructure that emerged after 1940, the American Negro Exposition anticipated much local cultural history to follow. . . . Some of its individual and institutional constituents reemerged in later years. Some faded from view, together with memories of the grand commemoration itself. But its broader ambition—that blacks rework the story of their race's presence within the modern nation—proved more resilient than did its reputation."[51] For Taylor Goss and her ACG cohorts, actively "rework[ing] the story" would prove a lifelong pursuit.

Such rewards but also struggles converged at the May 1941 dedication of the South Side Community Art Center. Alain Locke had also helped organize that effort in September 1940. The newly established Art Center board made inquiries for bringing Eleanor Roosevelt, who was perceived to have been a key force in the establishment of the FAP. With the prospect of a national media storm and crowds in the hundreds lining South Michigan Avenue, the Art Center board must have gained a heightened self-consciousness about its image as it planned its programs for the day. With this spotlight about to shine, tensions between artists, board members, and sponsors rose to the foreground. Divisions within Bronzeville at large played out. Tensions between "respectable" society and the "less savory" elements came to the forefront in true Bronzeville fashion, exposing the inextricable weave of a social fabric that depended upon a local economy of "policy," Chicago's version of the numbers lottery, as well as other illegal or unsavory enterprises, to support black businesses and cultural productions. According to Davarian L. Baldwin, "All black people shared relative positions of marginality within Chicago's socioeconomic structure, but community members drew lines of distinction around markers of refinement and, most important, respectability."[52] Even so, reformist-minded individuals such as Ida B. Wells would cross these lines at times (for instance, by supporting the policy-backed Pekin Inn, a popular black-owned nightclub), a move which Taylor Goss, a longtime admirer of the anti-lynching champion, likely noted.[53]

Burroughs recounted such tensions herself, looking back many years later. In 1991, the fiftieth anniversary of the Art Center, she retold the story of how Bronzeville's J. Levert Kelly, president of the Waiters and Bartenders association and, according to Burroughs, "a well-known gentleman around town whose activities caused him to be considered not quite in the pale of society by some people," was excluded from the banquet honoring Mrs. Roosevelt.[54] Burroughs wrote, "Mr. Kelly had the undisputable honor of being the first 'Life' member of the South Side Community Art Center. He had unhesitatingly plumped down $100! Certainly, one would

assume that the first life member would be one of the first persons to receive an invitation to the Dedication Banquet. He should have received
a seat at the Speaker's Table." But the "society ladies" who planned the
event excluded him out of fear of offending the First Lady. When Kelly
discovered his pending exclusion, he let people know he was going to attend and "that he might just break up the whole party, First Lady or no."
But Chicago police, "by some miraculous coincidence," picked up Kelly
two hours before the First Lady's arrival in town, and he was not released
until the ceremonies were completed and Roosevelt had departed.[55]

Burroughs drew a comparison between Kelly's fate and that of the
artists being shut out of speaking at the dedication ceremony. Both the
artists and Kelly had threatened to disrupt the day's events as a response
to the "society ladies" whose decisions held sway. Burroughs wrote, "Mr.
Kelly was not the only one shut out of the Dedication Ceremonies. We
artists were just about shut out as well. However, because of the fact that
(we) the artists also threatened to disrupt the proceeding, one David Ross
was granted five minutes to deliver the following statement which I had
prepared on behalf of the artist."[56] While Kelly did not succeed with his
protest, courtesy of the Chicago police, the artists did manage a modest
victory, perhaps in some recognition of their invaluable work at the Art
Center. The speech written by Taylor Goss contains often-cited passages
that illustrate her keen political consciousness about the role of art and
the community. In particular, she made a point to address stereotypes
that she likely viewed the "society" people as holding regarding art and
artists. It is worth repeating here:

> We were not then and are not now complimented by the people
> who had the romantic notion that we liked to live in garrets,
> wear "off" [quotes added] clothes and go around with emaciated
> faces, painting for fun; living until the day we died and hoping
> that our paintings would be discovered in some dusty attic fifty
> years later and then we would be famous. . . . We believed that
> the purpose of art was to record the times. As young black
> artists, we looked around and recorded in our various media
> what we saw. It was not from our imagination that we painted
> slums and ghettos, or sad, hollow-eyed black men, women, and
> children. There [sic] were the people around us.

We were part of them. They were us. Thus, the coming of this
Community Art Center has opened up new hope and vistas to
all of us.[57]

Despite these tensions, the inauguration of the Art Center was considered an enormous success and still stands as a significant milestone
in local African American history. Its first year of operations was, according to Burroughs, an "auspicious start," with twenty-five exhibitions
seen by twenty-eight thousand visitors, along with twelve thousand children and adults attending art classes.[58] The Art Center continued to be a
place where everyone from Bronzeville and beyond, rich or poor, white or
black, of various ethnicities and political persuasions, could meet, mingle,
and come together for the sake of community. As the famed photographer
and Art Center artist Gordon Parks remembered, "It seemed that half of
Chicago was there [for his 1941 exhibit]. The elite, dressed in their furs
and finery, rubbed elbows with some of the people I had photographed in
the poor quarter; I had invited as many of them as I could find."[59]

The establishment of the Art Center marked a turning point in Taylor
Goss's life and work. Her commitments to and visions of what in 1941
she called, echoing the CPUSA's Popular Front campaign, a "defense of
culture," had borne much fruit. This accomplishment drove home to her
just how powerfully the actions of a relative few could influence a greater
population. At the young age of twenty-one, Taylor Goss was already
launched not only as an artist but also as a key organizer for a major arts
institution. When singling out Burroughs as a figure of great achievement,
it is just as important to understand how her accomplishments were intertwined with her organizing and collective efforts. Without this important
social and historical context, it is far too easy to view her story as a heroic
overcoming of odds by her own efforts alone, as with the Horatio Alger
myth. Burroughs was simultaneously singularly talented *and* a part of a
larger cultural development, namely the remaking of black identity in
the urban North. She was one of thousands not only in Chicago but
across the country who took the idea of the "New Negro" to heart, and
in doing so demonstrated that African Americans possessed the agency
and imagination to develop identities that they themselves could shape.
For Burroughs, being a leading force in this shaping of identity would
continue to present both opportunities and challenges in the years ahead.

THREE

CROSSING INTO WAR

No matter how long or how far Dr. B and I continued to walk in the humid August heat, we did not go unrecognized for more than brief moments. The litany of gratitude and praise surrounded us in a cloud of hero worship that I had never before experienced. As Dr. B and I approached the next historical landmark, I began to see her with newly appreciative eyes, wondering what it would be like to be beloved by so many for the impact one had on others' lives.

Growing up in the south suburbs of the city, far away from the daily lives of the famous, wealthy, and powerful, I had had little firsthand contact with individuals of any public stature. Even into my adult life, the only times I crossed paths with any notables were in fleeting glimpses at O'Hare Airport or, in New York, on the streets of Greenwich Village, gawking at some remove at the appearance, gestures, and expressions of well-known faces. Chicago as a rule has always struck me as less a paparazzi stakeout and more a get-your-hands-dirty-and-rise-through-your-work sort of place than other major cities. Even now, when I frequent Chicago's downtown and its close-by neighborhoods, the last thought I have is whether I might run into Oprah or (these days) Jennifer Hudson, Rahm Emmanuel, or the Obamas. Chicago is the kind of place where the well-known can easily disappear, whether because the harsh weather discourages much strolling about or because, like me, few really expect to spot any "names" without going to great lengths to find them.

So to have witnessed these endless expressions of gratitude, which continue even beyond Dr. B's passing in 2010, remains a true marvel. For instance, in fall 2014, as I walked back to my table near the hotel breakfast buffet in Ann Arbor, Michigan, a couple stopped me to inquire about the T-shirt I was wearing, emblazoned with Dr. B's image and the DuSable

Museum's logo. Once they knew I was writing about Dr. B, they invited me to pull up a chair and listen to their Dr. B stories. Another such incident had occurred earlier that year at Soul Veg restaurant on South Indiana Avenue on Chicago's South Side. Accompanying Dr. B's longtime friend, the prison minister Queen Mother Helen Sinclair, for her weekly luncheon, I discovered that many patrons had a story to tell about Dr. B, who was also Queen Mother's companion on weekly trips to the Stateville and Joliet prisons. One enthusiast even handed me his cell phone at one point, urging me to talk to his sister in Jacksonville, Florida, for her recollections of that teacher who wore a "natural" at a time when such styles marked one as "crazy."

Dr. B continued to accept the recognition on our walk with smiles and nodding head, pausing only briefly before moving forward. Maybe it was the intensely humid, sun-drenched heat that spurred her on, but more likely she was determined to fulfill our mission of visiting local landmarks, including those housing her own historical heroes. She led me across the refurbished walkways and green spaces of Wendell Phillips High School, an institution which, founded in 1904, had survived even longer than she had. It was the first predominantly African American high school in the city and carries that legacy even today. Its graduates include notables such as Nat King Cole, Margaret's own friend and "fellow traveler" Timuel Black, Dinah Washington, and the founder of Johnson Publishing, John H. Johnson.[1] Another icon, Alfreda Duster, daughter of the anti-lynching advocate Ida B. Wells, was also a graduate, as well as a friend of Dr. B. As always, Dr. B's focus remained on historical education. Heroes mattered little without understanding their impact on the lives of others.

Clearly those who stopped and greeted Dr. B that day knew her as a teacher, a neighbor, and, to a lesser degree, as someone who had done a lot for folks on the South Side. But as her grandson Eric Toller observed, many in the neighborhood, including her students, did not know her work as an artist and activist, work that placed her not only on a national but an international stage. To most of them she was just Dr. Burroughs, emblazoned primarily in the memories of her DuSable High School students as that teacher who had worn a natural and taught them to take pride in their unique histories as African Americans. She did not do much to alter these impressions, since she was less concerned that people know her work than that they should know the leaders of African

American history. For example, her conversations during our Bronzeville tour always focused on whoever greeted her; self-promotion was simply not something she embraced. At the same time, the numerous published and videotaped interviews with Dr. B over the years attest to how much it mattered to her that she provide a positive role model and source of inspiration for others. Furthermore, she was deeply concerned and motivated to document and preserve her generation's legacies for younger people in years to come.

Some blocks later as we continued on Pershing Avenue and then up to Thirty-Seventh Street, we arrived at a cluster of four-story brick row houses. A sign in the lawn announced the "Ida B. Wells Garden Apartments."[2] I found myself suddenly glancing around, breath quickened, mind alert. The name on the sign registered as one of those I distantly remembered hearing on the local news as one of the public-housing "projects," and "projects" were, in my white-flight suburban understanding, never a good place to be. Yet, as I continued to take in the scene, the ordinariness of it had a calming effect—the grass was trimmed; laundry was hung and drying; kids' toys were scattered here and there. Dr. B noted how these homes, when first constructed in 1939, were much sought-after places with vibrant, active communities. And of course, a public-housing project being named after the anti-lynching activist and journalist Ida B. Wells was no small feat in 1939, in this city of heated political and racial struggle.

This was not a stop on the tour that I had anticipated and, in hindsight, I'm not sure I would have chosen it, given the haunting, even horrific images of public housing I carried from my childhood. But seeing the place firsthand, I was able to readily imagine how, once upon a time, this had been a beacon and refuge for so many African Americans who were otherwise steered by housing covenants and widespread racism into low-quality housing. This allowed me to perceive how "those people" in housing projects lived everyday lives, wanting many of the same things I wanted, namely a safe and comfortable place to call home. These sturdy, well-designed townhomes were a far cry from the more notorious high-rise projects that sprang up along the Dan Ryan Expressway during my childhood and that gave rise to even more menacing media images: children falling out of unsecured windows; broken elevators; hallways littered with broken glass. The Ida B. Wells "gardens" in their prime looked like a place I could have imagined living. In addition to affordable, well-constructed and maintained buildings, many social services, cultural events, and educational opportunities were available on the premises. A newspaper, *Community News*, was published by and for the tenants of "Wellstown." Teenage girls were crowned queens of Wellstown, while young children formed bands in music classes taught there. Classes in radio operation were among the wide variety of on-site offerings. A youth government elected its own mayor. A nursery provided day care, while a hospital offered residents much-needed medical care.[3] Far from the images I had grown up with regarding public housing projects, the Ida B. Wells apartments provided much more than subsistence living; in fact, the place supported a standard of living that my own South Side ancestors likely would have found enviable.

Seeing this place firsthand only reinforced Dr. B's insistence on truth coming from experience: "Find out for yourself," she liked to say about countries such as Cuba and the Soviet Union that carried less-than-stellar reputations as communist strongholds. She, of course, had very different stories to tell stemming from her own educational tours of those and dozens of other countries around the world. But that's what she was about—finding out the truth for oneself, never mind what the so-called "mainstream" had to say, whether fellow African Americans or white-dominated culture.

"Where next?" she asked.

It was only a few blocks more to Thirty-Sixth Street and King Drive, where we reached the home of Ida B. Wells-Barnett. Unlike the Ida B. Wells apartments, this was a scheduled stop on my tour, an official Chicago architectural landmark as well as a source of Bronzeville pride. I was gratified to see a city historical sign marking the house from the curbside. Such markers existed all along King Drive, all part of a push to maintain Bronzeville's identity in the face of a two-fisted opponent—empty lots and wealthy developers eager to extend the ongoing South Loop gentrification into the heart of the South Side. Dr. B had earlier commented on the newly built police station at Thirty-Fifth Street and Michigan Avenue as a bellwether of things to come; the police, she asserted, were not there to protect the current residents as much as those future ones with expensive new investments.

The Wells home itself, built in 1895, on what was then known as Grand Avenue, exuded the solidity and grandeur of similar castle-like row homes on the block, built during a blossoming of white wealth and business that generated an early Gold Coast environment. King Drive's broad boulevard still possessed a parklike atmosphere despite signs of decay all around. Dr. B's own home a few blocks away on Thirty-Eighth Street and Michigan held an even greater majesty as a larger residence on a grander lot. However, the pervasiveness of vacant lots close by under-mined the area's sense of permanence. Ida B. Wells's home, however, was still protected by existing, mostly well-maintained structures all around. At one point in its transition, the neighborhood may originally have em-braced some racial integration. But as Alfreda Duster, daughter of Ida, noted, hers was one of the first African American families to move east of State Street in the early 1900s; the first African American family to live at 3624 was that of the renowned actor Richard B. Harrison.[4] According to Duster, the white woman who owned the home at that time sought "retaliation" against her neighbors for various grievances by placing the Harrison family in that home. Once Ida learned of the availability of this property, she quickly made an offer for the "three-story, fourteen-room house [with] four baths, Italian marble, sink and all for $8,000."[5] The family lived in this roomy dwelling until 1929; Alfreda attended Wendell Phillips High School and later the University of Chicago.

In my south suburban neighborhood, structures built prior to the 1950s, when my parents and so many other young white couples left the city limits for former cornfields and prairies where they built their middle-class dreams, were rare. I took for granted the new construction, the white neighbors with ethnic surnames like Sokolowski, Strezo, Spell-man, Vogel, Garvey, and Sadler, and the vegetation-covered vacant lots we called "prairies." However, as I grew older and began to look around, along with my architecturally obsessed older brother, I started to develop a fierce old house envy, as in "Why couldn't we live in one of those big, roomy, wood-paneled nineteenth-century mansions?" not understanding, of course, the circumstances around why such places were sold off for a pittance and left their burdened owners to take in boarders in order to make ends meet.

Having developed a keen curatorial sense of the importance not only of historical fact but also the physical landmarks of history, Dr. B had the foresight to ensure that her own home at 3806 S. Michigan became a historic landmark, never to be torn down. Similarly, the South Side Com-munity Art Center, just across the street, was also designated a landmark. In contrast, I came of age in a sea of open space, not from demolitions of past dwellings but from the imposition of sprawling suburban tracts upon farm and prairie. History didn't seem to matter because my historical imagination posited that these flat expanses were a blank slate just waiting for people like my family to place their footprints upon it.

For Ida B. Wells and her family, however, their residence in a neighborhood not previously welcoming to her people was a matter of exerting leadership. She drilled one important hole in the larger dam that kept African Americans from escaping slumlord extortion and social ostracism south of downtown's Loop, a role that in our current times can be hard to fathom, since it was so full of daring and resolve, as was all of her life, which she spent speaking out against lynching and other injustices.

Dr. B stood quietly while I snapped a few photos. Even as I found myself bonding with my extraordinary companion over our shared interests in historic preservation, a part of me wondered what good it would do to preserve and curate this place if Bronzeville continued its decline. What difference did a single home, statue, boulevard, business, church, school, or community center make? Weren't memory, books, and relationships more important? Why put such resources into preserving a physical past that current generations of young people seemed to neither know nor care about?

As Omowale Ketu Oladuwa, a community leader in Fort Wayne, Indiana, has noted, the legacy of slavery put a premium on land ownership for African American families after the Civil War.[6] But even beyond that deep desire for one's own place, Dr. B understood the embodiment of history in its material guises. Certainly, as an artist she appreciated the importance of curating housing and other physical artifacts that convey expression as well as experience. Furthermore, in an interview with the historian John E. Fleming, she noted the importance of having "a living monument" to a Chicago founder, the black fur trader and Haitian immigrant Jean Baptiste Point Du Sable, through the museum she and her second husband would go on to found in their home.[7] As a teacher, she understood what it meant to bring history alive to students by providing a direct experience of an otherwise abstract past. And in their apparent permanence, such items represented a communal value and investment in specific people, places, and ideals. A Bronzeville school was named after Ida; in 2011, a campaign began to place a statue of her on the grounds of the housing project named after her. Such efforts might seem small and scattered, and even at times dwarfed by the building of big-box stores and the persistence of gaping, empty lots on the South Side, but they speak to a determination within and around the community to hang on to the legacies that help define the present, holding out hope for making the unimaginable once more possible.

As we moved on, Dr. B disclosed that she had had the honor and pleasure of reading some of Wells's journals, courtesy of her daughter, Alfreda. She described what an inspiration Ida had been and still was. Copies of Dr. B's linoleum print of Wells circulated widely, even into the hands of her Stateville prison "boys."

Even as evidence of Bronzeville's efforts to secure its accomplished past unfolded while we continued our walk up King Drive, threats to that legacy were disturbingly visible. I wondered how many young people, black, white, or any other color, knew of the enormous intelligence, willpower, and courage of Ida B. Wells and her impact on their own lives.

We moved steadily north in the hot afternoon sun, and as Dr. B continued to greet well-wishers and comment on community history through such landmarks, I felt the heat of my doubts being cooled by her large presence long enough to imagine how relics of the past, at that moment so visibly fading from memory and from view, could readily be revived. It could happen. Dr. B had faced as bad, if not worse, odds in her long, productive life.

My walk with Dr. B that afternoon was wrapped in the presence of Ida B. Wells-Barnett and her daughter, Alfreda. My fears of "the projects" faded in the recollection of a thriving, well-planned community that, although originally planned to maintain a segregated "separate but equal" housing site on the South Side of Chicago, turned out to be a "route to success" for hundreds of African Americans, many of whom found some semblance of a promised land after struggling under Jim Crow in the South. Dr. B became a living, breathing connection to the namesake of this housing as she recalled her long friendship with Alfreda, who had also lived close by in Bronzeville, and described reading her mother's diaries. No doubt those diaries were an absorbing read. Ida and her family's home had been preserved and prominently marked with street signs and historical plaques guiding visitors from around the world to a place where they could remember, dream, and imagine what had been, as well as what might still be. Without such places or people to inspire, guide, and even challenge us, how can we, in fact, carry on with meaning, purpose, and connection—to ourselves, to others, and to the earth?

Through the founding of the South Side Community Art Center, Margaret Taylor Goss learned how a relatively small group of organized, determined, and visible people could have an immense impact on their community and beyond. She also learned the value of having a dedicated space in which to meet. Her lessons earlier in life had solidified her commitments to organize with others in the pursuit of art and social justice. Although first and foremost an artist, Burroughs recognized early on that her own sense of identity and self-worth depended upon a fuller historical understanding than the one currently presented to her in a white-dominated world. She also grasped even more firmly the merits of interracial unity as a powerful force for social change. Her early experiences with supportive white female teachers had laid the groundwork for her to recognize the opportunities inherent in the Popular Front launched in the 1930s by the Communist Party, which, in an effort to expand its rapidly growing base, had reached out to African Americans nationwide but had found an especially eager audience in Chicago. Burroughs also found "fellow travelers" in older white artists such as Si Gordon, who gave her a book about Harriet Tubman.[8] Burroughs would later produce a linocut of Tubman after studying that printmaking medium in Mexico with pupils of the artists Leopoldo Mendéz and Diego Rivera. Burroughs's race philosophy developed, in part, because of the frequent and intense interactions between artists, writers, laborers, organizers, and intellectuals fostered by the Communist Party's Popular Front. And in addition to the Popular Front, there were the broader cross-currents of promoting racial pride by other "race women," including Ida B. Wells, that surely caught up Taylor Goss in their flow. And finally, there was the shift of economics toward local, black-driven enterprises that opened up more humane workplace opportunities outside of the grueling industrial and domestic service spheres, and which paved the way for Burroughs to find popular purchase in creating and teaching the fine arts.

This broad cross-section of individuals and groups was, in the mid-1930s, sought out by the Communist Party to join together around issues of mutual importance, particularly those around work and jobs, but also basic human rights. The parallel Negro People's Front also drew from this exchange. As Bill Mullen observed, the use of Popular Front rhetoric by individuals such as the prominent scholar Alain Locke "also echoed both the Left's post-1936 cultural front policy and [party leaders such as] James Ford's recurring references to black cultural workers as the vanguard of the 'democratic front.'"[9] At the same time, white artists began to seek out black artists who were growing increasingly more visible and respected as the "vanguard" of the cultural front: "Through the creation of the South Side Community Art Center, the Negro Exposition, and follow-up shows at the Library of Congress and Howard University, Chicago became the vibrant center of African American culture."[10]

Although Burroughs, like her role model, Paul Robeson, never actually joined the Communist Party, she too fell in with these popular fronts, fusing her artistic pursuits with political ones, accepting the roles of blacks in joining with other identity groups to forge a new democratic experience for those oppressed by race and class. For Robeson and for her, there was no separation between art and politics: "[Robeson] perceived art as such a direct instrument of revolutionary change that any dichotomy between the cultural and political would be meaningless and false before his system of thought."[11]

Once Margaret Taylor's eyes had been opened at age seventeen to a strong, positive image of black identity in the figure of the world-renowned actor-singer-activist, she vowed throughout her life to follow in his footsteps. An uncle had brought her to a concert and afterward a reception where she met this electrifying man face to face.[12] Even in high school, Taylor, drawing from Robeson's life and words, had challenged the negative views of the Soviet Union put forth by her social science teacher at the time. As she recounted in her autobiography:

> "They don't have Jim Crow in the Soviet Union like we do here," I declared.
> She asked, "And how do you know? You've never been there."
> "Paul Robeson said so!" I said. "He's been there and furthermore, he left his son there to go to school so he would get a good education."[13]

Beyond Margaret's early role models in white art teachers such as Mary Ryan and Kathleen Blackshear, along with white immigrant artist-teachers such as Morris Topchevsky and Si Gordon, Robeson's example of interracial, interethnic, and interclass unity was even more profound. And when he was vilified for his communist sympathies and his support of the Soviet Union, Burroughs, steadfast in her support, faced the challenge of her life; she had to decide whether to stick with her ideals and Robeson or abandon him and otherwise silence herself. As a result, the lessons of legacy–passing on the knowledge and values of who and what has come before–were deeply etched in her by midlife. She seldom, if ever, seemed to doubt her commitments or question whether she should stand up for herself; it was simply a matter of how to survive the pressures she was placed under and continue with her work.

Taylor also found much support and solidarity leading up to her work at the Art Center with friends and fellow artists such as her high school companion and fellow Art Crafts Guild member Charles White, who was also an enthusiastic Robeson supporter, and later, Elizabeth Catlett. Taylor and White supported each other's infusion of progressive politics into their artistic pursuits. Both were involved in the National Negro Congress, a labor-oriented group that included artists among its participants, joining forces with union organizers who later helped establish the Chicago Artists Union. These activities cemented Taylor's and White's commitments to art as the means to establish a democratic space for expression, organization, and action, first at the Abraham Lincoln Center and later at the Art Center itself.[14]

With the establishment of the Art Center, long-held aspirations to create space to bring together art and activism, along with a historical perspective on race and class, took shape rapidly and intensely. According to Erik Gellman, "In its first year, the art center staff organized two-dozen exhibitions, which twenty-eight thousand people saw, and enrolled twelve thousand members of the community in classes." The center also hosted many political events, including a 1941 "folk party" sponsored by the National Negro Congress to raise money for its civil rights work.[15]

The significant cultural and artistic impact that the Art Center exerted was not lost on Burroughs; her career, like many of her contemporaries, took wing during this period. The 1940 American Negro Exposition, headed by Alain Locke, the opening of the Art Center, and follow-up exhibitions brought awards, recognition, and a wider audience to Burroughs as an artist. Many writers and artists who gathered at the Art Center for classes and to teach went on to prominent careers, including Burroughs's childhood friend Gwendolyn Brooks, whose poetry blossomed under the tutelage of a white Gold Coast resident and the manuscript reviewer of *Poetry* magazine, Inez Cunningham Starks, who was also an Art Center instructor. The award-winning photographer Gordon Parks set up a studio in the Art Center. Burroughs's own writing, after she discovered in her Art Center classes that it was not suitable for formalist verse, strengthened under the tutelage of the Cleveland Hall librarian Charlemae Rollins, from whom she eventually took a class at Roosevelt University.[16] Burroughs went on to publish *Jasper the Drumming Boy* with the New York publisher Viking, along with other books. She also began writing columns and articles for various black-oriented periodicals. And of course, her art, influenced as it was by cross-cultural artists such as Topchevsky, who had introduced her to contemporary Mexican art, found ready acceptance across a wide variety of groups. Timuel Black remembered how he and other non-artists, including those in the labor movement, had developed an appreciation for artistic production because of the fertile conversations and contacts that the Popular Front and Negro People's Front had helped facilitate. This legacy of learning and teaching, gathering knowledge with respected teachers and then immediately turning around and passing it on, shaped Burroughs's entire life, along with those illustrious others with whom she shared the Art Center experience.

For the few years that the Works Progress Administration funded the Art Center, the amount and quality of participation—both in exhibitions and classes—were profound. An explicit interracial aim in its mission statement guaranteed that the Art Center would not be isolated within the black community, but instead would gain purchase across diverse city neighborhoods and beyond. Perhaps it was this sort of border-crossing that helped Taylor Goss and the other artists maintain a certain momentum even after the Japanese bombing of Pearl Harbor in 1941, when many artists left Chicago for either the battlefield or other, more career-oriented or politically sheltered locations.

Just before and during America's involvement in World War II, Margaret Taylor's life went through significant changes and upheavals even as her artistic career took hold. She and fellow artist Bernard Goss met in the late 1930s, brought together by art and eventually the push to found the Art Center. Burroughs described meeting Goss: "It was during one of those Saturday night 'house rent' parties that we artists often gave to raise much-needed revenue. The parties allowed us to promote our work and to network with other artists in the city."[17] At the time, Taylor was still taking classes at the Chicago Normal School, and she was intent on becoming an art teacher. Goss was from out of town, a native of Kansas City and a newly minted graduate of the University of Iowa. He had come to Chicago as part of the WPA, and was as handsome a man as Taylor had ever seen. She was smitten; she thought of him as a "Greek god."[18] Even the disapproval of her mentor, Mary Ryan, did not deter her from marrying this "god" in 1939. When the couple moved into 4342 S. Grand Boulevard (now King Drive), Taylor Goss's open house proclivities continued: "There were many poems and plays and lesson plans written on the dining room table of the coach house [by others]."[19]

Despite working long hours at mostly low-paying jobs, artists gathered on a regular basis for lively parties and incisive conversations. As Gwendolyn Brooks recounted in her autobiography, *Report from Part One*, every weekend gave way to a plethora of parties, both elaborate and modest, but always invigorating in the quality of talk as well as the cross-section of people who attended. The wealthy Evelyn Ganns bought a three-story house at Forty-Second Street and Drexel Avenue, a pioneering move into an otherwise white neighborhood, and set out bountiful buffets for her guests. The Gosses held a perpetual "open house" in their carriage house apartment. As Brooks described it:

> Three people would "fall in." Then three more. Before evening
> deepened there might be twelve. There would be your "party."
> You might meet *any Pers*onality [*sic*] there, white or black. You
> might meet Paul Robeson. You might meet Peter Pollack. On
> any night you might meet Frank Marshall Davis, the poet, Rob-
> ert A. Davis, the actor, artists Eldzier Cortor, Hughie Lee-Smith,
> Charles White, Elizabeth Catlett, sculptor Marion Perkins . . . ;
> once every couple of years you might get lucky enough to
> run into [the poet] Margaret Walker. Many of the painters
> were as familiar as the cushions in the place. Margaret, unlike
> Evelyn, did *not* spend huge sums on her parties. . . . The talk
> was fantastic—and it might survive not only the dawning, but
> next day's breakfast and lunch. In Margaret's barn apartment
> sculpture, rich fabrics, books, paintings and paint addressed you
> everywhere. Margaret, then a rebel, *lived up from the root.*[20]

Such a vigorous and lively social life had been part of Taylor's experience even as a young child, when she recalled entertaining guests at her uncle's bathtub gin parties and sharing living spaces with her extended family. Later the members of the Art Crafts Guild would meet regularly at each other's homes to paint, exhibit, and socialize, seamlessly weaving their works and lives together. Of course, necessity was the mother of this particular invention, given that African American artists were largely confined to Bronzeville and other South Side neighborhoods and had few options for gathering together in a public way. The Art Center, of course, continued this tradition as well. Burroughs had learned early on that being an artist, especially one of color, meant that the primary spaces for sharing work with fellow artists would necessarily be in one's own dwelling.

Even after Margaret Taylor married Bernard Goss and settled into a modest carriage house described by the art critic Willard Motley as "a barn of a place," the parties continued. Motley went on to describe just how humble yet vibrant a space the Gosses occupied: "a rude, hand-fashioned fireplace with its stove-pipe chimney and a large coal-burning kitchen stove cannot warm them all in winter. The water is fetched in a pail, the dishes are washed in a clothes-tub. But the studio, a large room, blends the artistic, the Bohemian, and the economic charmingly."[21] Later, when the divorced Taylor Goss met and subsequently married Charles Burroughs in 1949, another carriage house barn, and subsequently the main house on South Michigan Avenue, provided decades of similarly fluid "parties" and open houses. Such invitations clearly boosted the cultural scene among artists and their audiences in immeasurable ways. Bronzeville thus developed a distinct sense of itself as a community. Burroughs spent her entire life learning how such community-building took place on a grassroots level.

But as the Great Depression gave way to World War II, Art Center activists very quickly found themselves on the defensive to justify the center's existence. Conservative forces challenged arts funding nationwide and, by 1942, had all but suspended it. Indeed, not only did the Art Center receive challenges to its artists' liberal, even radical, agenda; it also shifted its focus to the war effort and its implications for the black citizens who were taking up arms for the nation's cause.

Before 1941, African Americans across the country had taken up many differing, sometimes conflicting positions regarding the war as it developed in Europe and the Pacific Rim. Robeson's questioning of U.S. involvement in a war that, in 1939, did not seem to provide any benefit for Africans and other ethnic and racial groups oppressed by Western colonial powers, reflected black nationalists' positions that this was not a war by or for blacks:

> A Western triumph in a subsequent conflict with the Soviet
> Union would, in Robeson's opinion, mean the continuing
> domination of a colonial spirit scornful of Asians and Africans
> and devoted to maintaining oppressive foreign control over
> their countries. He could see no reason, therefore, for blacks
> anywhere, or for the United States as a nation, to take part in
> a dispute that was lining up fascist versus communist.[22]

Robeson's experiences traveling the globe lent greater credibility to his perspectives for many blacks, including Taylor Goss.

But as Nazi Germany overran much of Europe from 1938 on, Robeson and those whom he supported on the radical Left began to come under fire for their critique of imperialism and that critique's apparent threat to "freedom" in Western capitalist economies. Robeson continued to support the National Negro Congress even as that organization started to divide between those who wanted to work with the Roosevelt administration on issues such as anti-lynching legislation and those who took a stand against American entry into the war and favored union-based approaches such as those of the CIO to address problems of injustice and racism.[23] By 1940, Robeson and the progressive wing of the National Negro Congress were calling for American blacks to focus their energies not on the "struggle between rival imperialist powers" but instead on "the struggle for rights within the United States."[24] Taylor Goss heard this call loud and clear.

Ironically, it was the Popular and Negro People's Fronts' focus on racial unity that, after the U.S. entry into the war in 1941, became a divisive weapon wielded by conservatives who were determined to stamp out any whiff of "communistic" aims, as well as any tears in the supposed fabric of national unity. Paul Robeson's sympathy for the Soviet Union, along with his personal interest in scores of cultural, ethnic, racial, and labor groups, positioned him as a lightning rod for a growing Red Scare. Taylor Goss's support of Robeson would put her on an eventual collision course with her beloved Art Center.

Taylor Goss and other Art Center artist-founders discovered that the war effort quickly began to limit their more radical positions. Peter Pollack, head of the Illinois Art Project, took a decidedly patriotic turn during the struggle to maintain funding for the Art Center: "Before leaving for the army, Pollack, in an attempt to sustain the [Art Center], pitched the center as important to African American morale and convinced the WPA and later Office of Civil Defense (OCD) to fund the production of war-related art."[25] This turn led some of the artists to produce war propaganda for the government in exchange for funding. Taylor Goss instead followed Robeson and the NNC's progressive wing's lead and focused her efforts on civil rights for blacks serving in the military. As Burroughs recounted, when she began to write a newsletter called *Life with Margaret* for her many friends in the military, their responses included many hair-raising stories of racial discrimination within the ranks.[26] In response, she began to write numerous articles and editorials, as well as a column for the *Chicago Defender*, the Associated Negro Press, and other publications such as *Freedomways*, *Negro Digest*, *Opportunity*, and *Negro Story*. The illustrious writer Frank Marshall Davis invited her to write for his Associated Negro Press column.[27] Thus, Taylor Goss vigorously pursued Robeson's insistence on civil rights at home even as the American war effort geared up. The hypocrisy of U.S. acceptance of blatant racial discrimination on its own soil while at the same time requiring its black citizens to fight for freedom abroad was not lost on Taylor Goss and many of her fellow artists.

Despite the increasingly conservative chill, Taylor Goss and her fellow artists' progressive political efforts continued, expanding rapidly across the community as well as across color, class, and geographical lines, with effects in the community that were widespread and profound: "In the same period of cultural and financial retrenchment at the Art Center, its most progressive vanguard . . . began to reinstitute ties with other South Side institutions similarly situated."[28] By 1944, the Art Center and the Abraham Lincoln Center had established the only "free spaces" in the city for "interracial cultural expression in that year."[29] As Mullen noted, "The symbiotic relationship of the Lincoln School and the Art Center was in 1944 definitive, if belated, evidence of the fluid rapprochement of radical political thought and black cultural production the 1936 opening of Chicago's Negro People's Front had aspired to."[30] This relationship culminated in an "Interracial South Side Cultural Conference" that explored "The Present Day Problems of South Side Poets, Writers, Painters, Sculptors, Dancers, Singers, Musicians, Actors, Entertainers, and Playwrights."[31] Taylor Goss served on the organizing committee.

The cultural and civil rights fronts during World War II were not the first "fronts" that Taylor Goss had entered as her commitments to art as politics found an ever-widening audience and mission. But they did have an immediate and profound impact on her relationship with her beloved Art Center, as would her affiliations with left-wing activists and artists such as Paul Robeson and, later, her second husband, Charles Burroughs. As the war continued, the divisions at the Art Center between the monied, middle- and upper-class patrons and the artists and their followers deepened as funds for the Art Center disappeared with the curtailment of the FAP. The artists continued to push for hosting progressive political events, providing a platform for left-wing artists, and generally maintaining an equal say in the operations of the Art Center. The more conservative elements at the Art Center grew increasingly wary of these "radical" moves, distancing themselves from them and even at times denouncing them. But because of the efforts of a core group of women spearheaded by Pauline Kigh Reed and Fern Gayden, class divisions were at least in part mended and, after funding dried up, these remarkable women formed a "Committee of 100 Women" and rolled up their sleeves to make sure the Art Center's doors stayed open.[32] Burroughs was one of these women. The writer Fern Gayden paid for heating and electric bills for the Art Center out of her own pocket.[33]

Along with the collapse of the WPA's funding for the Federal Art Project in 1943, including support for the South Side Community Art Center, Taylor Goss's personal life took similarly challenging turns. Her priorities as an artist had been forced to shift with her first marriage in 1939 and her subsequent motherhood. Marriage and motherhood meant that she had to scale back on her artistic production, but she found new outlets for creative expression, particularly as a writer, which, unlike much of her art, could help pay the bills.

No doubt becoming a single mother was the last thing Taylor Goss expected from her union with Bernard Goss. She had married this fellow Art Center founder and painter in 1939, but not long after their vows, the union began to struggle. As she recalled, "Bernard and I began to have problems almost immediately. We were young, and we hadn't thought about the fact that as artists, we wouldn't have a reliable income between us. . . . Bernard quickly made it clear that he would not give up his full-time devotion to painting, so it had to be me putting the art aside in exchange for a steady salary."[34] Thus, Taylor Goss went to work as a substitute teacher in the Chicago public schools. Shortly thereafter, she became pregnant with their daughter, Gayle.

Burroughs recounted in a tongue-in-cheek "fictional" account entitled "My First Husband & His Four Wives" (self-published in booklet form after Bernard's death in 1965) how she arrived home one day to find Bernard ("Leonardo") in bed with "my best friend and high school chum [Mildred]," to whom she had offered a room rental in their carriage-house apartment to help make ends meet. At that moment Margaret encountered perhaps her most difficult challenge to date: leaving Bernard and moving in with her widowed mother to face single motherhood and the pressure to improve her economic status for the sake of her child.

In the process, Margaret learned how to redirect her creative energies into securing stable work and income while at the same time maintaining a public presence as an artist, arts educator, and activist-organizer, as she would do for the rest of her life. Before her marriage to Goss, she had attended Chicago Normal College (now Chicago State University) for a three-year certificate in art education. However, as she explained, that credential had distinct limitations: "After three years you got a certificate, and some people could go right into teaching, but at that time there were long waiting lists. There were five hundred students there, out of whom there were ten Blacks. Most of the white girls were able to go on to the University of Chicago and get their degrees. Most of the black students couldn't, so they started a course which they called 'cadet teaching,' which meant that you went out and taught under a master teacher."[35]

After returning to work under her former elementary teacher, Mary Ryan, Taylor Goss was qualified to substitute teach. But to teach full-time would require a final year of bachelor's-level work. Had her marriage with Goss not begun to fall apart after barely a year, only to divorce in 1947 after years of estrangement, Margaret might not have had to work roughly six more years, taking classes part-time at the Art Institute of Chicago, before she could qualify for full-time teaching. She would continue to press on in her education, likely fulfilling not only her economic but also creative and intellectual needs, and completing a master's degree in arts education at the Art Institute of Chicago in 1948.

Until her marriage to Charles Burroughs in 1949, Taylor Goss shoul-
dered very weighty responsibilities mostly alone, utilizing every creative
fiber in her being not only to find a way to stick with her artistic program,
but even more importantly, to carry on with her life. In addition, the emotional burdens that Bernard's betrayal had placed upon her were enormous, burdens that this young wife and new mother struggled beneath.
Burroughs recounted in somber tones: "During Rosalind's [Gayle's] first
year, I was a most miserable human being. Often, in my loneliness, I
would dress Rosalind up in a pretty dress. Blue was her favorite color and
we would ride the 'El' back and forth from Sixty-Third Street and Stony
Island Avenue to the end of the line at Howard Street north. Several times
I felt so low that only my strong will power prevented me from going over
to the lake and jumping in, me, Rosalind and all. Now that really would
have been a waste."[36]

During the war years, even as Taylor Goss struggled, she continued
to join up with other artists and intellectuals in various causes and find
voice in her art and her publications. But clearly she still keenly felt the
challenges of balancing her home, art, work, and community life. In a
poem written to her daughter Gayle, "Apology to My Little Daughter for
Apparent Neglect," Burroughs reflected on the choices she made:

> My little one, when I am away from you
> Believe me I've been busy, not playing bridge
> Or sipping tea or gossip mongering
> I've been busy thinking and doing and working just for you.
>
> For you, I lift my voice too long with the
> Multi-many others black and white in this
> Constant cry against oppression.
>
> For you, in rain or snow, in sleet or fog
> I walk determinedly on the picket line of life
> Demanding bread, demanding jobs and homes,
> Protesting war, beseeching peace.
>
> For you I proudly bear these bruises
> Lashed upon me by the relentless whips
> Of the opposers of the people's progress.

In this regard, Taylor Goss was very much a woman *of* her time but also *before* her time, since she never shrank from maintaining a commitment to social justice as part of, rather than in spite of, her duties as a mother. She found ways to, if not seamlessly or perfectly, then humanly, weave together a life of art, justice, and politics along with family and home life. At the time this far surpassed the efforts of many other women in her immediate social sphere, and she was as vulnerable as any of them to questions regarding her morals and values. As the poem continues, she states an unshakable will to pursue what she believes is right:

> For you in face of all, I'll stand my ground,
> I'll make no confusion twixt wrong and right,
> Twixt those few who have and all who haven't
> I'll stand my ground, I won't turn back.
>
> For you I give of mind, of body, of self, of thought, of life,
> To create for you a better world.
> So, my little one and all children,
> When I am away from you,
> Believe me, I've been busy, not playing bridge.[37]

It appears that just as Taylor Goss's artistic career began to take off, and her educational opportunities, most notably to study for a master's degree at the Art Institute of Chicago, opened up, her personal life became more challenging. But clearly this did not deter her from producing art and writing that maintained and deepened her work for social change. If anything, having a child perhaps motivated her even more. But the "bruises" still came.

During the war, Taylor Goss and other "fellow travelers" continued their work with the National Negro Congress, even as the divisions that would eventually dissolve the organization mounted. Taylor Goss and other NNC activists concurrently began a drive to educate African American children about their history, forming in 1945 the National Negro Museum and Historical Foundation (NNMHF).[38] This cultural front—to educate blacks about their own unique history—found a footing during the war as a more viable approach to resisting white supremacy at a time when the national agenda was to tamp down any resistance to fighting the war against fascism. At the same time, as Erin P. Cohn observes, this drive for historical awareness "did not emerge in a vacuum. . . . American culture in the 1930s was marked by a collective obsession with finding a 'usable past' that would offer solace and hope in the face of a crippling economic depression."[39] Cohn cites the development of Colonial Williamsburg and the National Archives as examples of projects that "actively engaged in national identity-building through historical preservation and interpretation."[40] Thus, the NNMHF's efforts coincided with other, national trends.

However, developing African Americans' historical awareness and resources was also an effort that reached back to the historian Carter G. Woodson in Chicago in 1915, when he had founded the Association for the Study of Negro Life and History.[41] Taylor Goss, a frequent visitor to the Cleveland Hall branch of the Chicago Public Library, most certainly had been influenced at a young age by the efforts of "the early black history movement" to instill racial pride as well as protest ongoing inequalities and injustices around race.[42] Taylor Goss would also participate in the NNMHF's establishment of Negro History Week and take up the call of black newspapers across the country to know "Your History."[43] These and other cultural institutions and events also served to maintain the NNC's ties with labor groups at the Packinghouse Labor Center.[44] In fact, for the rest of Taylor Goss's life, she would promote African American historical education even at the risk of crossing swords with school administrators during her tenure as an art teacher at DuSable High School.

Perhaps because of Woodson and the significant efforts of artists such as Taylor Goss to use art as historical education, the NNMHF's establishment of Negro History Week in Chicago was recognized as one of the more "prominent traditions" of the city, picking up where its umbrella organization, the National Negro Congress, in some ways left off. In the face of growing anticommunist sentiments in society at large, Burroughs and her cohorts shifted to a more pointed focus "on art and education even more intensely as a means of maintaining a presence in the African American community within the constraints of McCarthyism."[45] This was a path that Burroughs would pursue for the rest of her life, using education and art as powerful instruments not only for maintaining a community presence, but for providing a sense of identity and pride to many others, particularly the young and impressionable. And as Ian Rocksborough-Smith observes, while many black communists and fellow travelers were crushed or silenced by government suppression, Taylor Goss and the NNMHF were able to survive and grow. In large part, according to the sociologist St. Clair Drake, this was because the ten-member group, with Taylor Goss as financial secretary, found a pragmatic political path through the Chicago Democratic machine's black leadership. They never "got into a real local fight [with the machine] but they went in for the study of Negro history."[46]

Erik Gellman illuminates this singular political path even more closely, citing Drake's observation that the NNC/NNMHF group "was the result of a backroom deal between prominent black leftists and the political head of the black Democratic machine in Chicago, William Dawson."[47] The deal, according to Drake, was that the local (anticommunist) "red squad" would not harass the artists if they limited their protests to a "strict cultural nationalist line."[48] Artists such as Taylor Goss and White would use their art to join the call for a southern civil rights movement, making it clear that "militancy and self-sacrifice for freedom is the tradition of American progress, and the Negro's struggle has strengthened it, kept it alive."[49] Thus, the radical voices of Taylor Goss and her fellow artists and travelers found a way to continue to be heard despite the gathering storm against such protests with the postwar Red Scare.

For the rest of her days, Burroughs would similarly seek an accommodation with, and resources from, the local Democratic political machine, her focus being on meeting specific goals and achieving visible projects; the latter included, by 1973, a Chicago Park District home for the Du-Sable Museum of African American History from Mayor Richard J. Daley. While she did not openly identify as a communist and never claimed party membership, her work and words clearly spoke to her commitment to social justice. It would seem that the growing wave of McCarthyism in the postwar years only taught her how to artfully walk a line between speaking her truth and getting things done, a pragmatic yet still principled approach that led her in 1975 to accept an award from Daley for starting the DuSable Museum of African American History. While she was less apt during this wartime period to hit the streets in protest, she was, as she stated herself, simply preoccupied with her cultural activism.

Taylor Goss's development as a writer and community voice acceler-
ated dramatically after World War II began. In part, this may have
been the result of a growing need for extra income due to her new family
responsibilities. But clearly her early successes informed her understanding of the power of expression to sway public opinion as well as action.
Even as she continued her work as an artist, her writing and publication
positioned her as an important voice, even as a young woman in her
twenties.

Much of her early publication addressed the war effort, and particularly an ongoing theme of how the British and French, and eventually
the American, claims to fight for democracy underscored the lack of democracy in those countries with regard to racism. Her voice joined many
others in the Negro People's Front of the early 1940s in its continued call
for unity, both within and across races and classes. At the same time, her
position on blacks' involvement in the war appears to have modulated as
the war progressed. For instance, in a pre–U.S. engagement feature article
in the *Chicago Defender* dated August 31, 1940, she gave a capsule history
of the role of black people in wars waged by whites who, despite the
contributions of black soldiers, continued to discriminate against them
during and even after the wars. She then went on to ask, "Why should
a Negro mother of today sacrifice her sons to the war god? Why should
the Negro mother be sympathetic to the other side? This is not our war."
At this point in time, Taylor Goss, like Robeson, was critical of blacks'
engagement in the European war.

She continued her article by criticizing the colonial exploits of the British and French, questioning how they now claimed to be fighting for
democracy when their national histories illustrated a serious lack of democratic values in their colonial rule. Instead of contrasting the Axis and
Allied powers, she condemned both sides as equal-opportunity exploiters
of black people: "The British and French imperialists are fighting the
German imperialists. The people pay the price." She concluded, "Instead
of wasting our men and our money on imperialist war mongers who cry,
'For Democracy,' why shouldn't we utilize our men, our money, and our
cultural heritage by making DEMOCRACY work in our own country?"
She noted how black mothers would willingly sacrifice their men to fight
for democracy at home: "We have a DEMOCRACY right here, only
it isn't functioning quite properly." Rather than cheer on the Allies and
rally her readers around their war effort in Europe, Taylor Goss used a

class- and race-based critique of the history of war to contextualize the current conflict as an extension of imperialism and its exploitation of "the people."[50] This critique would underlie much of her later writing during and after the war.

If we take her at her word when she wrote, "When faced by grave decisions, I would often ask myself, 'Now what would Paul Robeson do in this case? Now, on what side is Paul Robeson?' Whatever I concluded that Paul would do, that is what I did," then it is likely that Taylor Goss followed Robeson's ventures around Europe and the Soviet Union in the run-up to the war, and weighed her own positions against his.[51] She supported Robeson's embrace of Soviet antiracist laws and his visit to Spain during the Civil War there to lend support and encouragement to the Republican army; among that army's units was the Abraham Lincoln Brigade, which included American blacks who had taken up arms against Franco's forces. According to Robeson's son, Paul Robeson Jr., his father took an anti-imperialist stance, critiquing the racist practices of self-described democracies as well as their opposition to the antiracist Soviet state, which Taylor Goss echoed in her 1940 *Defender* article. Even as Stalin's reign turned into one of terror in the mid-1930s, and Robeson became more and more concerned for the safety of his son, who was enrolled in school there, along with other family members and friends, he never backed down from his support of the Soviet people and their inclusiveness, since they were the ones with whom he found common cause. As an entertainer, he saw his role as one of supporting people, not war.

Similarly, throughout her life, Burroughs never backed down from her support of Soviet society and culture. She would later marry Charles Burroughs, who, like Paul Jr., was schooled in the Soviet system to avoid the racism he would have otherwise faced in the United States. Just as Robeson carried on a critique of imperialist racism across the globe, while at the same time he supported the Allied troops by performing for them in Europe, Taylor Goss also maintained a dual position regarding the war, supporting the people who fought it while criticizing the wealthy and powerful backers who exploited them.

Once the United States entered the war in 1941, and African Americans started serving in the armed forces in significant numbers, Taylor Goss began to openly support the war, perhaps more overtly than Robeson, who was walking a fine line between his commitments to making his art work for justice, his ability to develop and sustain an audience, and his inclinations toward black nationalism. Taylor Goss at this point was in her late twenties, a newly single mother, struggling to make ends meet, but with deep commitments to "her people" that propelled her into the public arena again and again. So, in 1942 or 1943, she wrote an extended opinion piece for the *N.Y.P.S.* (Negro Youth Photo-Script) *Magazine*, a journal started by the Chicago teacher, short-story writer, socialite, and Art Center activist Alice Browning.[52] In this piece, entitled "This Is Our War," Burroughs countered some arguments against supporting the war effort by pointing out that speculations that "Japan would be kindly disposed toward the Negro peoples should she win the war, since Japan is classed as a darker race" and that "America would be no worse for the Negro under Hitler than it is for them now" were "dangerous lies" springing from "Axis propaganda." Instead, she argued, this was a "people's war of national liberation," comparing blacks' participation in the U.S. Civil War as a parallel to their efforts in the current world war: "During this struggle, when Union soldiers made themselves more active in kicking colored men out of their camps than in shooting rebels, when even Lincoln told the Negro that he was the cause of the war, Frederick Douglass, a great Negro leader, believed that the mission of the Civil War was the liberation of the slaves as well as the salvation of the Union."[53] Thus, Taylor Goss adjusted her primary position; she continued to critique imperialism, but she also supported those fighting its war, and she recast the war as a global struggle for oppressed people's liberation, one that could also continue within the imperialist societies themselves.

The Popular Front slogan "Black and White, Unite!" carried on into Taylor Goss's work throughout the war and for the rest of her life by connecting the struggle of African Americans for equality and justice with the struggle of all humanity. She commented on how democracy had been a work in progress ever since the Revolutionary War, and she noted that some progress had been made. She used figures such as boxing champion Joe Louis as an example of how whites were coming around to appreciate the abilities and accomplishments of blacks. At the same time, she did not hesitate to critique both her fellow African Americans and whites for what she perceived as short-sightedness in their visions of how to advance the cause of social justice. Her lifelong exhortation to "be positive" meant that she stayed connected to those whom she critiqued if they shared her larger goals. As Bill Mullen noted, "During the Negro People's Front, Marxists and black capitalists undertook different paths toward the same goal: making the system 'more responsive to poor people and Blacks.' Hence their strategies, resources, and personnel invariably overlapped."[54] Taylor Goss typically stayed "positive" about such shared goals even when she disagreed with how others wanted to reach them.

In many of her publications during this period, Taylor Goss maintained a steady drumbeat of identifying, critiquing, and offering solutions for the racism that hobbled African American soldiers as well as those toiling away on the home front. While she never seems to have openly disavowed Paul Robeson's early distancing of himself from the war based on black nationalists' perception of its lack of relevance to African Americans, she nonetheless found a way to maintain her connections to Robeson's more general vision of racial and ethnic unity by supporting a war of liberation, including the Spanish Civil War front against fascism, while urging a similarly liberatory impulse on the home front. It is doubtful that Taylor Goss would have seen herself as in any way contradicting her role model—not out of simplistic hero worship but from a more nuanced understanding of his and her own position in relation to the global stage, namely that oppressed peoples across the world had to see themselves as sharing a common purpose in overcoming discrimination on all levels.

While she was an active voice in shaping public opinion about the war before 1941, after the United States entered the war, her involvement soon shifted toward African American soldiers. She started corresponding with friends and family who were fighting overseas, including her close friend, the artist Charles White, and her estranged husband, Bernard Goss. She noted how after a while, she had so many letters to write and so many queries about news from home that she began a newsletter, *Life with Margaret*. This newsletter spread so widely among the troops that she received many letters in response, telling her not only of the bravery of African American soldiers and their contributions to the war effort, but also registering complaints regarding the segregation of black troops and the inequalities that resulted.[55] She thus had many sources for what was happening overseas that told a story unlike the mainstream newspapers. As she would find throughout her life, such firsthand experiences with people on the ground proved more reliable, from her perspective, than any newspaper accounts. As she urged so many others, "Find out for yourself." Her "boys" helped her do that while she remained stateside.

Keenly aware of the racism that followed the troops overseas, she wrote steadily and persistently about the need to recognize the patriotism and service of African Americans as a way to bring unity and equality between blacks and whites and avoid playing into Hitler's desire for internal conflict among his enemies. For example, in a column published during the war, she repeated a story by another columnist, Drew Pearson, about what happened when a Mississippi congressional delegation met with one of their state's war heroes in Washington, D.C. The young soldier was asked how he "got along with Negroes over there." The entire delegation "were set back on their heels when the lieutenant stated that he had fought with the Negro boys and had found them just as good fighters as the white boys." The soldier offered how he and many of his fellow white southern fighters had changed their opinions about Negroes because of their war experiences together.[56] In this way, Taylor Goss used the war to highlight the positive aspects of her people as contributors to a fight she nonetheless saw as an imperialist enterprise, though one, as the war went on, that working people could appropriate as a global fight for justice and equality for all.

As the war in Europe drew to a close, she focused on collecting the letters black soldiers had sent her, citing a call from the Schomburg Collection of Negro Literature in Harlem to collect such artifacts as part of the historical record.[57] Perhaps such calls influenced her own powerful drive to collect as many artifacts to document African American history as she could for the museum she would eventually found in her home. She also wrote about what soldiers had told her they most wanted when they returned home: "One thing that is mentioned most in the letters home is sleep. . . . One GI notes that he plans to come home, store up a supply of food and bolt the door. He plans to be quite alone with his wife and the babe that he has only seen photographs of. He wants to come back to the Southside of Chicago and open a bookstore that will have everyone reading from grandpa to junior." She goes on to describe others' plans to take advantage of the GI Bill, such as training to be an electrical engineer, getting involved in organizations to help combat social problems, and, instead of looking for jobs, obtaining Veterans Administration loans and starting their own businesses.[58] In this way, she continued to support those who had served by rallying those at home to appreciate the seriousness of returning soldiers' plans and to assist them in their fulfillment.

In addition to her personal connections to the soldiers and their struggles, she was also quite active in the Negro People's Front during and after the war, focusing heavily on the need to desegregate the armed forces, a national effort that, in 1948, succeeded in pressuring President Truman to do so. By the early 1940s, she had found a platform for her opinions in Claude Barnett's Associated Negro Press, for which she wrote numerous columns, features, and op-ed pieces. While the pay was likely marginal at best, the satisfaction of contributing to the collective voice of the Negro People's Front, along with making her own individual voice heard across the nation in syndicated African American newspapers, must have been profound. She also published letters in the *Chicago Defender*'s column, "What the People Say," during and after the war and throughout her life. In a 1942 piece, she first identified the war abroad as a fight against the "racial superiority" touted by Axis powers before she then segued into connecting a war victory to the victory needed at home to stop racism: "We in America have been working toward a unity of all Americans for the common defense. Certainly, all slurs on racial groups should be cut out of American life if this unity is to be achieved. Of course, it isn't. Every day there are flagrant instances of this type of abuse against the Negro people. We find it in the newspapers, periodicals, cartoon comics and—especially in so many instances—in the movies." She went on to cite a recent example of a movie with offensive stereotypical characters.[59] She often combined cultural critiques of this sort with efforts to support the war and the troops. For her, fighting the Axis powers and fighting racism were one and the same struggle, a sentiment ultimately shared by Robeson, who, like Taylor Goss, saw the Soviet people as freedom fighters undeserving of the suspicion placed upon them by the U.S. government and many of its people.

Over the years during and after the war, some of her Associated Negro Press columns ventured into cultural critiques of radio commercials, including the misguided psychology of ads claiming that children would grow up unhappy and develop "frustration complexes" if their parents did not purchase televisions for them.[60] She also put out a call to action to lessen or even curtail excessive commercial time on the airwaves, rallying readers to complain to the Federal Communications Commission.[61] After race riots in Detroit and Beaumont, Texas, she called for peace: "It will only be by sticking together that we will secure the peace that we have so dearly won. Already there are rumors going the rounds concerning racial strife after the war. We must not let that be."[62] She also wrote a review of a pamphlet, "The Races of Mankind," by Columbia University anthropologists Ruth Benedict and Gene Weltfish, who argued that "scientifically, intelligence does not depend on race, nationality or color. What racial differences there are, are attributed to locality, climate, and environmental surroundings." Taylor Goss used their argument to highlight Soviet laws that made racial discrimination and persecution illegal.[63] She also noted the provocative conclusion reached by the authors, namely that "no European is a pure anything. A country has a diverse population, not a race," directly countering Hitler's claims for racial purity but also opening the door to a globalism and racial diversity that had previously been unthinkable.[64]

Even as she wrote steadily for newspapers, Taylor Goss was also keeping her creative fires lit by writing stories and essays for journals with roots in the South Side, including *Negro Story*, started by the Art Center writers and teachers Fern Gayden and Alice Browning, and *Ebony* founder John H. Johnson's *Negro Digest*, which modeled itself on the monthly *Reader's Digest*. It seems incredible that all this writerly activity coincided with the breakup of her first marriage, the birth of her daughter, going to school and working, and still producing art. She also maintained an active presence in the community, working on projects through the Art Center, including the 1944 "Interracial South Side Cultural Conference" from which *Negro Story* sprang.[65]

While she would still write and publish or distribute her poetry throughout her life, during this period prose seems to have dominated. This was no accident, given that shifting political winds gave way to the development of the short story as a form that served multiple purposes, politically, socially, and culturally. Even as white America had been exploring the small press and little magazine phenomena in the previous decades, black America, particularly the South Side of Chicago, found a corresponding response to New York–based, mainstream commercial publishing. But beyond the racial boundaries drawn by commercial presses of the time, the war had, as previously noted, dampened the radical voices of the popular fronts of the 1930s as calls for national unity against Axis powers took precedence. As Mullen noted, "Attempted repression of the black press's most militant voices had begun as early as 1942, when [poet] Archibald MacLeish, director of the Office of Facts and Figures for the Roosevelt administration, had convened a conference of black newspaper editors to ask that they tone down calls for racial reform in respect for national wartime unity."[66]

But the short story, most prominently showcased in the short-lived *Negro Story* magazine from 1944 to 1946, provided a generic flexibility that helped writers like Taylor Goss to have her say, reach thousands of readers, and yet elude the worst of the anticommunist backlash to come later during the Cold War of the 1950s. As Mullen described, "By exploiting the short story's distinctive generic conventions such as its spatial economy, its accessibility to 'amateurs,' its comparability to popular forms like newspaper articles, and its untapped potential for both creating and shaping 'mass' literary markets of black writers and readers, the genre helped forge a new (black) market for the production and consumption of periodic protest culture."[67] For Taylor Goss, this genre, along with newspaper columns and journal articles, offered her a way to creatively unify otherwise divergent strands of her life, including her creative expression, political voice, and breadwinning role. Rather than back away from her more radical political commitments, she followed Robeson's lead and found a way to use her creative powers to further those positions in the face of increasing repression.

For example, in her 1944 short story "Private Jeff Johnson," Taylor Goss brought together several of her ongoing themes regarding race relations, the war, and the need for national unity through equality. Jeff Johnson, a twenty-five-year-old black man born in the South who had migrated to the North, returns south after his induction into the army for boot camp. "He hated white folks," Taylor Goss wrote, and this hatred sets up Johnson's internal struggle between his urge to fight against whites, who he expected would challenge him at some point, and his inclination to "not bother anybody so long as no one bothered him."[68] Johnson's resolve to keep to himself is tested one night at an off-base club, when a white MP "accidentally" knocks off Johnson's cap. After this first slight, Johnson accepts the MP's apology, quieting his friends' urgings to fight. But after the second "accidental" cap episode, Johnson's friends see red and badger him to fight and not be a coward. Perhaps remembering the white doctor from the story's opening, who, speaking as the story's conscience, in line with the author's viewpoint, says, "Don't you know what the war is all about? This is a people's war. Your folks will have a better chance if we win this war all together," Private Johnson struggles but ultimately does not retaliate.[69] His friends criticize him until, shortly after the MP leaves, a group of armed white soldiers burst into the canteen, looking for the race riot they were certain their fellow MP would have ignited. By not getting into the wrong fight, Johnson gains the respect of his black peers by saving their and his lives. The doctor's prescription, so to speak, for a "people's war" proves to Johnson that racial bias can lead to the destruction of all and the betterment of none.

Even as Taylor Goss wrote steadily critical articles and stories about racism in the United States, she also urged her fellow blacks to, like Johnson, look at the bigger picture, that is, winning the global war against racism and injustice by refraining from attacking the white provocateurs in race riots. She acknowledged that the sources of such anger were understandable and genuine, and she was careful to place responsibility on the heads of political leaders and government to address "economic and social sores that cause the fostering of racial strife and unrest in America."[70]

As some scholars have observed, the United States' entry into the war placed a huge damper on the liberal and radical fronts that had gained so much traction in the 1930s. As noted earlier, when funding dried up for artists, those associated with the Art Center turned to supporting the war in order to support themselves. In addition, the government began to cast antiracist voices as a threat to national unity and security, in the buildup to the Red Scare era. Eventually even Taylor Goss's beloved slogan, "Black and White, Unite!" would be seen as suspect. It is possible, then, to argue that Taylor Goss herself succumbed to this suppression by shifting to a strong and openly supportive stance for the war, one that her role model Robeson himself did not adopt. Given that her personal life took a turn for the worse just before the war, making her vulnerable to financial, cultural, and social backlash in ways that she as a single woman, dedicated first to her art and her people, would feel keenly affected by, it is plausible to conclude that she shifted for the sake of her livelihood.

However, her extensive paper trail of articles, columns, stories, and letters to the editor, as well as the arc of her life's story as someone who did not back down from controversy but rather met it, provide much evidence to the contrary. As much as she agreed with some black nationalists and their separatist impulses, she simply did not, in the end, agree with an across-the-board cutting off of relationships with whites. For her, if whites wanted to join the struggle, then everyone would be stronger in the long run. Thus, her embrace of the war as "the people's war" can be read as an extension of, rather than a divergence from, her involvement in the Negro People's and Popular Fronts of the 1930s. They shared a common enemy, racism, that was embodied both abroad and at home. Fighting together rather than fighting apart would move the cause ahead just that much sooner.

Margaret Burroughs before her home at 3806 S. Michigan,
the first site of the DuSable Museum, 2005.

Photo by the author.

Murals inside Margaret and Charles Burroughses' home,
painted for the original Ebony Museum.

Photos by the author.

Margaret and her beloved Siamese cat, Humphrey
Bogart, 1994.

Photo courtesy of Arcilla Stahl, South Side Community Art Center.

In front of the DuSable Museum for the Harambee Soirée, 1994.

Photo courtesy of Chief Condra Ridley.

Burroughs in front of the South Side Community Art Center, one of two arts institutions she helped found, 2005.

Photo by the author.

Charles and Margaret Burroughs, embraced by Haki Madhubuti, founder and publisher of the Third World Press, in 1987, the twentieth anniversary of the press.

Copyright © Dr. Haki R. Madhubuti.

Margaret Burroughs with her eldest grandson, Eric Toller, on a trip to Côte d'Ivoire, 1996.

Photo courtesy of Eric Toller.

Original South Side Community Art Center board member
Thelma (Kirkpatrick) Wheaton, acclaimed photographer Gordon
Parks, Margaret Burroughs, and Marva Jolly, a much-beloved
ceramicist and supporter of the Art Center, 1994.

Photo courtesy of Arcilla Stahl, South Side Community Art Center.

At the South Side Community Art Center with board member
Diane Dinkins Carr (*standing, right*) and Gloria Latimore Peace
(*seated, left*), early 2000s.

Photo courtesy of Arcilla Stahl, South Side Community Art Center.

Margaret Burroughs (*right*) with board member Elaine Moragne at one of many fund-raisers for the South Side Community Art Center, 2005.

Photo courtesy of Arcilla Stahl, South Side Community Art Center.

Burroughs lecturing in Côte d'Ivoire, 1996, during one of her many trips abroad.

Photo courtesy of Eric Toller.

Traveling in style in Côte d'Ivoire, 1996.

Photo courtesy of Eric Toller.

In Fort Wayne, Indiana, with Margaret Burroughs (*center*), the author (*on Burroughs's right*), Omowale Ketu Oladuwa (*on author's right*), and members and friends of the Three Rivers Jenbe Ensemble, who welcomed Burroughs to Fort Wayne with a performance, 2004.

Photo by the author.

Teaching a writing workshop at Weisser Park Community Center in Fort Wayne, Indiana, 2004.

Photo by the author.

In Fort Wayne, Indiana, with Chief Condra Ridley
and her daughter, Najah, 2004.

Photo courtesy of Chief Condra Ridley.

Prior to receiving the Legends and Legacies award from the School of the Art Institute of Chicago, 2010.

Photo courtesy of Eric Toller.

Hands of the artist.

Photo courtesy of Eric Toller.

FOUR

BORDER CROSSINGS

As we continued our walk up King Drive, the outlines of a statue in the median began to emerge. Dr. B did not have to prompt me to stop and take a photo while she narrated the significance of the Victory Monument at Thirty-Fifth Street. Monuments to war heroes are a common sight around Chicago, and so as I snapped a picture, I was intrigued to learn that this statue was not just another holdover from wealthy whites who once populated the former Grand Boulevard. Instead, the Victory Monument was the "first state-sponsored memorial to African-American veterans of World War I" honoring the Eighth Regiment of the Illinois National Guard, an African American unit that served in France during World War I as part of the 370th U.S. Infantry.[1] Dr. B's commentary seemed aimed less at glorifying war and war heroes and more at making the point that African Americans had served in World War I despite the discrimination they faced on their home turf, and they were now, remarkably, publicly and tangibly memorialized. As a proponent of public art, Dr. B never lost an opportunity to praise any art, public or private, that provided evidence of significant African American contributions and achievements. It is not an overstatement to say that she was on a mission to ensure such histories were well preserved and easily accessible, especially to "her" people. She understood how maintaining a cultural memory, as well as securing social justice, were ongoing endeavors, not a final outcome.

Across the boulevard on the east side was a building in some state of disrepair or renovation. Dr. B pointed out the Supreme Life Building, which had once housed an important black-initiated and black-run business. Such businesses were key to Bronzeville's eventual turn away from white-owned operations that often preyed upon the vulnerable Black

Belt. While Dr. B in her "liv[ing] up to the root" lifestyle, was, I guessed, unlikely to seek out the services of a life insurance company, she nonetheless understood the historical significance and positive image projected by a successfully run black-owned enterprise. She noted how this was the first company to offer life insurance to African Americans in the northern United States, and at one point had been the largest African American–owned business in the North. Blacks had been routinely denied insurance by white-owned companies, and so Supreme Life achieved amazing success once it was launched in 1919.

I reflected upon my own ancestors' entry into Bronzeville to make a living, starting during the Great Depression. My mother's father, the son of German and Polish immigrants, scrambled to find work during the 1930s. He had grown up in an ethnic German neighborhood in Chicago in the early years of the twentieth century, and he told stories about territorial skirmishes with Irish immigrants—what we might think of today as gang wars. No doubt he knew about the Black Belt from his early years close by that part of the city. Whether it was because he lost his job as a milkman or simply had an entrepreneurial itch in the late 1930s or early '40s, he turned to self-employment after learning that a commercial bakery, the Patsy Ann Cookie Company in Blue Island, sold bags of broken cookies on the cheap. Like many whites, he saw an opportunity to sell discounted goods to people who lacked the funds or access to buy the mainstream product. So, out of his car trunk, he began to sell these goods to corner mom-and-pop stores, many of them black-owned businesses. His business grew; he bought a truck and brought his son, my uncle, into the business, added candy and notions, and forged solid relationships with store owners and their families. My mother and her sister recalled how he attended weddings, funerals, and other family-oriented gatherings hosted by his customers.

Was this a "predatory" relationship? Systemically speaking, my grandfather fit the profile of many whites who took advantage of racist attitudes that prevented blacks from shopping in white-owned stores in white neighborhoods. He did not relocate his home and family to the Black Belt, but rather came to that area and offered products that store owners saw a market for, again, in part because of their limited access to such resources due to race. My grandfather's orientation to Chicago's neighborhoods, which were balkanized by ethnicity, race, or class, perhaps led him to conclude that selling to blacks directly was worth taking a risk to enter "those neighborhoods" for the sake of turning a handsome profit. During the postwar years, he moved his family to a larger, middle-class house that he had had built, and he enjoyed such luxuries as a baby grand piano to indulge his self-taught musical talent.

Standing on King Drive with a Bronzeville giant like Dr. B made me consider how much my family's prosperity owed directly to this neighborhood, these people and their ancestors. My uncle, who bought out my grandfather in the 1950s, was still servicing a small store two blocks from Dr. B's home at Thirty-Eighth Street and Michigan even as late as the early 2000s, when he was in his mid-seventies. Racism made my mother's family's livelihood possible. It also brought my grandfather into relatively close relationship with blacks, many of whom were impoverished or struggling economically. His stories and descriptions of these experiences formed very powerful images of African Americans that were passed on to his children and grandchildren, including me. Suffice it to say that racism strongly tinged those images, yet the picture remains more complicated; unlike in the Deep South, the individual interactions were not overtly unequal ones. My grandfather was a salesman, and his customers were store owners. They met on a somewhat equal commercial ground, rather than strictly boss-to-worker terms.

The "success" of the King Drive renovations appeared to be as patchworked as the Supreme Life Building's current structure. The building's grand 1921 stone and brick walls, cornices, and corners were quite visible, but a chain-link fence separated viewers from whatever work was under way on it, if, in fact, there was any. The Black Metropolis Convention and Tourism Council had bought the building, which had also received landmark status in 1998, and was in the process of renovation.[2] But at that moment, change looked more uncertain. While this particular section of Bronzeville showed some signs of development, that progress seemed more halting and less solid than in more affluent parts of the city where new construction moved at a much faster pace, with more resources invested. It was sort of like those broken cookies that my grandfather sold, and most likely shared with his own family as well—second best was better than nothing. And who cared what a cookie looked like as long as it tasted good? But the patchwork nature of progress also continues to symbolize the South Side's struggles, for better or worse.

As we approached the intersection of King Drive and Thirty-Fifth Street, distinctly new historical markers, similar to those at the Ida B.

Wells-Barnett home on Thirty-Sixth Street, greeted us from the median. The afternoon heat was beginning to take its toll on my attention span, however, and the appeal of reading more detailed signage was quickly dwindling. I shot a glance at my companion. She moved forward steadily, without pause, eager and curious and, most likely, proud of this signifi- cant community achievement of keeping the past alive. Feeling a little like an inattentive school child, I shook off my wandering gaze and focused on the goal ahead.

Dr. B seemed as curious as any child regarding these landmarks, as if seeing them for the first time. That may have been the case; she may have ridden by on the city buses that she valued so highly for the free rides she got on them as a senior citizen, or in the chauffeured car that took her to meetings as a Chicago Park District commissioner, without ever viewing up close the final products that she had in so many ways helped shep- herd to completion. She made sure that I continued to take photos, later asking me to send her copies for her records, which I discovered while doing research for this book were enormous and even, one might say, indiscriminate in what was saved; everything was of importance, down to a single ticket stub for a conference registration. She knew too well how such records had been invaluable for African American historians who found tangible evidence of African and African American achievements that would fly in the face of white supremacist narratives that blacks "had no history" or contributions of any value beyond their propensity for physical toil.

So despite my lagging energy, despite my internalized dislike of war monuments and business enterprises, despite the patchwork images of progress that challenged me to visualize the "beloved community" so familiar to Dr. B, I kept going. As the Bronzeville gateway pavilion mate- rialized in the thick, humid air, I actually began to regain my excitement. The gateway's festive red roof with contrasting green sides beckoned like a street fair and was intended to greet visitors like me as well as tourists from all over the world and orient them to the splendors of this neighbor- hood's remarkable past.

This gateway and the entire King Drive corridor was, indeed, a fairly recent development for Bronzeville. Dr. B did not indicate that she per- sonally had had a hand in this project, but it was clear that she took pride and felt gratification that her long-held vision of projecting positive images of locals and preserving evidence of historic achievements had been realized in a very visible and accessible format. It was only a few years prior to this, in 1998, that 1.5 miles of King Drive had received landmark status, and a $10.5 million beautification project began to transform the previously derelict boulevard. These new markers, along with the Convention and Tourist Council's acquisition of the Supreme Life Building, were clearly intended to make this street a destination for visitors of all kinds.

On the ground near the pavilion was a bronze map of the area that had been named "Bronzeville," an honorific generated by the journalist James J. Gentry in 1932 to counter the negative stereotypes of the Black Belt as well as serve as a promotional campaign for the *Chicago Bee* and later the *Chicago Defender*. When I had asked Dr. B in an earlier meeting where Bronzeville existed, she had replied, "Wherever black people live." However, this particular map had fixed a specific area in its metal embrace: south to Fifty-Seventh Street and the DuSable Museum, a bit east of Drexel Boulevard, north to near Cermak and Twenty-Second Street, and west to just past the Dan Ryan Expressway. Other maps, both historical and current, illustrate somewhat different boundaries for the neighborhood. Dr. B might have included her own neighborhood near Englewood High School, around Sixty-Third Street and the Dan Ryan Expressway, despite the fact that at the time her family had been one of the few black families in the area, a situation made famous by Lorraine Hansberry's Pulitzer Prize–winning play *A Raisin in the Sun*. But as we stood in the middle of King Drive, Dr. B did not seem interested in arguing the point. Boundaries, she knew all too well, were fluid. How else could one push for change?

"Where to next?" she asked. If Dr. B wanted to continue, who was I to question her?

"Olivet Baptist Church," I answered. Given Dr. B's orientation toward a socialist ideology and her pointed critique earlier in our walk regarding money-loving pastors who did little to assist the congregations from whom they gladly accepted tithes, I wondered how she would respond to a landmark I had somewhat randomly drawn from a tour guide as a significant piece of architecture as well as a historic church. Although raised by Catholic parents, Dr. B did not indicate any current religious affiliations, something I could relate to myself as a former Catholic.

Dr. B directed me to the east side of the street, toward the airy white Lake Meadows apartments. She commented on the art fair she had helped found there in the 1950s when she and fellow African American artists in

Chicago found they were shut out of Hyde Park and other city art fairs. "It's still going to this day," she said, with satisfaction. I nodded, trying to take in yet another legacy generated by this remarkable woman and her community. As we walked north past the rows of apartment buildings in some much-needed leafy shade, our eyes were drawn to yet more bronze-colored markers in the sidewalk, part of the Bronzeville Walk of Fame. Every few feet, a new marker appeared, naming and describing former and current Bronzeville residents of note. Dr. B, of course, knew many of them personally, having hosted them at her home for decades of parties and kitchen-table talk of art and politics.

"Where is your plaque?" I asked. I expected a bit of a reprimand; Dr. B always insisted that whatever she did, she did with the help of many others.

I don't remember her exact response, though I do seem to recall a hint of a smile coming through.

She might never have imagined that in 2015, the Thirty-First Street Harbor, site of the 1919 race riots, now a beautiful beachfront park drawing people of many races, ethnicities, and cultures, would be named for her. However, no plaque for her on the Walk of Fame has appeared—yet.

As we passed Lake Meadows, I commented on how modern and fresh the high-rise buildings looked, similar to pricey lake-viewing apartments farther north. Who lived there, I wondered? Then, when I asked, Dr. B informed me that these buildings still provided affordable housing, despite the push for gentrification in and around Bronzeville, a pressure felt even more as I write over a decade later.

An elderly man coming from the opposite direction greeted Dr. B warmly. They chatted about his experience at the South Side Community Art Center. As before, Dr. B took the attention in stride, literally and figuratively.

Nonetheless, as we left the shade and made our way up to Thirty-First Street, I fretted a bit over my companion's well-being. While she made it clear that she expected to be treated with dignity and not fussed over like some helpless invalid, I still worried about the effect of such a long walk in high heat and humidity on her eighty-eight-year-old body. I didn't know her well enough to determine if she was just too proud to back down or if she really was that resilient. For a fleeting moment, I pictured her collapsing on the ground, many people rushing to her aid, glaring at me for letting this awful scene come to pass.

I shouldn't have worried. I was the one feeling the heat more than she. A metaphor, perhaps, for how I felt in one of the rare moments in my life when I was clearly a minority race.

As we approached the intersection of Thirty-First Street and King Drive, the procession of well-wishers repeated itself; when Dr. B stopped in front of Olivet Baptist Church to recount some of its history, she was interrupted several times to field greetings and thanks. I had to keep reminding myself that this was Chicago, an enormous city, on a major boulevard, where anonymity is usually understood as synonymous with social isolation. Nothing could be further from the truth with Dr. B.

Olivet Baptist Church boasts a long, venerable history, first as a stop on the Underground Railroad but also as the oldest African American Baptist church in Chicago, and the second oldest black church in the city.[3] During the 1919 race riots, Olivet provided safe haven and helped maintain peace.[4] During the first wave of the Great Migration in the early twentieth century, the church hosted forty different social, cultural, and economic groups, and also undertook activism to push for education and housing.[5] At one point its membership swelled to twenty thousand members, and it was known by migrants as a "one-stop shop" to assist them in their transitions to northern urban living.

What Dr. B had to say about the church, however, was not so much about its glories as its foibles, specifically the tenure of the head of the church from 1940 to 1990, the Reverend Joseph Harrison Jackson, or "Joe Jackson" as she called him.

"In the '60s, Joe Jackson preached against King's work," she stated. Her disapproving tone positioned the reverend on the wrong side of the civil rights movement. She went on to say how he had cooperated with Mayor Richard J. Daley to work against King's efforts to equalize housing and instead emphasized civil rights through law and order as opposed to civil disobedience. Jackson's position was part of a huge rift in the community that lasted until the 1990s, when he died after nearly fifty years at the helm of the church. Like his predecessor, Lacey Kirk Williams, Reverend Jackson adhered to Booker T. Washington's philosophy of racial uplift, fearing that confrontations with whites could adversely affect court struggles for equality.[6]

Jackson certainly had articulated what many Bronzeville residents believed. But Dr. B likely took him to task for his leadership in swaying people against King. Her whole life had been dedicated to maintaining unity with other African Americans as well as other minority groups. Her Popular Front slogan, "Black and White, Unite!" extended that call for unity across the racial divide. But this did not mean she withheld criticism from those whom she perceived as taking the wrong position on an issue. As friends such as Timuel Black recalled, Dr. B was the person others turned to when controversies sprang up. She was the trusted one. She could and did speak her mind and yet at the same time would not tolerate negativity toward her own or other peoples.[7] "Be positive" was her mantra. She was a firm believer but perhaps an even firmer enforcer. So, for instance, over lunch at Pearl's Place during our first meeting, when I asked about tensions during the 1960s between black businesspeople and black radicals, she waved me off, suggesting that any differences paled in comparison to the unity that remained.

Time would prove King, as well as Dr. B, correct. Olivet's congregation dwindled, and to this day it still struggles to attract new and young members. The church's massive early childhood education programs that had begun in 1919 ceased operation in 1980.[8] In contrast, its rival during the civil rights movement and a proponent of Dr. King, Pilgrim Baptist Church, continued to thrive. Noteworthy as the birthplace of contemporary gospel music under the direction of Thomas E. Dorsey, this church building (originally designed as a synagogue by Louis Sullivan and Dankmar Adler) was listed on the National Register of Historic Places in 1973 and was designated a Chicago historic landmark in 1981, many years before the landmark status of King Drive.[9]

As we took in the majestic church architecture, and I snapped more photos, Dr. B continued to appear resilient and eager in the brutal heat. She did, however, suggest that we stop for water at a hardware store back up on Thirty-Fifth Street. I marveled at how cool and fresh she remained while I was dripping in sweat and breathing hard—and I considered myself in fine physical shape!

The metaphor here speaks to Dr. B's ability to weather the heat of controversies and still emerge as a figure of respect, admiration, and love. She displayed a rare talent for speaking her mind forcefully and clearly and yet finding a way to maintain unity and positivity throughout her life. No doubt her vision of a unified humanity was a major factor in her ability to move between cultures, races, classes, and ideologies, as well as neighborhoods, states, and countries, with relative ease. Unlike her role model, Paul Robeson, she was increasingly celebrated as she aged. But she was far from the public figure he was, and she was female to boot. Who knows what her fate might have been had she been as visible in the public eye as he had been in his prime years?

It may well have been her vision of unity that not only shielded her from negative repercussions during the McCarthy era, but also led her more deeply into creative expression. With Paul Robeson as a guiding presence in her life, Margaret Taylor Goss was clear in her views regarding basic human rights and social justice even though her art and activism put her on a trajectory that landed her, about a decade later, in the crosshairs of the Art Center's anticommunist board. Her politics also set her up for a confrontation with the Chicago Board of Education, thereby threatening her livelihood as a teacher at DuSable High School. With so much at stake, one could understand why someone in Taylor Goss's shoes might back off and at least suppress her beliefs for the sake of survival. But she did not back down. She was a force to be reckoned with.

Nonetheless, with the onset of anticommunist politics after World War II, her views, linked as they were to interracial collaboration, forced her to learn some hard lessons about survival in the face of serious threats to her and her family's existence.

As Taylor Goss knew, the radical push to rally around interracial and ethnic unity was viewed by many Americans, including politicians, as a "communistic" ideology and thus a threat to perceived "American" ways of life. Such thinly veiled white supremacist attacks in the name of national security did not escape Taylor Goss's or her cohorts' notice. Burroughs later wrote,

> Since the government felt that it had to quash all socialist views, its solution was to offer us the unpleasant choice of renouncing socialist leanings in order to win greater civil rights freedoms—which seemed a near acknowledgment that civil rights was our only goal in the first place, but it was useless to fight on those grounds. In fact, it was useless to fight at all. How could we trust this sharp-toothed government, slinking around us in the shadows? Yet if we refused, we were branded as communists—which was to be branded un-American, traitorous, and black as night.[10]

After the 1938 establishment of the House Un-American Activities Committee (HUAC), the persistent efforts during the Popular and Negro

People's Fronts to work across color and other identity lines met with more and more resistance. "Black and White, Unite!" retreated from its very public, very visible presence in the black community at large.

But even such retreats did not extinguish the ongoing socializing, organizing, and commingling that Taylor Goss and her fellow travelers enjoyed. If anything, the private gatherings they retreated into only amplified the sustaining effects of the artist-activist community while also providing a much-needed refuge that lay under the radar, so to speak, from probing authorities who, as FBI documents have shown, were certainly eager to find any incriminating scrap of evidence. As Bill Mullen and Ian Rocksborough-Smith have pointed out, while the war and its attendant conservative backlash against the social movements of the 1930s chilled many in the African American community, Taylor Goss and her crowd persevered and even thrived to some extent, keeping the fires of radicalism burning even into the McCarthy period of the 1950s. It was Burroughs and Bronzeville that maintained a sense of purpose and action that paved the way for the next generation of South Side artist-activists in the Black Arts Movement, OBAC, and AfriCOBRA.

Yet this contribution of Burroughs and others of her generation on the South Side was often eclipsed by the apparent collapse of African American cultural fronts elsewhere during and after the war. In contrast to the Harlem Renaissance, the Chicago black cultural renaissance persisted, according to Robert Bone and Richard Courage, as late as 1950.[11] This persistence and dedication is a significant aspect of Burroughs's legacy to future generations. While other artists moved away to more lucrative venues like New York (as did Charles White) or left the country for more hospitable cultural and political environments (like Elizabeth Catlett), Burroughs stayed on in Chicago, maintaining her ties with the South Side Community Art Center as well as continuing to open her home to a weekly stream of guests around her kitchen table salon. If the radical party was, literally and figuratively, over in Chicago, she had not heard the news.

After Taylor Goss left Bernard Goss and began raising their daughter by herself, she may not have been as able to host the studio parties she had grown accustomed to prior to marriage and motherhood. She did, however, remain active in attending many private as well as civic events and meetings. It was her meeting and subsequent marriage to Charles Burroughs that propelled her back into her open house tradition. In him she found a life partner who would encourage and support her work on all levels. If her house parties had been a place to gather, with Charles their home became *the* place, a salon for everyone, from the greatest to the humblest, to share. Without Charles, the Margaret Burroughs we celebrate today might very likely not have emerged as such a strong and powerful artist and leader. As she was apt to do, she always credited whatever success she had to others who had worked with her. Charles was certainly a major key to those successes.

Charles Burroughs came into Taylor Goss's life by way of their mutual interests in radical politics. As Charles recalled, when he returned to the United States after spending much of his youth in the Soviet Union, he began lecturing about Russia for the International Workers Order (IWO), an interethnic cultural organization with both Russian and Negro chapters.

> There was an organization called the International Workers
> Order, which was made up of many ethnic groups which were
> Independent [*sic*] but in the same organization. It was the kind
> of fraternal organization that had cheap insurance. It started out
> as a Jewish organization for immigrants who needed help. Each
> chapter had a representative in the overall administration. It was
> also a cultural organization that would have speakers on various
> subjects. It was considered to be a communist-run organization,
> which it really wasn't. The Russian chapter asked me if I would
> go on a lecture tour to their chapters in various cities all over
> the country. They sent me to Philadelphia, Boston, Cleveland,
> Columbus, and Chicago. Although the Russian chapter sponsored it, they invited other chapters to attend. At this time, they
> had a Negro chapter, and when I spoke to the Negro chapter in
> Cleveland a lot of people came. Margaret was a member of the
> Negro chapter in Chicago. She was the ticket-taker.[12]

Although Charles did not remember much about Margaret at that first meeting, when they met again at a New Jersey summer camp for children where Charles worked as a night watchman and Margaret came to visit a friend, "we started a conversation through the neighboring wall" and found a mutual interest in art and politics.[13]

Taylor Goss's extended social network proved once again to be a boon here; Charles White and his first wife, Elizabeth Catlett, had moved to the East Coast and were deeply involved in radical political work that was reflected in their art. White had invited Taylor Goss to participate in the IWO's summer camp, called the Workers' Children's Camp, or Wo-Chi-Ca, in which "interracial and interethnic respect was emphasized."[14] The camp focused on the children of ethnic union members who were part of "mutual benefit societies" with ties to the Communist Party.[15] The goal was to integrate the Marxist principles of unity, equality, and democracy, which Taylor Goss largely supported, into family life. The camp's directors "worked hard to recruit African American staff and campers" and were successful in drawing a diverse group of participants from across the racial and ethnic spectrum.[16] One camper recalled a verse sung at camp that drew from these principles: "'Where the children of the workers / Live as one big family / Black and white we are united / In a true democracy."[17] But the biggest draw for Taylor Goss, as well as for her friends White and Catlett, was certainly the fact that the camp "made the visual arts an integral part of the camp's overall mission."[18] No doubt, reconnecting with Charles Burroughs after his IWO talk in Chicago proved even more of an incentive for Taylor Goss to spend a summer at the camp. As she recalled, she and Charles maintained a relationship via letter writing until one day, when she decided to propose to him.[19] They wed on December 23, 1949.

Meeting and then marrying Charles turned out to be a pivotal event for Taylor Goss. Not only did she admire his erudition as a speaker of Russian and a student of its literature, but she also found great inspiration in his knowledge of African and African American history. He was a global citizen of the time and had a unique context through which to view his unusual experiences growing up and attending boarding school in the Soviet Union before and during the war. At the same time, Burroughs was the helpmate and supporter that Taylor Goss had hoped for in Bernard Goss, but with Burroughs she found someone willing to share her dreams as well. When it came time to begin the Ebony Museum in their living room, Charles couldn't have been more willing. Finally, Margaret had a partner whom she loved and on whom she could count.

Charles's unapologetic cultural identification with the Soviet Union fascinated Margaret. What Margaret had heard from Paul Robeson regarding his experience with the Soviet treatment of blacks and other racial and ethnic groups was amplified by Charles's own first-person stories. Her grandson Eric Toller recalled a portrait of Stalin in the family kitchen on South Michigan, along with Russian conversation, performers from the Russian circus, and of course, the imbibing of copious amounts of vodka.[20] Paul Robeson had certainly prepared Margaret to be interested in a person with Charles's unusual background and interests. As she wrote, "I think all of these men [Charles, Robeson, Langston Hughes, W. E. B. Du Bois, Claude McKay] traveled as much to obtain the proper perspective of distance, of 'away-ness,' as to gain a particular foreign perspective, in order to give them a vantage from which to consider the developing—or deteriorating—aspects of social and cultural life for black Americans at home."[21]

Charles Burroughs had lived much of his early life in New York, where his mother was a schoolteacher and activist and his father a postal worker with Shakespearean theater training and literary education. A member of the Communist Party, Williana Burroughs decided early on that her four children would not suffer a Jim Crow–style education. She sent nine-year-old Charles to a Moscow boarding school, where he became fluent in Russian. Although he maintained his American citizenship, he identified primarily as Russian by the time he finished high school. During the Depression, his mother stood up at a school board meeting to criticize its discriminatory practices against young teachers of all races and was subsequently fired. She later joined her son, working for the national English-language radio and also as a party representative. She stayed in the Soviet Union for most of the rest of her life.[22]

Charles remembered receiving a solid, even privileged education during his younger years at the Soviet boarding school that his mother, Williana, had endeavored to secure for him.[23] His unusual status among the Russians illustrates a broad tolerance and even strong acceptance of his unusual complexion in otherwise white Moscow. His experiences going to school in the Soviet Union echo much of the positive experience chronicled by Robeson (and later his son Paul, who was also schooled there) when visiting and touring that country. Burroughs found the Soviet people to be fascinated with African-descended people, to the point of his being given "preferential treatment" because so few blacks lived in Moscow. At the same time, a significant population of blacks lived in the country and had been there for over 1,500 years. As Burroughs noted:

They live near the Black Sea. It's not exactly determined how they got there, but the Greeks had conquered that territory, so probably a lot of these Blacks got there with the Greeks as soldiers. There were various peoples coming from Egypt to the north, so the idea is that most of them probably came up that way as troops. They all intermarried with Europeans. In the circuses in Moscow, you would see people who were obviously Negroid. Their features were like the local people in the Caucasus, but they were very dark and had kinky hair.[24]

Charles Burroughs named several African American contemporaries who also came to Russia and found the kind of high-level employment and honors that were denied them in the United States. Burroughs himself had no trouble finding gainful employment right out of high school. His mother had always discouraged college in favor of working for a while:

> My mother had this background of always having to work hard
> like her mother did. She said, "The trouble with many of the
> Negroes is they get a college education and forget their roots."
> She was saying that black people were really working people.
> They come from the land or are workers in the cities. She
> had no use for the black bourgeoisie. She told me that I could
> always attend college, but that if I worked for a year or two, I
> would appreciate my origins.[25]

Charles subsequently worked in the Stalin Automobile Plant in Moscow for two years and then drove a truck. For a short while he was also enrolled in the Soviet circus school, where he was recruited as a truck driver. Later, during the war, he had wanted to serve in the Russian military, but his U.S. citizenship precluded enlisting in a foreign army. Then in 1945 the United States embassy gave him notice to serve. Just as he was inducted into the U.S. Army in Teheran in 1945, he was called back to the States, via Cairo. But before he entered active duty, the war ended. He still received basic training, and once the war with Japan ended, he was sent to Germany for two years as part of the postwar occupation.[26]

Burroughs never forgot the exceptional treatment he received at the hands of the Soviets, and he refused to renounce what he knew even after he returned to the United States at the start of the Cold War and McCarthyism. Like Robeson, Burroughs remained a staunch supporter of the Soviet Union. As his grandson Eric Toller recalled, Charles told stories about meeting Stalin as a youth and sitting on his knee.[27] Even after learning how Stalin's purges affected his friends and fellow minorities, Robeson remained similarly staunch in his support of the country and its people. Margaret Burroughs would find a credible witness in Charles's firsthand experience in the Soviet Union. By 1968 the couple would begin their treks to that country despite continued Cold War tensions.

In Charles, Margaret found a person comfortable with people from a broad range of backgrounds and experiences as well as a seasoned traveler, reminiscent of the cross-cultural discussions held at her parents' table in St. Rose, Louisiana. Together they would roam the globe until his death in 1994. Charles's keen interest in languages and literature, including master's degree courses in Slavic languages from the University of Illinois at Chicago, paralleled Robeson's voracious appetite for learning languages, music, and literature. The poet Haki Madhubuti recalled how it was Charles, not Margaret, who took him under his wing when Madhubuti, then Don L. Lee, a disaffected army soldier in the early 1960s, showed up at the Burroughses' door hungry for intellectual companionship.[28] Charles loved his Russian culture and language and shared it with anyone who cared to listen, singing the praises of his adopted country as a place where he did not suffer the kinds of discrimination endured by his wife. For Margaret, Charles embodied the "go see for yourself" type of discovery that she embraced.

After Margaret married Charles Burroughs, she readily returned to her habits of "open house," only now even more regularly and intensely in the carriage house of 3806 S. Michigan, the former Quincy Club for black Pullman porters. The tradition of providing food and shelter for travelers that the Quincy Club had embodied continued with the Burroughses' household for decades. Generations were raised up at the picnic table in the Burroughses' kitchen where visitors might eat eggs and toast on a Sunday morning and discuss current events, art, and local, national, and international politics.

The former South Side Community Art Center board president and board member Diane Dinkins Carr remembered her parents requiring her presence at these salons, where she was expected to be seen and not heard, and to learn from her elders. Her father, Fitzhugh Dinkins, a prominent graphic designer for *Ebony* magazine and art director at Johnson Publishing Company, had been among the artists who helped found and teach at the Art Center and had sat on its steps in protest in the early

1950s when its board, in a move to stifle rumors about "un-American activities" taking place there, banished certain artists and their associates, including Taylor Goss.[29] Dinkins Carr says that her career as a promoter and collector of African American art was directly influenced by Margaret Burroughs, who passionately promoted the idea of everyone owning and displaying African and African American art in their homes and businesses.[30]

Margaret Burroughs would not escape the wrath of the authorities for long. Her ties to radical groups, her outspokenness and protests, and her cultural front work drew the attention not only of fellow Bronzevillians but also of her employer, the Chicago Board of Education. She had a reputation, according to her longtime friend Clarice Durham, for her radical stances and her open resistance to racist and classist ideology.[31] Her 1949 marriage to Charles Burroughs, who was under governmental scrutiny for his ties to the Soviet Union, only intensified suspicions around her. By 1951, while teaching art at DuSable High School and surreptitiously offering lessons in her classes on African American history, she received a letter from the Chicago Board of Education requiring her to testify before them.

As Burroughs recalled, her radical politics, including her activism at the Art Center, contributed to her reputation as a "militant" teacher at DuSable High School, where she had found full-time employment. She speculated that when she arranged for the Art Center to host Paul Robeson, and the Art Center's board was split in its decision, the Chicago Board of Education decided to look more closely at her political inclinations: "Some person from the arts center had reported to the Board of Education that I was instrumental in having Paul Robeson invited to come to the arts center."[32] Furthermore, as an "outspoken" member of the DuSable High School faculty, Burroughs stated, "I would always be the one at lunch time in the teacher's lunchroom. I'd be preaching this and preaching that and . . . 'Free the Scottsboro boys . . . Free Willie McGee'— whatever. 'Free Earl Browder . . .' so you know."[33] Like the other teachers, she had to sign a loyalty oath in order to receive her paycheck. But this did not stop her from speaking up to end discrimination or the need to include black history, which she had already found a way to do below the scrutiny of school authorities:

I just couldn't see myself standing in front of a group of eager-
eyed young black people and not being able to tell them something very positive about themselves. There was one guy who
taught, I think he taught commercial law, but he was telling
these kids, 'You're nothing. You're not going to be anything.
I don't see why you are wasting your time coming to school.'
I mean it was just totally negative. So I began to dig out information about our people and share it. And I still remember we
had this white principal—at that time most of our principals were
Anglos—so I would be teaching art . . . and while the kids were
drawing, I'd be telling them about Harriet Tubman, Frederick
Douglass, and so forth and so on like that. And then I'd look up
and there would be the principal at the door. And I said, "And
yes, students, as I was saying, remember how Betsy Ross sewed
that flag. She did a really good job sewing that flag, didn't she?"
And when he went away we went back on talking about black
history. It was bootlegging it.[34]

Eventually the Board of Education ordered the principal to call Burroughs down to its office for questioning. Burroughs retold her story
of this face-off many times, including to me during my visits, and some
persistent themes and events are repeated. The encounter was clearly a
turning point in her life, not simply because her livelihood and reputation were threatened, but because, as she found out later, she had been
singled out among all her fellow teachers and was the only one who had
to respond to charges of being communist and who was asked to identify
colleagues as such.

She went into the meeting clear in her positions about freedom of
thought, her admiration of Robeson, her ties to CPUSA groups, and her
activism, including writing a letter to free Earl Browder, who was then
chairman of the Communist Party.[35] Even as she did not back down from
her core beliefs, she did not directly challenge the questioners for asking
such slanted questions but rather reframed them to align with broader
democratic principles, much in the way that the National Negro Museum
and Historical Foundation steered its agenda toward cultural fronts rather
than direct action in the streets after the war began. At first she tried to
bring with her a teachers' union representative, but this was quickly rejected. She alone had to face a "long table" filled by a committee, with the

superintendent of employment at its head, and answer questions that she readily surmised were aimed at trapping her into some sort of confession or, at the very least, pressuring her into fingering other teachers. Her letter in support of Earl Browder was questioned. Her answers to that and other questions illustrate how Burroughs's long-standing commitments and her willingness to express them shaped her responses, which were coherent and firm in their values: "'Well, why did you write such a letter?' 'Because,' I said, 'I don't think anybody ought to be put in jail on account of their politics or their religion. They ought to have freedom of thought.'"[36]

Burroughs offered a similar defense in her support of Paul Robeson:

> Then they asked what I thought of Paul Robeson. I said, "I think Paul Robeson's the finest American artist we have . . ." "Well, didn't he send his son to go to school over in Russia?" I said, "I suppose he did. I should think he'd have the right to send his son to school wherever he wanted him to go." "Well, isn't he supposed to be a communist?" I said, "I don't know. I don't know what his religion or politics were."[37]

In Burroughs's multiple accounts of this confrontation, she focused on her and others' rights to freedom of thought and speech. She also expressed admiration for Robeson without attaching that admiration to his politics or religion, in this case claiming to be ignorant of them—no doubt a move to deflect further questioning. Nor did she directly disclose any of her own political alliances or positions. When she was finally asked the "key question"—"If you were a member of the teacher's union or any organization of teachers, would you be able to point out who was a communist and who was not?"—she answered in the negative, stating that "I don't look at people like that," and the committee accused her of being evasive. But in fact, given Burroughs's track record on civil and human rights, her answer was less a dodge and more a reflection of her deeply held beliefs in how she really did see people.

Feeling the pressure mounting, Burroughs, whether strategically or just genuinely feeling distressed, "pulled a nut role and I got real hysterical like, because sometimes you got to pull a nut down here."[38] She succeeded in throwing off the committee's questions and further scrutiny. But to her the message was clear—her job and her livelihood were under a cloud. She had seen so many others, including Robeson, subjected to similar or worse pressures, to sometimes tragic ends. She had evaded such consequences, with her head held high, but she was shaken to the core. Once more, she turned to art for answers.

Burroughs's interest in Mexican art, which led her to study with Leopoldo Mendéz in Mexico City in 1952, along with her friends Elizabeth Catlett and Charles White, very likely started when she was a young artist. The cultural stage was set shortly after she was born. In 1925 Jane Addams, the founder of Hull House, which the South Side Settlement House was modeled after, went to Mexico to study how art was being used to further education and that country's left-wing politics.[39] She discovered how murals and prints were produced easily and cheaply to teach people about their heritage as well as to communicate about current events. Furthermore, a general trend in the 1920s and '30s among collectors was to collect preindustrial folk art. The Art Institute of Chicago and smaller galleries also routinely displayed Mexican art from the 1920s to the 1950s.

Margaret Taylor's own teachers at the South Side Settlement House and the Abraham Lincoln Center were already eager audiences for the emerging global folk art movement, including that in Mexico. The radical artist Morris Topchevsky was one of the first artists to travel to postrevolutionary Mexico in 1925, befriending Diego Rivera and staying for two years, and returning thereafter for frequent visits. He and fellow Chicago Artists Union members used their gallery for political ends, in particular to fight fascism in the 1930s.[40] Many other artists traveled to Mexico as well, pursuing shared interests around collecting folk culture, admiring Mexican modernism, and sharing political sympathies.[41]

Given the rich and pervasive cultural exchange between Chicago artists and those in Mexico, Taylor could not have escaped that particular influence. No doubt she would have seen a 1931 exhibit, "Mexican Arts," at the Art Institute of Chicago.[42] Other opportunities for young Margaret to see Mexican art included Katharine Kuh's work as a collector and art historian at the Art Institute. In 1936 Kuh opened a North Michigan gallery to show Mexican modernist art. The gallery owner, Illinois Art Project director, and Art Center cofounder Peter Pollack brought Leopoldo Mendéz's art to the Art Center.

During the summer of 1951, when she was teaching art full-time at DuSable High School, Burroughs collected her family and set out for a bus trip to Mexico. She chronicled that experience for Chicagoan Claude Barnett's Associated Negro Press in a series of articles published throughout the United States. One prominent theme was the contrast between Mexico and the Jim Crow experience north of the border, particularly as Burroughs's Greyhound bus passed south of the Mason-Dixon line. She described how, once they had reached St. Louis, the public facilities became separate and unequal. Her introductory article ended with a call to action: "As a positive action, we have decided to write protests to the Greyhound Motor Coach Co., against the inferior types of facilities accorded Negro passengers who travel on their lines. It may not help much, but if enough letters bombard their offices, perhaps something will be done."[43]

Another, contrasting theme was how at home she felt as a woman of color among the Mexican people: "Most impressive to us was the fact that being Negroes, we rather melted right in with the rest of the population. No one stared at us when we went to eat at the fancier places. We received the best and cordial service. And we were welcomed wherever we went."[44] She also did not hesitate to editorialize some conclusions that she drew along the way:

> I am sure few of us Negroes can imagine what it feels like to
> walk around, anywhere, all over a beautiful city, to be wel-
> comed all over, without feeling one's color as a badge of shame.
> This is a wonderful feeling. And I am sure that if more Negro
> Americans could have this experience it would make them more
> determined than ever to make our America the democracy that
> our forefathers planned it to be.[45]

Burroughs also described the diverse racial mix in Mexico and how white American gringos were in the minority, along with their prejudicial attitudes. Mexico, like the Soviet Union, held firm against importing imperialist intolerance, according to Burroughs: "Thank God they have not been able to bring their anti-Negro practices into this beautiful country. I understand that they have tried in some places but the Mexican government would tolerate none of it. Hurrah for them."[46]

Yet another theme was the beauty of the land, its people, and their art. She described side trips to Taxco, the "Silver Center of Mexico," and that town's spectacular silver jewelry, along with its beautiful setting, inspired Burroughs to wax a bit poetic: "Taxco is a beautiful town which seems as if it was just flung up against the mountainside. It was beautiful to see as we left it at dusk, with thousands of lights twinkling on the mountainside, spangling it with wonder."[47] She also described a visit to Toluca, another mountainside village, famous for its markets featuring baskets, weaving, and food sold by indigenous people. She extolled the virtues of historical sites such as the Palace of Chapultepec, one of many sites adorned with art to mark the country's history. At the palace were "paintings, murals, and actual objects" that told the "story of the fight for Mexican independence."[48] At the Palace of Fine Arts in Mexico City, she noted how the mural that Diego Rivera had originally created for Rockefeller Center in New York was "drawn too one-sided to be hanging in a building which is a bastion of capitalism." She proudly stated how "a constant procession of people pass[ed] before it" and how its controversial message "doesn't bother the Mexicans."[49] If the Mexican people were, as she wrote, inclined to see Negroes through certain North American stereotypes, albeit with more compassion than their gringo compatriots, Burroughs, in her chronicle, sought to dispel stereotypes of Mexico and Mexicans held by her fellow African Americans.

So when the time came for Burroughs to find an escape from the pressure cooker that her job and her community had become in 1952, she had already found a place where, as other artists had told her, "If you ever go there, you will not be happy away from there."[50] Fortunately for her, she already knew of a place that was not only friendly to people of color, but also a treasure trove of art and history. She could do what other artists similarly pressured by Red Scare tactics did—she picked up and moved her family to Mexico for a year's paid sabbatical from teaching. Burroughs described it this way:

> One of the places I was always hearing about was Mexico—what a colorful place it was, particularly when you'd see the paintings and the arts and crafts that people would bring back from Mexico. Seeing all these colorful things and seeing all these beautiful posters—travel posters—about Mexico and talking with people who had been there, I decided that maybe, being an artist, I should like to visit. So Charlie and I saved up our money and in 1952 I asked for a sabbatical leave from teaching because

there was an awful lot of pressure put on anybody who was the least bit militant. They'd claim that you were a Communist and would try to take your job away from you. So I asked for this sabbatical and got it for 1952.[51]

Fortunately for her and for her art, she experienced what she herself considered to be the most important year of her life in Mexico, a year when she developed not only artistically but also morally and intellectually.[52] By turning to her passion for art during a period in which she and everyone around her were targets of right-wing persecution, she not only found refuge in Mexico but also camaraderie, artistic exchange and growth, and a resolve to fight back against what oppressed her. As a polestar of her life, art inspired her to discover that she could and would risk more than she might have initially thought possible.

As a result of trusting her art, her leadership blossomed even as her art rose to new levels of achievement and audience. Many of her best-known works draw upon the linocut techniques, along with the practices of inexpensive mass distribution, which she learned at the Taller de Gráfica Popular. Later in life she would freely give out her prints as rewards to those who had helped further her work and activism.[53] Art had been her chief pursuit ever since her mother released her from dishwashing duties, recognizing its value in helping young Margaret realize her multifaceted capacities for aesthetics, politics, and leadership in the community and eventually across the globe.

In Mexico, through her good friends and fellow artist-activists Elizabeth Catlett and Charles White, Burroughs was introduced to many artists from around the world who had sought refuge from political persecution. Other Chicago artists such as Hale Woodruff, John Wilson, and Lawrence Jones had sought refuge there.[54] She lived in an apartment building "with practically all Mexicans" where she acquired a working grasp of Spanish. Diego Rivera, one of the foremost muralists of that era, had already passed away, but many other artists, both Mexican and international, were there for her to mingle with and share art and stories. She recalled being highly influenced not only by Rivera but also by the muralists José Orozco and David Siqueiros, whom she visited while in Mexico. She toured many museums as well. To fulfill her sabbatical contract with

DuSable High School, she enrolled in La Esmeralda, the National School of Painting, Sculpture, and Printmaking in Mexico City.[55] Her contact with Leopoldo Mendéz as well as Catlett and White brought her into the Taller de Gráfica Popular, an artists' printmaking collective that Mendez had helped found in 1937.

This experience cemented her commitments that had already formed in the 1930s and '40s and which aimed at a fusion of art and political activism. Like Robeson, she made no distinction between the two. Also like Robeson, she sought out methods and means for making her art work for her people, "the little people," as she liked to say. While her childhood artwork used inexpensive materials because of a lack of funding, her adult pursuits were responsive to the revolutionary spirit of the Taller de Gráfica, which put the mass production of art at the center of its collective endeavor. To her final days, Burroughs would reproduce and distribute for little or no cost her linocut prints, booklets and pamphlets of her writing, and other "rewards" in her drive to bring everyone to appreciate and own art—specifically, art infused with deep, political consciousness about racial history, pride, and education.

In several accounts of her sabbatical time, Burroughs praised her Mexico experience for the exposure and education she received, which brought her to an even greater pitch of awareness of her role as an artist-activist in the world. She also recollected seeing "natural" hair on other women, many from Africa. Women in Mexico praised her hair for its natural curl. She found herself following suit in changing over to a hairstyle in which she could forgo hot combs and chemical straighteners.[56] For years afterward, her hair was the target of many comments—good, bad, or indifferent—and it inadvertently became a symbol of African American identity years before the slogan "Black Is Beautiful" was ever uttered in the streets. She claimed to have no message to convey at that point, instead seeking only to gain relief from the painful hair-straightening method.[57] Of course, later, when Afros became an important symbol of revolutionary consciousness, Burroughs would claim her "natural" as ahead of its time, as she and many of her fellow travelers had been in a social, political, and cultural sense.

That hairstyle ultimately became iconic in the eyes of her DuSable High School students, a visual lesson in being oneself and valuing one's heritage in the face of criticism. When offering memories of Burroughs as a teacher, almost everyone interviewed for this book brought up

Burroughs's "natural." One gentleman at the Original Soul Vegetarian restaurant on Seventy-Fifth Street and Indiana Avenue, for instance, explained how he had been taken to task by Burroughs for not completing an assignment. When he told his mother that Burroughs was that "crazy teacher with the natural," his mother backed off from her punishment. Others such as Moses Jones similarly recalled the powerful impact Burroughs's hairstyle had in communicating a message of racial pride and self-determination to students.[58] While Burroughs may not have initially intended to convey any message, she clearly understood, as an artist and educator, the power of the visual image in helping students to feel pride and confidence in themselves and their heritage.

Similarly, Burroughs may not have entered the Taller de Gráfica with a particular political agenda other than simply taking refuge among fellow radicals and the desire to improve her art and activism "for the little people." Her accounts indicate how strongly learning art through this collective process affected not only her sense of her art, but also her identity as someone who would "stand up" to all forms of oppression, particularly those aimed at people of African descent. In her refuge, she found a way to stand tall in the face of potentially crushing adversity. She became more fully what she had always aspired to—a woman who spoke her truth and helped bring others along with her.

Burroughs knew from early on the importance of surrounding herself with people she looked up to, people who "broke through" whatever obstacles or oppression stood in their and others' way. Paul Robeson clearly captured her imagination as well as her devotion. In a self-published booklet, Burroughs described in great detail her recollections of Robeson, his philosophy regarding life and art, his political perspectives, and his internationalism. She turned to his example over and over to help her in her own life's struggles:

> So it was when faced by grave decisions, I would often ask myself, now what would Paul Robeson do in this case? Now, on what side is Paul Robeson? Whatever I concluded that Paul would do, that is what I did. His guidance and direction sustained me through the thirties and the forties and left a lasting impression on me.[59]

In our contemporary moment, it is easy to deride the seemingly wor-shipful attitude held by Burroughs and others toward the iconic figure of Robeson even to the final days of her own life. One might accuse Bur-roughs of blindly following a man who was, after all, a human with flaws and blind spots, and capable of misjudgments, including his long-held support of Stalin. Yet Burroughs never wavered in her devotion to Robe-son not just as a man, but as a representative of all that she cared about, and in that, a tangible source of inspiration and guidance:

> I consider myself fortunate that my acquaintance with Paul
> Robeson grew into a friendship that withstood the strains and
> stresses of the McCarthy Witch Hunt period. When few homes
> were open to him, he was always welcome at our home. To
> buttress my pledge of fidelity, in his later years I vowed to place
> my talents and my time at the disposal and behest of Paul and
> Eslanda Robeson and this I have done.[60]

It is remarkable enough for any adult outside a religious or romantic context to "pledge fidelity" to anyone, let alone the lightning-rod figure that Robeson became over time. But what Burroughs seems to have un-derstood and subsequently aimed to pass on to others was the need for real people and places to turn to when facing one's own trials and tribu-lations. It mattered to her that someone who stood to teach her so much like Paul Robeson would spend time and share conversations with her as an equal. But it also mattered to her to preserve and have ready access to places like the Ida B. Wells homes had been in their heyday, a place where everyone knew that living there was "a route to success." It mattered that the deceased Ida B. Wells should remain present in the community in material ways—in the preservation of her home, in the naming of a South Side park, a school, and even in the naming of a distinguished professorship awarded to one of Margaret and Charles's mentees, Haki Madhubuti, at DePaul University.[61]

History can be kept alive when it remains present in our everyday lives in visible, tangible ways. Our connection to our collective pasts, to the stories of those who broke through, whether into formerly segregated neighborhoods, workplaces, museums, libraries, or schools, is strength-ened and affirmed in so many small but impactful ways. We become what we encounter, if we remain open to it. These were the lessons learned by

Margaret Burroughs that she strongly felt needed to be passed on. Her own life embodied those lessons. She, like Robeson, remained humble about her achievements and accomplishments, and at the same time she made sure that others could follow in her footsteps. It was always with and for others that made whatever she accomplished matter.

He Was Our Big Paul
The Man for Whom They Named a Mountain

He was our big Paul, the man for whom they named a mountain
He is the pride and joy of our people
He was our big Paul Robeson

. . .

For as long as his spirit lives, and it will—
Big Paul Robeson, the man for whom they named
A mountain will live.
He will live in my family,
He will live in your family,
He will live in our hearts.
For he is the pride and joy of our people
He is Big Paul Robeson, the man for whom
They named a mountain.[62]

—MARGARET BURROUGHS

FIVE

ART AS A PASSPORT
TO CROSSING

As the intense August sun continued its assault, Dr. B suggested an additional destination, in part to cool off, but also to view another landmark, one that was not on my tour list. We made our way back down King Drive, recrossing the Bronzeville Walk of Fame, with the Lake Meadows apartments beckoning us from our shaded path. As we approached Thirty-Fifth Street, I noticed that the Chicago Public Library branch, like the boulevard we traversed, was named after Dr. Martin Luther King Jr. This was yet another sign of how Bronzeville, guided by people such as Dr. B, had made important strides toward historical preservation while keeping the memory of such greats as King alive in a palpable way.

Dr. B's pace did not lag; in fact, she seemed even more resolute and purposeful in her stride. Fortunately, we were not stopped by further admirers in our quest for relief from the sun and the sweltering humidity. Yet as we crossed King Drive so that I could take a photo of the library's sign, we were greeted yet again, this time by a woman in a car at the stoplight at Thirty-Fifth Street. Then from still another vehicle, two other, younger women drew our attention. One held a book out the open passenger window while the other waved her arms to draw Dr. B's notice.

"Dr. B, Dr. B, I got your book!" one cried out.

I can't recall how Dr. B reacted, or if she even did, intent as she was on simply getting across that wide boulevard in one piece. Once safely on the other side, however, she explained to me that her autobiography, *Life with Margaret*, had just been published. She recommended that I might want to read it for further information.

As I wiped sweat from my forehead, I thought that this was quintessential Dr. B. She got us across the street without stopping to bask in the praise and then offered yet another resource for my research without ego attachment. She simply wanted to be of use to those she encountered, for the sake of her people and her community, here and around the world.

After taking my library photo, we crossed Thirty-Fifth Street and walked down to Meyers Ace Hardware. Although I was a little confused about Dr. B's plans for our destination, given the fast food venues nearby that would more likely provide us with the necessary refreshment, I trusted that Dr. B knew what she was doing. Meyers Ace Hardware is an unremarkable two-story brick building painted with the store's logo on the side. A circa-1960s sign juts out from the building's street side. The storefront windows were jammed with various and sundry items one might need for home repair, along with signs touting store specials. As we entered the cooler clime inside, I was struck by the narrow aisles and overflowing shelves of an old-time urban neighborhood business. Still, this hardly seemed the place for cool refreshment. Plungers they had in excess, but nary a hint of a soda machine or water fountain. I was hardly one to question Dr. B, but the heat and my growing thirst continued to challenge my patience.

It did not take long for Dr. B's logic to make itself known. As we stood at the front of the store, a man close to my own age, perhaps slightly older, approached to greet us, or should I say, Dr. B.

"Good to see you, Dr. Burroughs," he said and shook her hand. "What brings you here?"

"This young lady"—she pointed at me—"wants to see your historic landmark here."

The man turned to me. "David Meyers." He shook my hand, too.

"So this is a landmark of—?" I asked.

"My father bought this building in 1960 from Joe Glaser, Louis Armstrong's manager. It started as the Sunset Club and then became the Grand Terrace."

"A speakeasy?" I'd read a fair amount about Chicago's nightclubs, jazz and blues legacies, and the people who frequented them. I was hopeful I'd stumbled upon the real deal.

"It was a black-and-tan nightclub. Louis Armstrong, Cab Calloway, Fatha Earl Hines, lots of these musicians played here early on." He paused, looking around the store. "Just a minute. Let me take care of something and then I'll show you the bandstand with the original mural in the back. Can I bring you ladies a cold drink?"

Dr. B stood, patient as usual, while David Meyers settled his business elsewhere in the store. The cool air dried my face and arms. I scanned the shelves for signs of items other than the expected ones, looking for something by way of a souvenir. No such luck. Nothing camera-worthy, either, only displays such as quart-sized plastic drinking cups with lids and straws sporting Scooby-Doo's Great Dane grin.

David returned with lemonade in hand. I couldn't help but think that had I been alone, I would not have received this level of hospitality. Bronzeville certainly held this elder in highest esteem.

The Sunset Club was known as a "black and tan," one of the few types of places where blacks and whites could mingle together socially. The building's exterior had been remodeled when it became the Grand Terrace, though scant evidence of its once ornate entry remained. Glass bricks on the second floor hinted at an Art Deco design that the store sign's bold red-and-white typeface echoed, a respectfully tasteful marker overshadowing those large picture windows packed with merchandise.

David Meyers led us through the narrow aisles to the back of the store. "Tourists come in from all over the world," he said. Pointing to the black plungers on one shelf, he offered, "A group of German tourists came through. They all bought plungers! One of them hugged the pillar"—he pointed to a plain white square pole in the middle of the aisle—"and cried. The BBC filmed here." My puzzled look may have prompted more explanation: "Maybe the plungers looked like trumpet mutes! They asked us to autograph them." He smiled and nodded his head, clearly relishing the anecdote.

"And the pillars?"

"Like hugging their idols."

David found Dr. B a comfortable chair and then shepherded me into the nether regions of the business. David apologized yet again for the mess. "Home Depot is building across the street soon," he said ruefully. Would Meyers Ace Hardware survive, I wondered?[1]

Apparently, Dr. B did not require another tour, instead taking the time to rest. Would Dr. B have frequented this club back in its heyday? Had she listened to some of her beloved jazz greats here in person? But then, as a young woman, starving artist, and later mother and wife, would she have had the means to patronize an apparently luxurious club such as this one? One ticket in may have been through the reviews of musical acts she wrote for the Associated Negro Press. On the store's walls, photos and sketches of the Grand Terrace revealed a classy white-tablecloth cafe where women wore gowns and men wore black suits and ties. The plain pillar we had just navigated past had once been ornately decorated. Was this the kind of place Dr. B would have favored?

At the very back of the store, raised up about a foot, stood the old bandstand. David Meyers pointed out two staircases, one on either side of the stage, which led to the second floor. "Blocked off for security," he said. Back then, the stairs had led to practice rooms and restrooms. The dressing rooms may also have served multiple, unseemly purposes for the likes of sexual rendezvous, prostitution, and gambling.

The store's office had been built on the bandstand. David escorted me inside. Here were original murals from the club on the very back wall of the office, visible through steel shelves crammed with supplies. Suddenly the colors, shapes, and by extension, the sounds and flavors of the club leaped forth. In one mural, a tan woman with large clawed hands and feet, wearing only a tiger-striped loincloth, gripped a wide white drum-head reminiscent of African drums in one hand and a padded drum stick in the other. Her downcast eyes focused intently on her instrument like a tiger on its prey. Her bare thighs straddled the round drum eagerly, even playfully. Above the loincloth, her naked chest was small and muscular, her midsection taut and strong. The loincloth drooped below her waist like a tail. It echoed the curved lines of a white, U-shaped hand harp float-ing in the auburn spaces of the background behind her. The bold black outlines and dynamic, almost free-form shapes of the mural recalled as-pects of both African and modernist art. Later I would see that same harp in a Picasso sketch from around the same period.

The style of the mural surprised me. The Grand Terrace had been all classical elegance, gowns and suits, and palm-tree ease. The mural spoke in much rawer, more animated tones.

To the right, another figure, with lighter skin tones and white hands that looked almost gloved, played with pursed lips on some indistinguish-able instrument loosely held like a pole. Another, horizontal drum-like object, similar to a West African *dunun*, stood below. This was one cool cat, dressed in a black-lapeled jacket, with a side part and smooth hair. With eyes closed, his lips puckered like a kiss around the instrument's reed. Cool meets hot. Cool tones meet hot licks. Red, yellow, black, tan—all the calculus of a masterful painterly eye.

I should have asked Dr. B if she had known the muralist. She likely had.

"The City of Chicago made this building a landmark," David said. "If we got rid of this mural, we would pay $5,000 a day penalty."

"Pretty steep price to destroy history," I replied.

After I took photos, David ushered me behind the bandstand, where the former kitchen had stood. He pointed out an old iron rotisserie; overhead, the pressed tin panels of the original ceiling added an unexpectedly ornamental air to the otherwise dim back of the store. Then he led me up a sounder staircase to the second floor.

A hand-printed menu of much simpler fare than that suggested by the rotisserie greeted us on the wall: 25¢ HAM SANDWICH COCA COLA CHECK-ROOM GIN VODKA BOURBON SCOTCH BEER declared this fragile paper sign in bold capitals. Below in lighter print: ORANGE-LIME-SODA OR GINGER ALE WITH DRINKS. It seemed that a second, back-room operation had catered to simpler tastes.

We walked up to a chalk board painted in white lines.

"A policy board?" I asked. Policy was Bronzeville's version of the numbers game.

"More like a voting tally. Aldermen used to come on election nights. For a while, after the nightclub, this was a political center."

I squinted at the small, hand-printed letters. Words such as "Ward," "Precinct Capt.," and "No." came into view. So the local pols had made a headquarters here, in the upper realms, among the dressing rooms and all their goings on, probably drinking and smoking and wheeling and dealing. There were even ladies' and men's room signs to serve this shadowy patronage.

Downstairs, Dr. B sat patiently, taking in the moment. She rose upon seeing us. As we thanked David Meyers for his personal tour, Dr. B nudged me, and pointing to the display of Scooby-Doo travel cups, she suggested that I purchase two of them. And so I did.

I kept that cup until it cracked and fell apart, long after Dr. B's body had given out and cancer had taken her from this life. I'd like to think that she kept her cup, too. But most likely she gave it to someone else, a child perhaps, who would need it more.

Upon her return from Mexico in 1952, Margaret Burroughs was, "in her own words . . . 'in a fighting mood,'" after her confrontation with the Chicago Board of Education.[2] As Burroughs said, "I got strong. So when I got to the end of that job from t[hat sabbatical] year, I said, 'Hey, they're not going to take my job from me. I worked too hard for this job.' I came on back, went on back to work. Nobody ever said anything to me."[3] The camaraderie and artistry of her fellow travelers across the border had sparked a resolve, even a rejuvenation, in Burroughs that burst forth not only in her art, especially her inexpensive, mass-produced linocuts of African and African American subjects, but also in her work on the cultural fronts that she had been involved with since the 1930s. Through her continuing education as an artist, Burroughs found a compelling means of bringing art to "the little people," her people, and along with the skillfully rendered images, imparting valuable lessons in African American history.

Despite the duress under which she had traveled to Mexico, the experience proved to be a watershed moment in her life. Not only was she supported and even nurtured by her contacts and friendships with fellow travelers there, but she also found an even more powerful means of focusing the multiple activities in her life. Throughout her life, art had provided such a focus to seemingly disparate roles and efforts: as a student, then a teacher, a daughter, then a wife and mother, and (for several years) a single parent, a community organizer, an institution builder, a salon host and networker. But lessons from the Mexico sabbatical catapulted her into a new, more fiercely engaged effort to inscribe black history and culture as reality.

Nonetheless, Burroughs's livelihood, her teaching post at DuSable High School, remained on the line. No one may have openly challenged her after her confrontation with the Board of Education, but the surveillance continued. Ian Rocksborough-Smith commented on the pervasive surveillance of Chicago teachers, especially those with ties to left-wing politics:

> One scholar notes how many Chicago teachers faced "scrutiny from the Chicago Police Department's Subversive Unit, or 'Red Squad,' which started to investigate the political activities of all those who applied to or worked for the city, state, and county, and especially the Chicago public schools" in the 1940s and 1950s—information which the department then shared with the federal House Un-American Activities Committee (HUAC). A brief perusal of Burroughs's Red Squad file clearly indicates

the high level of surveillance she and no doubt many others were subjected to at the hands of the city's police department. It includes entries on seventy-four public events she allegedly attended and publications she authored or was mentioned in from local newspapers and publications between 1950 and 1968. Despite such surveillance and harassment, Burroughs would continue to teach art and black history—a vocation that became the cornerstone for her public history activism.[4]

At the same time, Burroughs also claimed that she was the only teacher she knew who was called before the Chicago Board of Education: "And then the key question was asked. . . . 'If you were a member of the teacher's union or any organization of the teachers, would you be able to point out who was a communist and who was not?'" Burroughs of course did not comply, perhaps ensuring that she would remain the only one to be questioned by the board.[5]

Various scholars have characterized the Cold War period for leftist African Americans as one of retreat, defeat, and sometimes compromise. In contrast to the robust and very public representations of a vitally alive black culture and community bound together by the twin villains of racism and classism during the 1930s Negro People's Front, blacks' activities in the postwar years and the 1950s are generally characterized as a scaling back and retrenchment of progressive cultural and political work. According to Rocksborough-Smith, those remaining "'left-influenced African American institutions of the 1940s largely disappeared during the Cold War,' and those that survived this moment such as the South Side Community Art Center and the *Chicago Defender* (like in the labor movement of the same period) purged or isolated many known leftists from their ranks."[6] He went on to note how

> in general, the 1950s and early 1960s in Chicago have generally been downplayed by civil rights historians. Many view the takeover of a militant protest-oriented leadership of the local NAACP chapter in 1957 and 1958 by Chicago's Democratic machine as a moment of decline for black activism and community vitality in that decade prior to the more widely recounted and beleaguered open housing and school desegregation movements of the 1960s in the urban North.[7]

Bill Mullen similarly observed how the Negro People's Front, which had worked side by side with the Communist Party's cultural front in the mid- to late 1930s, struggled to maintain an active, visible presence within Bronzeville in the late 1940s and throughout the 1950s.

At the same time, both Rocksborough-Smith and Mullen described the remaining cultural front, which included the Burroughses in Chicago, W. E. B. Du Bois, Shirley Graham, and of course, Paul Robeson, among others nationally, as remarkably strong and resilient, a far cry from the general purging, oppression, and defeat suffered by many other leftists, black and white alike, during this period. Chicago proved to be a particularly resilient location, despite the departure of luminaries such as Charles White, Frank London Brown, Richard Wright, Gordon Parks, Elizabeth Catlett, and others. Scholarly accounts raise interesting questions about how to regard the shift in leftist tactics, strategies, and public presence during the 1950s, questions that, depending on the answer, cast Margaret and Charles Burroughs in varied lights. Of course, nothing in these accounts can diminish the bravery and courage of the Burroughs and their fellow travelers during this period and beyond. But through closer scrutiny of their efforts, some important lessons about legacy and its transmission to the next generation—in this case, the Black Arts Movement, OBAC, AfriCOBRA, and even the Black Power and black nationalist movements of the 1960s, as well as the founding of the DuSable Museum—can be understood. Chicago politics would support a legacy that not only ushered in the establishment of the DuSable Museum but also the election of the city's first black mayor and an opponent of its long-established Democratic machine, Harold Washington.

Burroughs, like Paul Robeson and many others, did not distinguish between her art and activism at any point during her adult life. When the Red Squads of the 1950s began to attack left-wing activists mobilizing for civil rights as communists, many such people and groups had to switch tactics just to survive—if they did at all. So pervasive was the anticommunist sentiment that, according to Eugene Feldman, cofounder of the DuSable Museum, "in the 1950s when McCarthyism was on, everyone who advocated peace, love and friendship surely was thought of as a communist. Yes, there were those who said that anyone advocating desegregation, integration were communists."[8] Burroughs had begun to change course after her face-off with the Chicago Board of Education by joining fellow artists and fellow travelers in Mexico for a year's sabbatical. But upon her return in 1952, she found a much-changed cultural and political landscape, including changes at her beloved South Side Community Art Center. With the collapse of the National Negro Congress, along with the Popular and Negro People's Fronts of the 1930s, Burroughs shifted instead toward the kind of cultural and historical work that would, in some ways, operate under a lower and apparently less threatening profile than she had previously worked. As the 1950s came to a close and civil rights movements began to mature and become more visible on the national scene, Burroughs did not join up or actively promote such events.

This apparent lack of participation on Burroughs's part raises the question of why she seemed to change direction from her youthful rallies with the NAACP and her affinities with leftist labor, political, and other groups. Instead of pressing for better jobs, labor, and housing, Burroughs instead focused on using art to develop historical consciousness among African Americans. Instead of simply critiquing the Chicago Democratic machine's stranglehold on the South Side, she joined forces with some machine politicians in exchange for precious resources and social and political support. The broad strokes with which scholars have painted this period of retrenchment among African Americans during the postwar and Cold War years would seem to offer enough explanation for Burroughs's seeming shift toward "safer" cultural work. But such an explanation falls short when applied to Burroughs. Rather than view such shifts in tactics as a necessary compromise, it may be more accurate to see them as more of a continuation of previous activities, interests, and commitments, namely her early advocacy of creating a positive image of African American and African identity through artistic production and historical education. Following in the footsteps of so many female teachers, librarians, club members, and social service providers, Burroughs worked from a nexus of pan-Africanism, expressive arts, and social protest/activism that did not draw hard-and-fast distinctions between institutional activism and direct action protests, between creative and political expression, or between the nations of the black diaspora. She had from early on grasped Carter G. Woodson's call to create black history curricula for the schools and, along with other liked-minded teachers, would continue to do so. While others may have found themselves having to back down, move away, or even be imprisoned or, in the case of Paul Robeson, exiled for many years, Burroughs returned from her sabbatical leave in Mexico ready and eager to face down her adversaries. And as she had experienced during the creation of the Art Center, those adversaries existed not only outside her beloved community, but inside it as well.

Throughout the 1950s, Burroughs would continue to pay a price for her outspoken views on race and class. At the same time, she never lacked friends, support, and ideas. As her contemporaries attest, everyone knew everyone else, in part supported by Burroughs's kitchen table salons. So perhaps rather than assume that Burroughs took on cultural and historical work as a way to continue under the radar, so to speak, it might be more accurate to say that Burroughs simply continued on her path, even though the terrain around her had clearly shifted. While others may have viewed her activities as a move away from civil rights work, according to Rocksborough-Smith, Burroughs regarded her efforts as conjoined: "'We had sympathy with [the civil rights movement],' she noted, . . . 'I imagine a lot of Chicagoans participated in it. I spent my time working on black history work and didn't have time to work with them because of what I was working on.'"[9] Rocksborough-Smith continues: "Though they were parallel activities, civil rights activism and the cultural work she and others did on black museums, public history, and other heritage projects were quite connected. As Burroughs stated, 'I think it's the civil rights movement that made us realize it's important to know about and document the history. To know where you're going, you have to know from whence you came.'" Rocksborough-Smith concluded, "If not intimately involved in conventional civil rights activism such as sit-ins and direct action throughout the 1950s, Burroughs clearly saw her efforts to promote cultural heritage during the same period as vitally important for efforts at redressing racial discrimination."[10]

Well before the idea of starting an African American history museum in her own home entered Burroughs's thoughts, she had for years been fascinated with historical figures and scenes as subjects of her art. She also pursued her own education in African American and African history and culture with an all-consuming passion. While she worked within the National Negro Congress, that group had made Negro history and education one of its many projects; Burroughs had been on those committees. In turn, members of the NNC were also part of the National Negro Museum and Historical Foundation (NNMHF), including Burroughs. This foundation picked up where Carter Woodson left off in 1926 with the establishment of Negro History Week. As Rocksborough-Smith wrote, Burroughs was part of a group of ten black labor leaders, civic leaders, and teachers based mostly in Chicago who initiated the city's first significant attempt to establish an African American history museum in 1945, called the National Negro Museum and Historical Foundation. The NNMHF's members included Margaret and Charles Burroughs, as well as the community activist John Gray, the local Communist Party member and union activist Ishmael Flory, and the Associated Negro Press editor and writer Frank Marshall Davis. Other members were older, well-respected community figures such as the public school teacher Sam Stratton and John Bray of the Colored Episcopal Church. Margaret Burroughs was the NNMHF's financial secretary. Most of these members were also leading members of the National Negro Congress—a broad civil rights organization that became increasingly Communist-influenced, but was mainly composed of black labor activists with chapters in numerous American cities.[11]

The scholar St. Clair Drake in 1969 discussed the interwoven relationships between NNMHF activists and the powerful black Democratic machine politician William Dawson, claiming that an "entente," or informal alliance, had been reached between the group and that congressman. Instead of focusing on international issues of war, peace, and revolution, the NNMHF instead continued its efforts to promote the study of Negro history. In turn, Dawson leveraged this "entente" to persuade mayors and governors from the 1940s to the 1960s to "proclaim Negro History Week."[12] In this way, the activist base of the 1930s could still find a focal point and means for promoting civil rights. As a result, "Chicago's celebrations had become one of the more 'prominent traditions' of their city and consequently received due recognition from public officials."[13] Such alliances no doubt taught Margaret Burroughs the importance of garnering political support for future projects such as the DuSable Museum.

In 1955, perhaps encouraged by their relative success with the NNMHF, Burroughs, the labor leader Ishmael Flory, and other local teachers and community activists sought to resurrect the local chapter of Woodson's group, the Association for the Study of Negro Life and History (ASNLH). However, Cold War politics played against Burroughs and her fellow travelers from within the community, most significantly from a prominent clubwoman, Irene McCoy Gaines. Gaines was a Republican proponent of Booker T. Washington's more integrationist approach to civil rights. Like others in Bronzeville, she was wary of left-wing groups who maintained ties with communist leaders like Flory.[14] So when Burroughs and her cohorts applied for a renewal of the ASNLH chapter,

Gaines, an executive of the national organization, rejected Burroughs's application.

Gaines's rejection, difficult as it may have been to receive, would not be the only blow Burroughs would receive in her efforts on the cultural front. In 1956 Burroughs submitted her annual membership dues to the Art Center, only to be stung by its return shortly thereafter. As Burroughs recounted in her remarks for the Art Center's fortieth anniversary in 1981, relations between the Art Center board and its artists had always been rocky: "Looking back over 40 years, I reflect upon the many ups and downs that the artists had as they were tossed in and out of the Center by whoever the 'in' group was. One thing was certain, after the fury of battle had died down the artists were always around to pick up the pieces and put Humpty Dumpty together again."[15] However, unlike the marginalization of artists during the grand opening of the Art Center in 1941, this rejection was likely motivated by the larger political winds of the McCarthy era: "It would not be the last time I was persecuted for being a communist. One of the most appalling examples of this came in 1956, when my membership dues to the South Side Community Art Center, which I helped to create, were returned to me with a note that simply indicated I was no longer wanted as a member."[16] In the 1950s Burroughs had invited Paul Robeson to speak at the Art Center. While Robeson was hardly the first left-leaning guest there, his invitation appeared to spark a strong backlash among the Art Center board members:

> When Paul Robeson came—this was in the 50's in that
> McCarthy period—well, there was a real split in the board of
> directors about the fact that—I think I was chairman or some-
> thing then—that we permitted him to come. And this was
> criticized very harshly by some of the other board members.
> And I understand that one of the reasons why, as a teacher,
> a militant teacher, I was called before the Board of Education
> about my politics was because some person from the arts center
> had reported to the Board of Education that I was instrumental
> in having Paul Robeson invited to come to the arts center.[17]

As a result, Burroughs kept her distance from the Art Center for most of the rest of the decade. The artist Doug Williams recalled how, while he was living at the Art Center during the 1950s, Burroughs, his mentor and friend, would not come to see him there. "She got mad," he said. "No one at the Art Center would talk about what had happened." Williams kept asking her to come back, asking for her help. At one point, the Art Center's fence and storm windows needed to be replaced. Burroughs donated the fence and windows, and repainted the fence immediately. In this way, she stayed connected, albeit indirectly, during those years. As Williams speculated, perhaps it took years for those who had exiled her to either pass on or look the other way. Williams would later take up residence in the Burroughses' coach house at 3806 S. Michigan, just down the block from the Art Center, where in the 1960s he became the director. He attributed his success as an artist to Burroughs, "the den mother of the art world." Besides taking art classes with her on the weekends, he followed in her footsteps and took classes at the School of the Art Institute of Chicago. Burroughs's one-on-one time with him, along with being his go-to person whenever problems arose, helped give him an artist's life. Perhaps it could be said that Williams returned the favor by keeping her involved in her beloved Art Center, however distantly.[18]

No doubt drawing upon the resolve and motivation from her Mexican sabbatical, Burroughs, in conversation with other teachers, students, and fellow travelers, began to imagine starting a second institution, this one focusing on African American and African history. Such an idea likely had been in the air for some time; as Burroughs recalled, other ethnic museums had already appeared on the scene in Chicago.[19] Her travels had also awakened her to some out-of-the box thinking about museums:

> I had visited this professor at Howard [in the 1940s]. His home was practically an art museum. He had paintings hung around in the various rooms and all, and on weekends he would have it open for the public. And I saw that you could do this in a house. Then, I had been to New York and I had visited one of the museums started by the Rockefeller community, with primitive art . . . in a greystone building, three stories . . . And then also I had found out that 90 percent of the museums in the United States are small house museums. . . . It's only 10 percent that are [housed in] these great big edifices.[20]

Of course, Burroughs had for her entire life looked to ancestors and elders for inspiration and guidance, and was always quick to credit them for their legacies. Many historical figures who are now well recognized, such as the Underground Railroad freedom fighter Harriet Tubman, the former slaves and abolitionists Frederick Douglass and Sojourner Truth, and the first black man to die in the Revolutionary War, Crispus Attucks, were lifelong heroes for Burroughs, as well as subjects of her art. Lesser-known historical figures, gleaned from her inexhaustible hunger for knowledge about "her people," included King Afonso I of the Kongo in the sixteenth century, who resisted Portuguese colonization, and Queen Anna Nzinga, another African monarch who resisted the Portuguese. Burroughs was influenced, too, by the white abolitionist John Brown and the newspaper publisher William Lloyd Garrison.[21] Among contemporary influences, Paul Robeson towered over them all. In addition, Burroughs also found support, resources, and inspiration from the scholar-writers W. E. B. Du Bois and his wife, Shirley Graham. Over the years, Burroughs had worked on committees to bring Du Bois to Chicago. Graham had written a biography of Chicago's founding father, Jean Baptiste Point Du Sable, which resonated with Burroughs, who felt that Chicago had done an inadequate job of honoring this black man's legacy. Burroughs would eventually travel to New York City for doctoral work. While in residence there, she frequently attended lectures and receptions frequented by Du Bois and Graham while continuing to read their published work. Thus, during her darkest days in the 1950s, Burroughs found solace and strength in these stellar people.[22]

By this time the Burroughses had rented the carriage house of the mansion at 3806 S. Michigan, which was still occupied by the railroad porters' group, the Quincy Club. Margaret and Charles hosted many guests at their kitchen table salon, where sometimes the talk veered toward the absence of any institutions for African American history. Margaret had "bootlegged" such history lessons into her classrooms at DuSable High School for many years, but public access to books and artifacts on black American history to use as resources was haphazard at best. To assist others in their own research, Margaret began to collect materials, which she would then either lend out or invite people over to see.[23]

Renting the coach house, and then buying the front mansion at 3806 S. Michigan in 1959, was a turning point for the Burroughses. While Margaret herself had shared a similarly spacious dwelling with her first husband, Bernard Goss, nearby, and had hosted many "house rent parties" there on the weekends, the mansion she and Charles had bought quickly rose to the more elevated status of the "Chicago Salon," as friends, fellow artists, writers, intellectuals, and visiting luminaries began to regard it.[24] Some regular visitors, like Diane Dinkins Carr, remembered a home full of art and an endless conversation about art with other artists. Others, such as Clarice Durham, remembered a more political bent to the discussions.

Dinkins Carr, the former board chair and current member of the Art Center board, as well as an art collector and artist agent, grew up around that kitchen table. She recalled being required to accompany her parents, both artists, to the Burroughses' salon every Sunday. Years prior, Burroughs had introduced her parents to each other, both having come to Chicago from other cities. (Burroughs had helped make a number of significant matches, including Gwendolyn Brooks and her husband, Henry Blakely, as well as Elizabeth Catlett and Charles White.) Dinkins Carr's father, Fitzhugh Dinkins, had helped begin the South Side Community Art Center, along with Burroughs and Bernard Goss. When he and Burroughs were denied Art Center membership during the Red Scare era in the 1950s, Dinkins stood firm: "Before establishing a workshop across the street (at Burroughs's carriage house), artist Fitzhugh Dinkins and others protested the board's decision by sitting on the Center's steps, vigorously holding forth on the 'role of art in society.'"[25] Diane Dinkins Carr was thus immersed in art and politics from early on, with Margaret Burroughs providing lifelong guidance. Dinkins Carr remembered those Sundays as enforced social time. She had to go with her parents, having no choice in the matter: "You'd be tortured, you'd have to listen to what they were saying," she said.[26] She heard stories about art and artists all the time. She also remembered how people thought artists were communists; Charles Burroughs and her father were always being investigated. The Burroughses' "Chicago Salon" as it became known, doubtless helped maintain a sense of community in the aftermath of the Red Scare.[27]

Clarice Durham, a longtime friend of Burroughs as well as an early education teacher and fellow civil rights activist, along with her husband, radio writer Richard Durham, remembered the Burroughses' home as welcoming: "There was always food and a lot of talk, and she was interested in what was happening politically." Burroughs was not much for "chitchat" but instead discussed issues that people were concerned about. "You felt very comfortable in her home, very welcomed. So she was a good hostess." Durham recalled a table and "a large kitchen." People would sit around the table very informally. Margaret had a lot of cats: "She collected these cats . . . was devoted to those cats." Diverse groups of people came by, usually by invitation. Charles liked to cook, while Margaret "wasn't much of a cook or a housekeeper or anything like that." Before they purchased the big house, they lived in the coach house and it was "open door." Eventually Margaret would invite those she wanted to meet each other, whether for personal or other, more public reasons.[28]

As labor organizer and fellow traveler Timuel Black recalled, Burroughs invited students to her home, "particularly when artists came to town." When Gordon Parks, a *Life* magazine photographer and former Art Center artist, would visit, Burroughs had students and teachers come to meet him. This was a typical pattern. Burroughs's use of her artistic talents brought non-artists like Timuel Black into her sphere. As Black noted, an important part of her legacy was using art to bring diverse groups into a "universal" sphere that art made possible: "You see a better world through art and music. Artists and musicians communicate with each other through their work across continents. They understand each other pretty well, even though it may be China, Argentina, United States, Black Belt." For many years, that "universal sphere" included the Burroughses' kitchen table and later, other parts of their home.[29]

Eugene Pieter Feldman, one of the founders of the DuSable Museum, remembered the kitchen table as a place of serious exchange but also lively spirits, a "cuss and discuss" venue that drew from a wide swath of cultures, classes, races, and vocations.[30] Many educated or specially trained people "with something substantial to contribute" were invited. But in addition,

> there were also people self-educated who had not gone to
> school, college, but who had read and through their reading
> were very much "up" with things. From all of these Margaret
> Burroughs learned, from the men and women of the Marcus
> Garvey movement (who generally were carpenters, bricklayers,
> construction workers or dining car waiters but who read). . . .
> Here were great writers, published writers and unpublished.
> Here were poets, poets who told stark truths about Black
> life. . . . Here were artists painting and sculpting Black life as
> it was. Here were philosophers, ministers, teachers, librarians,
> bricklayers, factory workers, entertainers . . . all discussing,

commenting, advocating and mostly teaching. . . . Here were
Garveyites, socialists, communists, here were those affiliated to
the Democratic party and the Republican party. And Dr. Margaret Burroughs listened, offered more hot coffee, added some
of her own comments and mostly learned.[31]

When Feldman first arrived in Chicago in 1957, it did not take long
for others to steer him, a white Jew from Alabama with a keen interest
in black history, toward the Chicago Salon. His first visit left a lasting
impression:

Here I found a most unusual cultural scene. There was a fellow
there giving guitar lessons. Then Charles Burroughs, Margaret's husband, who had since boyhood gone to school in the
U.S.S.R., began giving lessons in Russian. After the "hellos"
they all made me welcome. I waited in a butterfly chair (I'd
never seen one before) in an apartment that served as a gallery
also. It had beautiful paintings, black and white sketches and
sculpture. It had a large wooden picnic table around which we
were, in many weeks, months, and years, to drink coffee and
give birth to projects including the building of a Museum.[32]

Grandson Eric Toller understood his grandmother's dedication to
knowing one's heritage; her belief was that progress could not be made
unless people knew where they came from. Burroughs took him on two
trips to West Africa, including the Ivory Coast and Ghana, while he was
growing up. Knowing one's origins and ancestors, Toller said, were part
of his grandmother's philosophy.[33] From a very early age, Burroughs relied on the history of her people to provide a sense of value and purpose.
This desire to know and expand her knowledge, as well as share it with
others, was a driving force in her life. Drawing from various African traditions, tribes, and cultures, Burroughs came to a similar conclusion as
her ancestors: art and history were, in fact, deeply intertwined.

The idea for another, historical institution was an ongoing topic at the
Chicago Salon. The Burroughses' family collection of art and books became more and more a public, not simply a personal, resource. Just coming over was an education in itself for those lucky enough to be invited
to the salon. What helped shift this trend of informal, invitation-only

resources into a full-fledged public museum was, according to Burroughs, predicated on a bit of humor. She claimed to have "liked the sound of the 'Ebony Museum of Negro History'" and, to "try it on for size," she listed it in the phone book with her and Charles's coach house number. One Saturday morning in 1960, the doorbell rang, and an elderly black minister stood before Burroughs, inquiring if the museum was open. As Burroughs recounted, "Now at that time, we didn't really have a museum, but somehow or another I got a quirk of humor and answered, 'Oh, yes sir. The museum is open today. Come right on up.'" She proceeded to show the man around the house, pointing out paintings, photographs, sculptures, and bookshelves full of books on black literature and history. As the man studied the room's contents, he asked if there was an admission charge, to which Burroughs responded, "Oh, no sir . . . Today is a free day. Please won't you register sir?" She then asked him to register in a notebook she put before him.[34]

Burroughs later told this story to many friends, who laughed at the pretense she had staged. But the joke eventually turned more serious: "The more I talked about it, the more real it seemed to become."[35]

But again, perhaps the most significant precipitating event in the move to begin the museum was Burroughs's exile from the South Side Community Art Center. While she was, indeed, hurt by her exile, she also wanted to keep educating others about African American and African influences. She did not see a museum as a competitor to the Art Center but rather as a complement:

> I'm not the kind of person—I don't go back trying to do any-
> thing against you. I keep moving straight ahead. About that
> time [after the board refused her membership] several of the
> school teachers came together and we decided, well, maybe
> there's room for us to have two cultural institutions. One that's
> devoted to history, and the arts center devoted to art. And it
> didn't mean that I would stop working with them, but I was
> going to help them along. And we decided to start the Museum
> of Negro History.[36]

Right around this time, after having moved into the coach house, the Burroughses were approached by a Quincy Club member, Ralph Turner, one of the few remaining resident members of the aging club, about purchasing the mansion. Turner had seen the artistic activity in the Burroughses' coach house, and he and fellow residents had supported their effort to bring African American art and history to others. Charles and Margaret purchased the mansion at 3806 S. Michigan Avenue in 1959. Turner eventually would join Margaret and Charles, Eugene Feldman, and others as founding board members for the Ebony Museum of Negro History and Art, which was founded in 1961 and was renamed the DuSable Museum of African American History in 1968.[37]

Once the Burroughses moved into the mansion, they immediately considered what to do with all the extra space. Having already surrounded herself with many people who shared her passion for African American history, including the relatively new arrival, Eugene Feldman, Burroughs sat down with some of them at the coffee table of 3806 S. Michigan and drew up an official charter to the secretary of state of Illinois in February 1961. Those who signed included the Burroughses, Ralph Turner, the librarian and collector of black history Marion Hadley, James O'Kennard, the Oxford scholar Wilberforce Jones, an auto worker, and a member of the automobile workers union. Hope Dunmore signed as a notary public.[38]

When the museum officially opened in the mansion in October 1961, Margaret Burroughs's work in attracting others interested in African American history and culture paid off. Donations poured in. As Eugene Feldman wrote,

> Even when we started we were given important collections. One of them was that of Captain Harry Dean, a Black sailing vessel Captain whose ship carried cargo along the coast of Africa. He was a friend of Harold Ickes, a member of Franklin Roosevelt's cabinet. . . . We received some papers and manuscripts of Langston Hughes, Dr. W. E. B. Du Bois, Paul Robeson and many others.[39]

Those who helped start the museum donated as well. Hope Dunmore, the notary public, provided materials about her and her family's lives as "old Black early settlers."[40] Another founder, Gerard N. Lew, a longtime civil rights activist, gave a powder horn used by his ancestors in the American Revolution. His family were also early settlers in Massachusetts and fought in the French and Indian War.

As Feldman noted, "It was Margaret Burroughs who served as the leader, the one who called us together, the inspirer, the motivator. She made it her business to get acquainted with like-minded, history-interested persons."[41] Her long-standing interests, activities, and relationships focused on African American history and art brought people together in this initial push to open a second institution down the street from the first institution she had worked so hard to establish.

Most people associated the new Ebony Museum (later the DuSable Museum) with Margaret, and to a lesser extent, Charles Burroughs. To this day, it is Margaret Burroughs who is hailed as its chief proponent and longtime director. However, Burroughs, always keenly aware of the strength in diversity she had seen throughout her entire adult life, was also quick to credit the "good white people" who offered assistance, resources, and support at critical junctures in her projects and in her life in general. The Art Center was the product of President Roosevelt's Works Progress Administration, along with black donors and workers from the community. And the DuSable Museum, according to Burroughs, depended upon more whites than blacks as donors: "My position is, 'Don't tell me how to run it. Don't tell me to keep white folks out unless you bring the money in, because the bulk of the money comes from white people. We always stress that the purposes of the museum are brotherhood, understanding, and bringing people closer together."[42] Burroughs also credited her white friends Shoshanna and Joe Hoffman for guiding her into the fund-raising aspects of starting the museum. Shoshanna had been a classmate, and Joe was the development officer for the Better Boys Foundation. Shoshanna "nagged" Joe into teaching Burroughs "how to write the proposals, how to raise money, and how to make a presentation."[43]

Of the many people, white or black, who Burroughs herself cites, Eugene Pieter Feldman stands out as a key figure in the museum's founding. "Black and White, Unite!" was more than an old slogan from Burroughs's cultural front days. It became a motto she lived by, and Feldman, who appreciated this, carried on when others dropped away. As a southern Jew with radical interests in African American history, Feldman had left his Alabama home for more hospitable cultural and racial climes up north, where he studied at the University of Wisconsin. Upon his return to Birmingham, Alabama, he began researching and writing about African American history and whites who supported black liberation. Because of this work, he and his family were, according to Burroughs, "marked and a cross was burned on his lawn. So he had to leave Birmingham in the dead of night and then he came up to Chicago."[44]

Feldman first met Burroughs at the Fifty-Seventh Street Art Fair in Hyde Park on the South Side in 1957. Feldman had recently arrived in Chicago and had inquired about people who were also interested in African American history. He had been pointed out to Burroughs by mutual acquaintances. At the art fair, he came up to Burroughs at her exhibit, and their connection was formed. She invited him by the house, and their discussions led to the idea of a museum. As Burroughs recalled, "Four or five of us got together and just talked about the idea of starting a museum of Negro history. And that's how it all came about. But he was instrumental in all of that, and I think everybody should know . . . that it wasn't just something that we African Americans thought up—we have allies."[45]

In the beginning, Margaret and Charles, along with Feldman and Burroughs's younger sister, Marion Hummons, paid for, staffed, and promoted the Ebony Museum. After clearing out all the furniture from the four first-floor rooms of their newly acquired mansion, Margaret and Charles set to work to organize the space. They sent out letters to museums asking for donations of display cases. They put up a sign in the window, "The Ebony Museum of Negro History. Welcome!" Charles served as "janitor, librarian, researcher and lecturer." Margaret was "director, secretary, fund raiser, lecturer, public relations person." All expenses were paid for by Margaret's wages as a teacher and Charles's laundry truck driving. Margaret and her fellow teachers developed a series, "How to Teach African American History," that quickly became very popular. According to Burroughs, school buses starting lining up in front of 3806 S. Michigan. Soon, the museum became so crowded that staff members would go onto buses and give lectures to the children while they waited their turn to go inside the museum.[46]

Word of the museum's opening, along with its need for volunteers, quickly spread. Just a few months after the opening, a young army soldier stationed at a missile base at Fort Sheridan read a notice in the *Chicago Defender* about the new museum while searching the ads for a used car. Don L. Lee had grown up mainly in Detroit with a single mother who, to put food on the table, took up as the mistress of a local pastor. Lee's life was school, work, and the lure of the streets. At the tender age of sixteen he found himself alone. But early on, he took to reading books as a way to address the problematic reality of being a black man. He saw no answers to his life's questions in the streets. When it came time to earn a living for himself, by himself, after finishing his schooling, he joined the army. Books followed him there; ideas did as well. He read many African American authors who spurred thoughts, feelings, and ideas that he desperately wanted to discuss. But his interests were, for the most part, discouraged, even threatened as anti-American, a common occurrence during the Cold War era. The army itself was not so friendly to black men, whom he saw routinely get into trouble. So when he read the notice in the *Defender*, desperate for intellectual conversation, he showed up at 3806 S. Michigan. He expected that anyone who would open such a museum must share many of the same questions about being black that he did. As he recalled, "This was a decision I needed to make to grow."[47]

Lee, who later changed his name to Haki Madhubuti, remembered his first encounter with Margaret and Charles Burroughs, whom he credits as early mentors. He was met at the door by Eugene Feldman on a Saturday afternoon and told Feldman that he wanted to meet Margaret Burroughs. As he approached her working on a linoleum cut print on the kitchen table, Lee was struck by her "natural" hairstyle. As he stared at her, she asked, "What you want, boy?" She was the first black woman he'd ever seen with natural hair. He told her he'd "devoured" all these books—Du Bois, Robeson, Wright, and so forth—but at the still-young age of eighteen he had no one to talk to about them. Burroughs recognized the searching in this young man, who had no idea how to put his ideas into action, or even how to converse about them. She told him she knew Du Bois, Robeson, and others whose work he admired.

"Go upstairs and talk to Charlie," she directed as she continued her printmaking.

Madhubuti recalled how Charles Burroughs was seated at a big desk, surrounded by books, reading and writing. He offered Lee a glass of clear liquid, which Lee drank, only to discover it was vodka. Charles, Madhubuti remembered, was poet and fluent in Russian. He introduced Lee to Russian literature, including Dostoevsky, Pushkin, and Mayakovsky, as well as Lenin and Trotsky. Charles was the first black male intellectual that Lee had ever met. He felt grateful that at such a young age he could learn from someone who read in the original Russian language, and he could gain insights that were not available in a university class. Charles also provided a strong political voice against which Madhubuti would argue for years. While Charles argued from class-based leftist positions formed during his early years in the Soviet Union, Lee found a leader in Malcolm X and a black nationalist movement that regarded white supremacy as the overarching oppression in the world.[48]

In contrast, Margaret "had an artist's temperament," Madhubuti recalled. Unlike Charles, she did not argue. She and Lee did not discuss politics. Her view of the world was that she needed to be in the forefront of developing a black presence on many levels. For her, "art was core to the development of all people." He learned from both Margaret Burroughs and Gwendolyn Brooks that to have a meaningful life, there must be art: "Strong, healthy and inquisitive people develop this way." The core of Margaret's being, according to Madhubuti, was art, which she produced her entire life.[49]

Margaret provided a strong counterpoint to the oppression and early death suffered by Lee's mother. Margaret stepped into a man's world, a black man's world, in which the major leaders were ministers, and she "challenged all that," claimed Madhubuti. Even with the male cofounders of the museum, she was the central figure. She was "the founder," according to Madhubuti; no museum would have happened without her. She also showed him how black women artists thought for themselves and held high standards: "I don't care what you bring, you better bring it high." She was the first liberated black woman he had ever known, including her "natural" hair. Along with Margaret's compatriots Barbara Sizemore and Gwendolyn Brooks, Madhubuti admiringly recalled being in the company of "some bad sisters. I wasn't going to mess with them."

Lee worked as a volunteer for the museum as an assistant curator from 1962 to 1966 or 1967. As an assistant, he cleaned up and did whatever else was necessary to keep the place running. Margaret trusted him with giving tours, which increased his own knowledge, because curatorial work involved "continuous study." This in turn helped him find a voice as a writer. He stayed on with the army until 1963, volunteering at the museum on the weekends. After 1966, other interests began to develop out of the museum, interests that would ultimately steer Madhubuti toward the Chicago literary movement OBAC, and later the founding of Third World Press and Afrocentric charter schools in the Chatham neighborhood of the South Side.

Like Margaret Burroughs, Madhubuti is quick to credit his forebears for the legacy they provided to find his way in the world as a black man. Madhubuti's experience with the Ebony Museum led him to a new interest in art and artists, but it also inspired him to strike out on his own and develop Afrocentric enterprises. Burroughs brought him into contact with the independent black publisher Dudley Randall in Detroit. The poet Gwendolyn Brooks, a childhood friend of Margaret's, took Madhubuti under her wing. He would eventually found the Gwendolyn Brooks Center for Literature at Chicago State University, where they both taught for many years—this university was the former Chicago Teachers College, where Margaret Burroughs had received her training as an art teacher. Inspired by the Burroughses' "you've got to build your own" attitude, Madhubuti maintained a commitment toward Afrocentric enterprises, education, art, writing, and culture throughout his adult life. It was Margaret who suggested that he start an independent black press by taking his poems to a printer and paying for their printing; she sold his books at the museum, and he himself went out into the streets to sell them, much like the Mile of Dimes campaign in the 1930s that jump-started the South Side Community Art Center. Like Margaret, artistic expression formed a core that Madhubuti then brought into the schools he founded and the teaching he did: "None of this would exist without me being a poet."

For twenty years, yellow school buses lined up on South Michigan Avenue, full of schoolchildren who would learn about their heritage through art, history, and historical artifacts. For the first time in the United States, an African American history museum had opened its doors. Just as with the opening of the South Side Community Art Center, the community proved to have a deep and abiding hunger for such knowledge. People from all over the country and the world contributed significant items to the museum's collection that likely would have otherwise been lost to posterity. Margaret and Charles traveled every summer to a new place, loaded with art upon their return. New generations began to take pride in their heritage. The mansion at 3806 S. Michigan had expanded its Chicago Salon into the community and beyond.

On the surface, the founding story of the DuSable Museum may appear deceptively simple, a "build-it-and-they-will-come Field of Dreams" tale. But building the museum was a decades-long commitment that occupied Margaret and Charles Burroughs on a daily basis and was woven into the fabric of their lives in the most intimate ways. Many people stepped up to help, but it is clear that without Margaret Burroughs herself, the museum would not have come into being. Eugene Feldman captured this sentiment well: "It was Dr. Burroughs who was the strong magnet to pull people in to help with the many tasks. Today we call this charisma, but she had it then and continued to have this important ingredient in her personality."[50] Of course, Margaret Burroughs was about more than charming people; she labored endlessly in pursuit of her goal to promote African American culture and history. But labor without vision does not necessarily equate with success. Burroughs had her eye on the bigger picture: "And you know, I always stress the point—if the purpose of our museum is really to bring diverse groups together in understanding, in fellowship, friendship, and through knowledge of the positive achievements of African American people, I stress bringing them together and I think that is very important. Because it's not a separate thing—it's not an all-black thing."[51]

Once the Ebony Museum's doors were opened, the Burroughses were faced with the task of not only soliciting and storing artifacts but also the all-important need for fund-raising. Just as the young Margaret Taylor Goss had stood on the street corner collecting a Mile of Dimes for the purchase of the South Side Community Art Center, she again put her shoulder to the wheel to foster this new institution. She wrote letters to friends, colleagues, and letters to the editor, asking for family letters, scrapbooks, genealogies, and so on. When individuals stopped in with artifacts to donate, she and her volunteers would "talk at the coffee table and learn more about the person's family."[52] She began the arduous and never-ending task of writing foundations and businesses for funds, which was a challenge for someone whose main fund-raising education had come through a WPA-funded project. Following the Art Center's example, she began a membership campaign that proved crucial in the early years of the museum, given the initial lack of response from other sources, and she once again modeled these activities on her experience at the Art Center, which had also solicited memberships.

One person who proved crucial to her early fund-raising was the intellectually minded Eugene Feldman. Feldman had even less experience with fund-raising than Burroughs, but Burroughs understood that in a racist, capitalist society, "the fact that I had this gentleman with me *of the other persuasion* gave them more confidence in what I was trying to do and what I said I was going to do. Because they figured that at least he'd be watching the money."[53] As previously noted, help from across the racial divide also came from her white schoolmate, Shoshanna Hoffman, and her husband, Joe, a development officer, who taught Burroughs how to write proposals, raise money, and make the all-important presentations.[54]

Within a few years of opening the doors of the museum, Burroughs's efforts began to result in some significant grants. The local Wieboldt Foundation provided the first substantial grant, boosting the spirits of the museum's founders and volunteers as well as raising the museum's profile in the community.[55] Other donations followed suit. In 1968, seven years after the opening of the Ebony Museum, another breakthrough grant came from the Field Museum of Natural History in Chicago. Burroughs had been reading magazines about museums; small donations to the Ebony Museum had fortunately provided subscription money that Burroughs herself lacked. When she spotted a notice about the availability of museum internships, she immediately applied to the Field Museum. At first, she was denied, in large part because the grant required that applicants maintain a salary from their home institutions during the internship. However, Margaret and Charles had been funding the museum from their own, modest salaries and thus had nothing for Margaret to claim on her grant application. But when the first awardee turned the internship down, a Field Museum official called Burroughs and, after discussing her financial situation, offered to write to the Washington grants office to make the case for Margaret to receive the internship so that she could help put the museum on such a financial footing that she and others on staff would eventually draw a salary. The request was accepted, and Burroughs was thrilled to be able to take a year off from teaching to study the ins and outs of museum operations.[56]

The Field Museum internship provided crucial support for Burroughs and the museum at a time when the Ebony Museum was reaching out into the community not only with its growing collection of artifacts but also with lectures, spontaneous coffee-table sessions, and, eventually, outreach to educators and other civic and business interests with the goal of promoting greater racial understanding and collaboration. The internship was a landmark as well; no blacks had ever been involved in a curatorial department at the Field Museum before Burroughs; as Burroughs noted, "in all those years, there were no blacks behind the scenes."[57] As part of the internship, Burroughs was also given a year of course work in Northwestern University's African Studies Department, including tuition and travel. She studied with well-known anthropologists and learned about every aspect of museum operations, from maintenance on up.[58] Her knowledge of fund-raising was also significantly enhanced through this program.

Around the same time, Burroughs had been giving some sixth graders a tour of the Ebony Museum, showing paintings of African scenes and teaching about the African continent, when a little boy asked if she had ever been there. When Burroughs replied that she hadn't but that she understood how it was, the boy persisted in asking how she knew. Burroughs heeded the call to action enunciated by this young child. Her remarkable web of contacts and connections led her to the American Forum for International Studies, which was offering scholarships to individuals—with preferences to teachers working in communities of color, minorities, and women—and applied. Charles could also accompany her once they secured a loan from the teachers' credit union, putting everything in their household up for collateral so they could take a six-week trip to Ghana that, according to Burroughs, "would [change] the whole course of my life."[59]

But even before these momentous events in the museum's founding, Burroughs had already been acquiring and passing on knowledge about arts institutions and their role in society for many years. Her commitment to using what she knew as a bridge for learning from others was already a well-established practice for her, both informally and formally. This kind of networking continued even more strongly after the Ebony Museum opened its doors. But one reason why the museum gained the momentum it did was because of Burroughs's constant seeking of new avenues to promote African American culture and history. For instance, in 1959, she and fellow black artists from across the country founded the National Conference of Negro Artists—later the National Conference of Artists (NCA)—at Atlanta University. Burroughs was well known at that point for her artwork, the art fairs she had helped begin and promote, and her writings on black culture. Bringing a national focus to the efforts of black artists only helped further the development of the Ebony Museum a few years later. As of 2012, her mentee Haki Madhubuti had taken over for Burroughs in the NCA. She was also involved in the founding of the African American Museum Association (AAMA), with Charles Wright of Detroit. This organization began in the mid-1960s as a way for similar institutions focused on black culture to exchange ideas as well as artifacts "to help each other out."[60]

For Margaret and Charles Burroughs, launching the Ebony Museum
was not a part-time, catch-as-you-can endeavor. Instead, it demanded their
full-time commitment, on top of their family life with two young children
and two full-time jobs to pay the bills. But because of Margaret's magnetism, a core group of supporters could be relied upon to pitch in, including Feldman, Margaret's sister Marion Hummons, Don L. Lee, and
the early board members Gerard Lew, Ralph Turner, and Jan Wittenber,
among others.[61] The fact that busloads of schoolchildren continued to
arrive at the museum was testament to how deeply rooted Burroughs
was in the educational community; she was known widely for her commitment to promoting black history and culture, and was a leader in
curriculum development.

There would be no resting on anyone's collective laurels as far as Margaret Burroughs was concerned. As the years passed, and artifacts and
grants rolled in, the question of space, along with the ongoing issue of
funding, began to loom large. While it was true that Burroughs exuded
a certain magnetism, she would not have been nearly as effective as an
institution builder if the Bronzeville community itself had not been so
tightly knit. Even today, among those who were interviewed for this
project, everyone had at least a passing acquaintance with their fellow
South Siders. For instance, as Clarice Durham explained, she and Burroughs were connected through her brother Charles Davis, who married
the dancer Rosalee Dorsey Davis, an elementary school friend and later
roommate of Burroughs at one point; both had helped with the Art Center's early development. Durham also knew Burroughs's two sisters, and
Margaret spoke at Durham's husband's funeral; Richard Durham was
a well-known radio writer and activist. Lawrence Kennon, a civil rights
lawyer and Art Center board member, became Burroughs's attorney
later in her life. Theresa Christopher, a volunteer and later registrar at
the museum, had a brother, Lewis, who worked in Kennon's law office.
The Art Center board member and previous president Dianne Dinkins
Carr was the daughter of the Johnson Publishing Company's art director
Fitzhugh Dinkins, who regularly brought his family to the Burroughses'
kitchen salon. Ramon Price, half-brother to Chicago's first black mayor,
Harold Washington, had been a student of Burroughs and later became
head curator of the museum; Harold Washington appointed Burroughs
a Chicago Park District commissioner. And so the web of relationships
goes on.

Throughout her teaching life, Burroughs supported a cadre of students whom she not only taught but who also taught her. It was students, once again, who took the lead in developing the museum. This time, in the early 1970s, Wilson Junior College (now Kennedy King Community College) students noticed that a former lockup facility for the Chicago Police Department in Washington Park had been vacated and boarded up.[62] Letters and petitions to the Chicago Parks Commission to reinhabit the property ensued, and the idea was born to house the expanding DuSable Museum in this building. Students wrote the superintendent and copied their letters to the mayor. As Burroughs recalled, "Luckily election year was coming up, and I guess the mayor [Richard J. Daley] figured it might look . . . good to see his picture in the paper presenting me with the keys to this building, for the black folks to see this."[63] Clarice Durham recalled how Burroughs approached the current alderman, Ralph Metcalfe, for help. He told her to write up a proposal, which Burroughs subsequently did. Unsatisfied with it, Metcalfe suggested that Burroughs take her draft to Clarice's husband, Richard, a well-known writer for radio. With Durham's tweaking, Metcalfe moved the proposal forward until Burroughs was invited to make the proposal in front of the Park District board.[64]

Obtaining this newer, larger space in 1973 was indeed a great triumph for the museum, although it was not universally praised within the community. As Lawrence Kennon observed, some of his fellow black nationalists regarded Burroughs's reliance upon the Park District as a sellout. Burroughs was more pragmatic; the city parks belonged to all citizens, so blacks deserved their fair share. Burroughs persisted in this approach and gained much acceptance.[65] However, the next challenge immediately presented itself: to renovate the building from a police facility to a modern cultural institution. Drawing upon a tip she'd learned from yet another "good white person" during her Field Museum internship in 1968, Burroughs found a state statute that required the state to offer tax levy funds to any private citizen who started a museum on state land. But the contract offered by the Park District expressly stated that the DuSable Museum would not receive any tax levy funds. "Even though I knew," remembered Burroughs, "I decided not to raise a fuss, because if I've learned one thing in life—you know, you've got to crawl before you can walk." At the time, the museum had enough money to begin renovations of the building—"one room at a time."[66]

As always, Burroughs persisted in pursuing this essential source of
funding. She wrote the Park District the following year, asking for assistance with the school outreach. As expected, the district shifted the question to the existing Chicago museum consortium, who, in response to
Burroughs's letter asking for a piece of the pie, came to visit the DuSable
Museum to see if it met their criteria for a museum. Burroughs and the
current board chair, Vernon Jarrett, were then invited to dinner at the
Museum of Science and Industry "to sound us out." Burroughs observed,
"I felt like they would not like to have black folks doing a demonstration
in the lobby of the Art Institute." But again, following the advice of "that
same good white person," Burroughs did not ask for a cut of the existing
funds; instead she focused on lobbying the state legislature to increase the
appropriation so that the existing members would not have to give up
their piece of the pie, and the DuSable Museum would finally be "on the
totem pole."[67]

As Eugene Feldman rightly observed, Burroughs's approach to this
work took much time and effort: "She was in so much contrast to a
few . . . who want instant growth as they want instant coffee or who say
history begins with them."[68] Instead of leaping at the first opportunity for
funding and risking the ire of her fellow museum directors, Burroughs
embarked upon the laborious task of lobbying state government. She
wrote more letters to black legislators, stating that since the other museums were requesting an increase, couldn't the DuSable Museum be
included? Luckily, she found a champion in Corneal Davis, the "dean
of the legislators," who called Burroughs to say, "'I'm going to tell them
when that bill comes up, if I don't see DuSable's name on it, I'm going
to filibuster it out of existence."[69] And Burroughs, being the community
builder, passed on what she had learned to others seeking to begin art
and history museums. For instance, when a Mexican American group,
following the DuSable Museum's example, found an underused property
to turn into a center, Burroughs advised them that calling their place a
center would not meet with Parks Commission approval; instead they
needed to call it a "museum," which they subsequently did. Burroughs's
attitude was "the more the merrier" in terms of the "ethnic enclaves" that
made up the city of Chicago and its neighborhoods: "these museums
cut across all that because they have the culture of all of us."[70] Again, the
bigger picture prevailed over "instant" results.

In the meantime, the DuSable Museum had gone through some changes prior to the move south to the building in Washington Park. *Ebony*, a Chicago-based magazine for African Americans, had written the Ebony Museum ordering them to stop using "their" name after mail between the two institutions began to be mixed up in delivery. While the museum's lawyer saw no claim to exclusivity on the word "ebony," Burroughs decided to change the museum's name to the Museum of Negro History. But when she wrote letters to African countries asking for artifacts, they would always reply by calling the museum "the Museum of African American History." This "got to [Burroughs's] head," and so she changed names yet again. Finally, "this good white person" at the Field Museum where Burroughs had been interning pointed out the importance of having a major institution named after the founder of Chicago, Jean Baptiste Point Du Sable, a black fur trader who plied his trade on the site near the river where Chicago was born. So in 1968, the DuSable Museum of African American History acquired its permanent name. As always, the advice of this one person led to further opportunities. Burroughs knew that the community had been lobbying the mayor to fund a museum dedicated to Jean Baptiste Point Du Sable. A task force was formed around the same time that the DuSable Museum moved into Washington Park. Ever alert to opportunity and at this point growing in political savvy, Burroughs contacted the mayor's office and offered them a ripe opportunity and "an easy way out of this problem." The museum subsequently received official status as a DuSable monument, along with $10,000.[71] This first major commitment to honoring Jean Baptiste Point Du Sable opened the door to other such landmarks being created in Chicago.

Burroughs would herself eventually be appointed a Chicago Park District commissioner in 1985 by the man whom she helped gain office, Mayor Harold Washington. Having learned so much about the impact of the Parks Commission on the life and welfare of its citizens, Burroughs was eager to exert her influence to assist others in developing their own cultural projects. As an educator, she recognized the opportunity to shift the Park District's sports-centric focus toward more arts education.[72] The trade-off was that she would become director emeritus at the DuSable Museum in order to avoid a conflict of interest. For Burroughs, the advantages outweighed the changing role she would play at the museum; as she put it, "Not being tied down to day-to-day operations, I have the time and freedom to help others who are trying to start other black history museums."[73] Indeed, such assistance and advice became a great part of her life's work in later years. Perhaps it is not too much to speculate that if it hadn't been for Dr. Margaret Burroughs, the Smithsonian Institution's new addition to the Washington, D.C., mall, the National Museum of African American History and Culture, which opened in 2016, might never have come into being. If only she could have been there for the grand opening! No doubt her friends and fellow travelers would count her there in spirit, a powerful presence made manifest in the shining jewel in the crown of the museums she helped found, and yet another example of her ultimate purpose: "to bring diverse groups together in understanding, in fellowship, friendship, and through knowledge of the positive achievements of African American people, I stress bringing them together and I think that is very important. Because it's not a separate thing—it's not an all-black thing."[74] Released from her day-to-day responsibilities at the museum, Burroughs would move on to other, even more diverse projects that would gain her recognition and acclaim across the globe.

SIX

ANCESTRAL CROSSINGS

W here next?" Dr. B asked.

I scanned my list of landmarks for ones we had not yet seen. Dr. B waited as if she had all the time in the world, a characteristic noted by many who knew her when she was in fact a very busy woman, busier than many people half her age.

This time, however, Dr. B's voice sounded weary, a bit more like, "How many more stops?" and lacked her earlier eagerness. When I named sites that would take us back toward her home, she brightened.

"The armory?" I wasn't exactly sure which direction it was, but Dr. B turned us west on Thirty-Fifth Street until we reached Giles Avenue. The venerable brick building had been renovated in the previous decade and now served as a military academy. For Dr. B, the pride she took was in a monument that preserved yet another piece of Bronzeville's history, namely that of the "fighting Eighth" Regiment, an all-black unit that had served in several conflicts, including World War I. She had described the unit to me earlier in front of the Victory monument on King Drive.

Dr. B's radical roots as an artist again struck me as disconnected to her apparent veneration of these military monuments. Of course, her love of historical preservation, along with her aesthetic appreciation, could not be denied. Furthermore, Dr. B's interests in the military were directly connected to her passion for justice. In the late 1940s, she had been a champion of the campaign to desegregate the armed forces under President Harry Truman. She had also promoted writing to and saving the letters of GIs for the historical record. She wanted black soldiers to be recognized for their service to a country that still treated them as second-class citizens. She personally knew many friends and fellow travelers who had willingly enlisted in the armed forces. Years later, her daughter's son,

Eric Toller, would also enter the military, just as many black men did in order to carve out a future when faced with scarce resources. And her beloved husband Charles had served as well.

Still, I wondered how she felt about the existence of a military academy in the heart of Bronzeville. I later imagined her answer would have been along similar lines, seeing an opportunity for better-quality education than was currently available. My own misgivings arose by just standing in front of the spotless glass-and-brass door, picturing how young people were being trained to support the imperialist actions of the U.S. government. Although Dr. B wouldn't necessarily disagree with my sentiments, I later thought that she would also point out that opportunities were opportunities, and she wasn't about to tell someone in need not to take them.

In any case, we lingered just long enough for me to take a few photos.

"Can you give me a copy of all those?" she asked as I returned the camera to its case.

By now I knew that whatever Dr. B asked for, I would comply.

"Yes, I'd be glad to," I replied. Years later, after she had passed on to another world, I would wonder what had become of those photos. As I would find out upon viewing some of her files and archives, she saved every last scrap of paper, in case it might be of interest to those who would no doubt keep her legacy alive.

As we slowly approached our last two stops, I considered all of the institutions and resources that lay within a brief walk from Dr. B's home. Compared to my more sprawling suburban life growing up, Bronzeville's community resources seemed deeply concentrated, with its academies, clubs, community art center, historical landmarks, museums, and the comprehensive resources of churches and housing developments. I discovered the mural projects that Dr. B and subsequent generations of artists representing diverse ethnicities and races had painted across the city's neighborhoods, and these murals were something as unthinkable as graffiti where I grew up.

I could imagine then, as I walked with Dr. B, what was at stake, what was always at risk of being lost: a sense of oneself as part of a larger endeavor.

Maybe it was the sun and heat, but when we stood in front of the Wabash Street YMCA, or the "Wabash Y" as Dr. B called it, I could barely register the importance that she placed on this institution as a gathering place, a meeting hall, and a residence for those who had had no other options in their travels as porters on the Pullman car trains, the same trains that my mother's mother's relatives had made a living cleaning inside. It was all so overwhelming, so unlike my own childhood. Even the Chicago Public Library books I'd read and reread had said nothing about such a place, such people. Just the idea that Bronzeville residents met outside their home, work, school, or church on a regular basis, to enjoy each other's company but also to promote a better vision of their world, was so totally foreign to my sense of what constituted "normal." My "normal" was home, school, shopping at the mall with parents, and visiting relatives. Church on Sunday. The public library every few weeks, waiting with my dad while my mom received her naprapathic treatments. Girl Scouts and Boy Scouts meetings. It had been stable, predictable, and, to most people, safe—a version of the American Dream in that democracy had already arrived; after the war, the struggles were over, and everyone could just get on with their lives.

But now Dr. B, who had grown up with her large extended Catholic family, who was out of the house and into the community from an early age, who even now could not imagine living without boarders, proudly stood before the Wabash Y, describing this place where people made things happen. All sorts of groups—labor, athletic, cultural, social, activist, spiritual—found a home and a voice to share a vision of what could be.

One more stop, I reminded myself. Just one more stop and this walk will end. I had that saturated feeling as when I'd been in the galleries of the Art Institute of Chicago and knew I couldn't look at one more painting, one more sculpture, one more piece of ancient Greek pottery. There is only so much that we humans can absorb at one time.

Dr. B shuffled forward in silence. If I asked a question, she answered it. But small talk was not her concern. My purposes, my past, my people mattered only insofar as they found common cause with hers. Silence joined us on this final leg of a journey that had taken us through more than two miles of sweltering heat, sunshine, and impromptu greetings and well wishes. Now, no one else approached. We had the street to ourselves.

Had I been alone on a street anywhere else in the city, my city radar would have risen up and I would be scanning all around, planning my next moves, considering possible hazards, checking my bag and making certain I had left nothing behind on my stops. I called such alertness my "city chops." It's how I confront the unknowns of the urban landscape, always anticipating what might or could happen.

But as Dr. B and I rounded the corner at Thirty-Ninth Street and Michigan, approaching the Bronzeville chapter of the Chicago Youth Center, our final destination, I realized that not once had my "city chops" turned on while I was with Dr. B. How remarkable that I would walk in a part of the city unfamiliar to me, guided by an eighty-eight-year-old woman in one of the busiest urban areas in the country, and not once turn my defenses on. As we approached the R. R. Donnelley Youth Center, the omnipresent yellow brick of Chicago postwar construction was enlivened by a colorful Egyptian-style mural to usher us inside: two women in profile poured water from decorative vessels that became ocean and wave, sun and moon, across the industrial doorway, transforming it into a lively scene of history and imagination.

Dr. B stood next to this mural as I snapped more photos. As she led the way inside, I recognized a deep hunger I'd had as a kid for art, for beauty, for knowledge of the past. I remembered the Egyptian mummy exhibit at the Field Museum, and how curious I'd been about the mysterious hieroglyphics, wondering if these people could ever have anticipated being an exhibit where schoolchildren and their parents would stare down at them. But here Egypt was a living part of history, still a part of culture, not simply a preserved relic. It was this hunger that I recognized as almost a betrayal. Who were my people, after all? And why had I been kept from this rich knowledge of others? I had recently discovered that my family's fortunes had been tightly bound up with those of the residents of Bronzeville. I had vaguely known this most of my life, but to drive around and see landmarks and people that I had begun to understand in a new and different light brought home that reality in a deeper way

As Dr. B and I entered the Youth Center, we were greeted with even more colorful banners in the WPA style of Charles White and Thomas Hart Benton, promoting community building and regard for the past. One banner read "HONOR. By the mighty arm of God and the wisdom of the elders we shall be liberated. RESPECT." Glancing at Dr. B, I saw once again the pride she took in not only this obvious example of the positive influence she herself had exerted but also in her role as an elder, as one worthy of honor and respect.

As Dr. B made a beeline for the front desk and struck up a conversation with the women working there, I recognized another betrayal, along with more anger–my elders had shown themselves to be in some significant ways unworthy of my honor and respect. I had been cheated of the kind of elder that I saw in Dr. B, one who stood up for the greater good, against the evils of her time.

I wondered what kind of life I would be living had this wall between the black and white worlds not existed.

Dr. B chatted for a while with the staff while I looked around. What would otherwise be the same kind of bland institutional setting as my old grammar school was rescued by the omnipresence of colorful art that depicted the values–the *morals*–which the Youth Center promoted in its programming. My Catholic grammar school had had 1960s pop art banners focused on Catholic values, along with more traditional symbols and vestments. But nothing as colorful and dynamic as this.

"Let's go outside." Dr. B took my elbow and steered me back through the front door.

On the Youth Center's side, a ground-to-roof-sized mural of the Great Migration dominated a playground that hosted equally colorful hand-carved totem poles of an Afro–Native American remix. On this large crumbling red brick wall, the entire sweep of decades of struggle, danger, turmoil, dreams, hopes, and joys was laid out before our eyes. The mural had been, of course, a collective effort: "A Chicago Public Art Group Project." Given Dr. B's all-pervasive influence on South Side art, I expect that these artists were no strangers to her artistic beneficence, her "den mothering" of all artists.

"That's the Great Migration," Dr. B offered. She was in full-fledged teacher mode. She showed me two other sculptures that lay outside the sandbox playground, both of which were equally elaborate, no doubt collective youth efforts: a plaster cone reminiscent of a teepee, with round plate faces and polka dots on a white background. A grotto-like structure made entirely of pebbles echoing the curved lines of some of the Eastern European–style churches I'd known growing up, all in shades of ivory, gray, white, beige, and blue.

What were they for? What did they mean? Dr. B shrugged. It didn't matter. They were there. They were art. They would endure.

In some ways, Margaret Burroughs's story is like the fairy tale "Hansel and Gretel." She left a trail of breadcrumbs–or in her case, countless interviews, art prints, paintings, sculptures, essays, letters, poems, stories, plays, murals, videos, and file cabinets full of the flotsam and jetsam of her long and productive life—as a guide back to our collective roots. She left hundreds of people who remember her energy, skill, determination, generosity, kindness, and selflessness, who would feel the urgency that Burroughs felt to create and maintain a legacy that would link past, present, and future generations in a strong chain of identity and truth, strong enough to resist the onslaughts of oppressions waiting at every turn.

When describing Burroughs, many who knew her used the term "renaissance woman." Even though beginning and maintaining a museum in her home was an all-consuming task, she continued not only to produce art but also to write and publish voluminously, as well as organize major events. To the end of her life, she knew how to stay active; she advised others that when their energy flagged on one task, they should switch to another. She was seldom without a project. Even while attending a Chicago Bears game at Soldier Field, she would be writing or otherwise occupying herself.[1] Her "use it or lose it" philosophy led her to take up roller skating in her last decades and to bowl weekly with a team. Indeed, tracking down all of Burroughs's activities and accomplishments is an ongoing project; so much of what she has left behind is scattered throughout the world. She, alas, was only marginally interested in organizing the many streams of her efforts into a comprehensive narrative.

While Burroughs's central project became the museum she founded in 1961, she also maintained a steady flow of writing and publication. Of particular interest was curricular reform after the desegregation of public schools in 1954 with the Supreme Court ruling in *Brown v. Board of Education*. The museum became a focal point of not only arts education but also African and African American history. In a 1966 *Negro Digest* essay, Burroughs argued for the necessity as well as the benefits of a curriculum that truthfully depicted the achievements and contributions of not only whites but blacks and other ethnic groups to the founding and development of the United States. As always, Burroughs linked such progress as beneficial to all, including whites, whose children had been previously deprived of such knowledge and, as a result, were also harmed:

> Thus, the white child grows into adulthood with a sense of false
> superiority based on the color of his skin alone. He feels that
> he does not have to try, that all he has to do is be white! This

concept ends in a rude disillusionment and mental upsets when
persons with this outlook come face to face with the realities
of life.[2]

The attorney Lawrence Kennon recalled Burroughs's strenuous campaign against "Willis Wagons" from 1962 to 1966. The Chicago school
superintendent Benjamin Willis had continued Chicago's segregation of
schools by race by enforcing rules for children to attend only neighborhood schools. To maintain this segregation, Willis proposed to buy "150
to 200 of the 20 × 36-foot aluminum mobile school units and install them
at existing schools and on vacant lots. Besides installing the portable units,
officials accommodated swelling ghetto pupil enrollments with double-
shift schedules, rented commercial space, and much new school construction."[3] Kennon and Burroughs were both part of "the Movement" for
civil rights at the time. When Willis Wagon protesters were arrested, it
fell to Kennon to bail them out and defend their cases.[4] Burroughs joined
in by writing articles, opinion pieces, and letters in support. She, along
with other teachers and community members, wrote and campaigned
heavily against Willis, the Board of Education, and the mayor in favor of
open enrollment in city schools.

An avid poet from her days in the South Side Community Art Center's writing groups, Burroughs penned what is perhaps her best-known
poem and overall publication, "What Shall I Tell My Children Who Are
Black?" Originally published in 1968 by the small press undertaken by
the Ebony Museum, this lengthy piece has circulated the nation and the
world many times. Burroughs commented that this poem "explains why
the museum got started in the first place."[5] With maternal care and racial
pride enveloping the tone of the speaker's voice, Burroughs chronicled
the linguistic traps of racial labels such as black and white, as well as their
emotional, psychological, social, physical, and other consequences. As a
counterpoint, she extolled the global achievements of blacks and cultivated a positive self-image for black people.

Many other poems and essays were unpublished or self-published as
giveaways. Like her artwork, she believed that poetry was for everyone.
Audiences who heard her read appreciated her down-to-earth style, humor, and humanity. To her audiences, she often distributed a brochure
with her poem "Legacy," and urged listeners to consider their own. She
used the Ebony Museum, later the DuSable Museum, to print and dis-

play many booklets containing her poems, essays, and other musings. These productions were inexpensively produced and were often tendered as "rewards" to deserving individuals and groups.

Burroughs's organizing did not stop at the threshold of the Ebony Museum. If anything, the museum propelled her even further into related projects such as the hundredth anniversary of the Emancipation Proclamation show in 1963. As Burroughs recounted, the state of Illinois had voted to offer $150,000 to put on a show at the McCormick Place exhibition center and formed a commission to review proposals. Burroughs put in a proposal for a series of paintings by black artists about black subjects, "The Negro in Illinois."[6] She was the only one to put in a bid for artwork. However, she grew concerned that most of the money would go to "a commercial exhibit of blown-up photographs," leaving nothing behind for posterity. Instead, she proposed that fifty artists create one hundred paintings of "great moments in the lives of black people in Illinois."[7] Because the exposition was held at McCormick Place, and was supervised by "crooks," most of the money went into their pockets rather than the exposition. The paintings commissioned by Burroughs were later claimed as state property and were shown around the state before being stored in Bloomington, Illinois. Burroughs then worried that the Ebony Museum would not have access to these pieces, so she put on her lobbying hat and contacted then state senator Corneal Davis, who helped prompt the State Museum in Springfield to pick out twelve paintings for itself and transfer the rest to the Ebony Museum on a ninety-nine-year loan. The works are periodically displayed at the Ebony Museum (now DuSable Museum) as part of the permanent collection.[8]

No one could have possibly thought the less of Burroughs had she decided to rest on her most impressive laurels and end her public life with the achievement of transplanting the DuSable Museum to its own, independent structure in Washington Park. Had she spent the rest of her days simply producing art, she might have become even better known as an artist and enjoyed some of the high-profile notoriety that her much-celebrated friend, the poet Gwendolyn Brooks, had won. She could have basked in the company of her children and grandchildren, marveling over every minuscule growth and change. Any one of these commitments could have absorbed all her time and energy had she so chosen. Instead, she kept moving and growing. All these people and activities in her life remained, but she grew larger to encompass them.

The cultural arts leader Omowale Ketu Oladuwa was a master's degree student at Northwestern University in the early 1980s when he first encountered Margaret Burroughs at the DuSable Museum. Oladuwa attributed Burroughs's focus on institution-building and art to her drive to develop places where the "double consciousness" described by W. E. B. Du Bois—that of being black in a white-dominated world—could find ongoing resolution. Burroughs, he claimed, was likely the premier institution builder of her generation. But those institutions existed because of Burroughs's identity as an artist; as Oladuwa observed, institution-building wasn't possible without artistic integrity. Such integrity allowed Burroughs to weather all the storms, disappointments, and rejections that would inevitably come her way. As an artist, she had a larger frame of reference than that of just an institution builder. Institutions, Oladuwa said, are "part of [artists'] artwork."[9]

Burroughs's sense of her art had deep roots in African sensibility, one that went beyond literal influence and into the genetic inheritance of her ancestry. It located itself in the interplay between the individual's vision and a collective consciousness. Its purpose was to build relationships. According to Oladuwa, "[African art] is not meant to dictate what something should be. It's meant to call forth something." Art made the "double gesture" of working both individually and collectively possible. It also drew from African groundedness in its everyday functionality: "Art is really geared to inspire and educate, to provoke the community toward a self-realization that just doesn't exist in any institutional regard."[10]

In this respect, it is clear why Burroughs did not simply retire to private life and individual achievement: her entire life had been about working against the dominant cultural paradigm that placed art and the artist outside and above society rather than as an instrument of ongoing change and a source of opposition to inert elements of the political status quo. According to Oladuwa, "Art is the ability to bring relevance and reality and practicality into your life, and to manifest reality and relevance in my life. That's what art is about. It's being able to tell a story that carries with it the life force of generations of people. . . . Good art attacks politics."[11]

The successful relocation of the DuSable Museum to Washington Park in 1981 most certainly provided Burroughs with a larger public platform and presence than she had ever known before. But to view this shift in her fame as ambitious and career-building would distort the true legacy that she had been steadily developing for so many years; namely, to use art as a means to connect. Of course, from an individualistic, market-driven perspective, her career as an artist was more widely recognized because of her position as director of the DuSable Museum. She networked even more broadly, could solicit greater resources, and received more invitations to lecture, give shows, and collaborate. Honors and awards began to accrue more rapidly. Yet as those who knew her well attest, she was, as Lawrence Kennon said, "the kind of person that nobody could own." Kennon also identified with her being a "race woman" who saw her individual achievements as important to her people, and vice versa.[12] Haki Madhubuti similarly concluded that Burroughs "could not be bought," a sense of integrity that he himself still aspires to.[13] So, while Burroughs definitely enjoyed a host of benefits from her position as cofounder and director of the museum, she channeled those benefits into an ever more inclusive vision of connecting people and places across the globe, as well as in her own backyard.

In 1979, Burroughs retired from a ten-year tenure at Kennedy King Community College as a professor of humanities, following nearly twenty-five years of teaching art and English at DuSable High School. Liberated from the need to earn a paycheck, Burroughs launched into projects that would further extend her ability to use art as a means of transforming the lives of her people and bringing understanding and mutual respect between groups and individuals. With the election of Harold Washington as the first black mayor of Chicago, Burroughs saw an opportunity not only to influence the distribution of tax levies for Chicago museums, but also to shape the Park District's curriculum toward more creative work. Washington appointed her a Park District commissioner in 1985, a post she maintained until just before her death in 2010. Upon her appointment, she left her position on the DuSable Museum board to avoid conflicts of interest, which relieved her of the day-to-day tasks of museum operations and allowed her to fund-raise on a broader scale. She continued her travels, charged with an even more relevant mission for the ever-expanding museum collection, including curatorial collaborations and exchanges. Around this time, in the mid-1980s, she also began an arts outreach program in the state prison system with her friend and fellow activist, Reverend "Queen Mother" Helen Sinclair. Burroughs continued to run the National Congress of Artists (NCA), the oldest professional organization of black artists in the country, of which she was a founding member, and to organize conferences. Along with Charles

Wright of Detroit, she cofounded the African American Museum Association. As Lonnie Bunch, founding director of the Smithsonian's National Museum of African American History and Culture, stated in a radio interview following her death, "Margaret was one of the leaders in creating the African-American Museums Association, which is really an important organization that encourages and supports the preservation of culture around the country. Margaret was the [main] leader."[14] And in the 1990s she went back to study art at her alma mater, the School of the Art Institute of Chicago.

These activities might seem impressive in and of themselves, but they represent only a fraction of the efforts Burroughs put forth in terms of travel and mentoring, not to mention her prolific output of artwork. Indeed, not only the number of people she touched but the depth and power of her mentoring relationships are in many ways the most profound and far-reaching aspects of her legacy. If a person was lucky enough to have known Burroughs, they most likely have a story of how she had helped them, or at least positively impressed them in some way or another. For some, the relationship was, quite literally, life-changing. For others, she left a path open that connected them to their heritage, their humanity, and their own legacies.

Burroughs's lifelong agenda to bring art into the lives and homes of all people did not stop at prison walls. She had a close acquaintance with men and women who had been incarcerated through her work at a nearby community correctional center where she helped individuals transition from prison life. Reverend "Queen Mother" Helen Sinclair recalled having visited the Ebony Museum in the Burroughses' home one day when Margaret Burroughs was busy working at that correctional center, and Charles showed Sinclair around. Not long after, a meeting about a recently closed work release center was held at a church across the street from the Burroughses' home, attended by Sinclair and Burroughs. At this meeting, Burroughs learned from Sinclair about her mother, Jessie "Ma" Houston, an activist with Operation PUSH, along with Jesse Jackson. Houston was best known as a prison chaplain, the first woman to bring a ministry to death row inmates. Prisoners affectionately named her "Ma" and later would name her daughter "Queen Mother." Following in her mother's footsteps, Sinclair became the first female chaplain allowed into a maximum-security prison for men. Burroughs subsequently declared her commitment to continue "Ma" Houston's legacy.

At the work release center meeting, Burroughs approached Sinclair with a question: "What do you think of work release centers?"

"We need 'em," Sinclair replied.

"Well, I'm with you," said Burroughs, and their friendship and long collaboration began, starting with the reopening of the work release center near the Burroughses' home.[15]

Burroughs had already been invited to work with Operation PUSH as an educator but, as Sinclair observed, the organization did not offer Burroughs enough work to occupy her fully. In the meantime, a businessman who had been successful in selling hair products invited Burroughs to help him quell black-on-black violence through soliciting and publishing the poems of prisoners in the Cook County Jail. In addition, Christine Johnson, the principal of a Muslim school on the South Side, invited Burroughs to join her on her trips to Joliet Correctional Facility. But when Burroughs learned that Sinclair was going there on a regular basis, she told Sinclair that she wanted to help maintain "Ma" Houston's legacy of prison work. She began calling Sinclair "Mama" despite the fact that she was several years older than Sinclair and put herself into the hands of her compatriot. Sinclair was one of the first black female cab drivers around the city; for years, she relished the hours of driving it took to reach their destinations. Every Tuesday on their way south to Joliet or Stateville prisons, they would stop at a Denny's Restaurant off the Dan Ryan Expressway, and Burroughs would tell Sinclair to decide what they would eat. Burroughs always bought their breakfasts and included anyone else who accompanied them.

Sinclair remembered that at first, she and Burroughs would caravan with two or three carloads of churchgoing women. Burroughs had already shared with Sinclair her story about leaving Catholicism: she had been moved from the Doolittle School (also attended by Sinclair a few years later) to Saint Elizabeth's Catholic school. However, the nuns there told her in no uncertain terms that she, a black child, would not be admitted to the Catholic high school, even though her parents were Catholic, and she had been raised one. Sinclair remembered a scene from a play about Burroughs which enacted that very scene, a foundational moment in Burroughs's life. Traveling with churchgoers, then, provoked some humor from Burroughs. Early on, she commented that everyone carried a "bee-bul" (Bible), and so on their next trip, she showed up with a book "just to have something in her hands," a line that she and Sinclair laughed over together.

The fact that Burroughs was not a churchgoer did not trouble Sinclair, who herself had stopped attending Sunday services once her prison ministry began. Initially her bishop in the Christian Methodist Episcopal Church had assigned her to the prisons. She saw her mission as bringing church to the people, so she began to go to the prisons on Sunday. Some chaplains, she noted wryly, have "other interests" on Sunday. Burroughs appreciated Sinclair's spiritual engagement, one that did not depend solely upon a minister and congregation. Burroughs gave her a book, *God Works the Night Shift*, in 1999, inscribed "to my best friend," which became Sinclair's "pattern for living." "She sure knew what she was doing" by giving Sinclair that book. Sinclair recalled it was not hymns but the Negro national anthem, "Lift Every Voice," that excited Burroughs and inspired her to share with others in the spirit of fighting for one's rights.[16]

Sinclair recalled that Burroughs "didn't do a lot of rapping" on their drives together over the years. Instead, they listened to jazz and some talk radio, including the sex therapist Laura Berman, who provoked many jokes and much laughter. They shared many an adventure during this time. When they began their weekly thirty-eight-mile trips, Burroughs was already without a driver's license. Sinclair remembered that they would sometimes get lost, and Burroughs would simply trust Sinclair to steer them back to the correct route. Those who knew them thought the two women were "crazy" for traveling through places where "people didn't look like us." But wherever they went, they found friendly faces and assistance. Once, a truck driver brought a flat tire to their attention. He escorted them to a gas station and radioed for a police officer to assist them. The tire was changed, and the men refused compensation. Similarly, the Denny's Restaurant staff where the pair were known regulars ("they served grits there") became "like family." Burroughs would, without any hesitation and great relish, consume all the cream on the table, along with their grits, biscuits, and sausage. Once during a snowstorm, Sinclair suggested they not travel that day, but Burroughs insisted that the prisoners were expecting them. Miraculously, they made the trip safely.

Sinclair's travels with Burroughs were not limited to statewide trips to the prisons. At the Burroughses' kitchen table, much talk about travel across the globe ensued. Sinclair found herself part of a group of Burroughs's family and friends who found their way to Cuba, likely arranged by Eleanor Chatman, Burroughs's travel agent and close friend for decades. Two of Sinclair's classmates from DuSable High School accompanied her to Cuba. Like all Burroughs ventures, this trip did not emphasize leisure time on the beach; instead, travelers educated themselves about a country and a people who were part of the diaspora. The tour group met teachers at all levels of education, along with artists, lawyers, and judges. They discovered through their contacts that African ancestry was more widely embraced at that time than when the Spaniards had ruled the island. Seeing for themselves what it meant to live as a Cuban, including a memorable visit to health care facilities, they discovered what Burroughs would often say about many of her global destinations: that one had to see for oneself the truth about a place and not rely only upon mainstream sources to represent the lives of others.

Margaret and Charles, and later Margaret alone, swept up many into the wake of their frequent and extensive international trips. Eleanor Chatman took more than fifty trips with Burroughs herself over thirty years, usually two trips per year. Burroughs had a "passion, almost an obsession" about bringing others to Africa, noted Chatman. According to a former DuSable student and longtime fellow traveler, Gloria Latimore Peace, Burroughs paid for many others' trips to Africa because she believed that everyone, no matter what their race, should visit the continent at least once. When it came to sharing what she knew, Burroughs's generosity knew no bounds.[17] Her later travels focused almost exclusively on the African diaspora, which, as Burroughs discovered, meant just about any country in the world. If there were people of African descent, Burroughs would find them and exchange her artwork, ideas, and historical knowledge with them. Founding a major arts institution gave her a very visible platform for doing so.

Ever since Charles Burroughs entered her life in the late 1940s, Margaret had lived awash in all things Soviet. Charles was a self-taught scholar of Russian literature and linguistics and was a fluent speaker of Russian, able to teach others who dropped by their Chicago Salon in impromptu lessons. His comrades in the Soviet circus would visit the Burroughses' home whenever they came to town, as did Russian diplomats. Paul Robeson's travels to the Soviet Union also caught Margaret's attention. In 1965 she took her first trip there as a tourist. The following year she organized a delegation of black artists for a month-long exchange with artists from across the Soviet Union, including Moscow, Leningrad, and Kazakhstan. While Burroughs had already come to terms with her "radical reputation" ever since her standoff with the Chicago Board of Education in 1952, the Cold War attitude was still powerful enough to deter other black artists from signing on to the trip, despite the fact that it was virtually free, requiring only the purchase of a one-way ticket—the rest of the trip was covered by the Soviet sponsors. In the end, eight artists joined her. What she discovered was that

> artists were artists the world over. We had the same interests, the same curiosities, even though we couldn't speak the same language. We found we were very much alike, regardless of the propaganda that's put out. We got an understanding of the motivation behind the work of Soviet artists, which appears sometimes as regimented. It's just that their art serves a purpose. . . . They still feel that art is communication and is used to teach the people.[18]

Having encountered similar sentiments during her sabbatical time in Mexico, Burroughs was doubly affirmed by her Russian experience in her aesthetic sensibilities and her insistence that direct experience was an invaluable teacher. She noted upon her return home that others did not want to hear "anything positive about the Soviets or their system, because then you become suspect."[19] Having lived under suspicion for so many years, Burroughs became fearless in her pursuit of the truth of black people's experience.

During this time of relative freedom from earning a living, Burroughs took her ideas regarding her own and others' legacies to a new level. Coming out of the postwar repressive era of the 1950s, she may have keenly felt the need to keep black art alive and accessible to the next generation. She succeeded in her task of providing continuity and pride in heritage that was later taken up by the Black Arts Movement (BAM) and its Chicago South Side extensions, the Organization of Black American Culture (OBAC) and AfriCOBRA. But she also had much work ahead to ensure that subsequent generations would understand themselves as part of a cultural and historical continuum that included elders such as herself.

The DuSable Museum provided a certain visibility and stature that she as an artist could use to build upon the work of cultural exchange and understanding. As Omowale Ketu Oladuwa notes, such Chicago institutions provided a place where people could "grow together" in collective work and action.[20] While political differences and agendas had always existed among Bronzeville dwellers, the 1960s saw a resurgence in black nationalism, which was directed particularly at establishing black independence and community-focused enterprises apart from mainstream white economic activity and culture. Sharing the "common enemy" of segregation, black nationalism found a renewed voice in Chicago in the mid-1960s.[21] While Margaret and Charles Burroughs were less connected to black nationalism (in contrast to Haki Madhubuti) than they were to a socialist orientation, Margaret would not concede any major differences or conflicts between these groups, since the core values that she had promoted were finally resurfacing after years of repression. However, she did take exception to some of the younger generation's claims on African American identity as something they had discovered independently of the previous generation. For instance, in a play entitled *But "We Hope Not Tomorrow,"* Burroughs pokes fun at a younger generation (the "Supreme Revolutionary Council of the Legion of Bad Blacks," or SRCLBB) who are planning the Black Revolution but who become so caught up in questions of style versus substance that they can't even agree what day of the week would be best for the revolution.[22] Burroughs cast a similarly comic eye at her fellow School of the Art Institute of Chicago students with their rainbow-colored hair, piercings, tattoos, and ripped and paint-spattered clothing during the 1990s: "I wondered to myself how long could I stand looking at that."[23] At the same time, she conceded how strange her "natural" hairstyle had looked in the 1950s and how she and her fellow artists wore "crazy get-ups" such as paint-encrusted jeans that "could stand up" on their own. Her sense of humor around aesthetic differences was irrepressible: "I imagine now they're framing [those jeans] and calling them soft sculpture or third-dimensional sculpture, because they just stand them up."[24] Eugene Feldman similarly took the younger generation to task for not recognizing the legacies of their elders: "In the last few years we have had a number of young people come up who said loudly in their poetry, story, music, oratory that they began Black culture. They are not willing to acknowledge their debt to others of the past. Some will acknowledge Margaret Burroughs."[25]

Despite the shortcomings she may have perceived in the younger generation, Burroughs was absolutely dedicated to helping them succeed, offering not only advice and personal connections, but also her home and other resources. "If she saw a need, she met the need," observed Gloria Latimore Peace. In addition to paying for others' trips to Africa, Burroughs paid for college tuition, a non-relative's funeral, and art supplies for her "boys" in Stateville, to name just a few of her many acts of generosity.[26] Clarice Durham recalled how Burroughs had inherited money from someone close to her and used it to take friends to Galena, Illinois, where she had a speaking engagement at a church associated with her daughter. She chartered a bus and arranged accommodations. "She always took the attitude that money was to help you do things, not to accumulate it or leave it for people to argue over," said Durham.[27] At the same time, Burroughs's own spending and needs were quite disciplined. Her philosophy was, "If you don't need it, don't buy it."[28] As many have commented, Burroughs lacked any ego with regard to her personal abilities and accomplishments, sometimes to her detriment. "Margaret was not a self-promoter. She was just down to earth, a regular person. She didn't toot her own horn, so to speak," said Durham. Because of this, people didn't appreciate her as much as they would someone who was always getting press coverage and promoting themselves. Durham commented that some people are in social groupings that are "always sort of in front." Many of them are highly educated or in high society. Burroughs was not a part of this. Instead she called them the "hoi polloi."[29]

Burroughs maintained a sense of herself as someone whose legacy went beyond fame and fortune, focused as it always was on working with and for her people. "She was very self-assured," said Durham, who offered an amusing anecdote to this effect: While traveling to Cuba around 1988 on one of her many educational ventures, Burroughs was with a group of young black women lawyers. They had initially just solicited her advice for the trip, but they wound up inviting her and other female educators, including Durham. While waiting to change planes in Miami, a few of the younger women discovered that the singer and activist Harry Belafonte and his wife were at the airport, waiting for the same flight. They wanted to go to him, but Burroughs said, "Bring him to me." And he came and met her. "That's the kind of person she was. 'Nobody's above me. We're equal,'" said Durham, chuckling.[30]

The famous Wall of Respect at Forty-Third Street and Langley Avenue, part of OBAC's mission to create public spaces where people could gather, plan, express, educate, and take action, may have tested Burroughs's patience with the younger generation. Some have suggested that Burroughs was unhappy that her image had not been included on the Wall of Respect, along with other luminaries such as Malcolm X and Stokely Carmichael, and, in later versions, her friend and fellow poet Gwendolyn Brooks. She knew all the artists involved in the project, so it was not for lack of recognition that she was overlooked; she herself had been working as a muralist on the South Side. Furthermore, OBAC's guiding principles echoed those of Burroughs and her contemporaries: "The artists and community debated and agreed [to] a list of black heroes to feature in the mural, using OBAC's definition–'any Black person who honestly reflects the beauty of black life and genius in his or her style'– and who demonstrated originality and social consciousness for other less fortunate black people."[31] On the other hand, the agreed-upon subjects of the mural's evolving images apparently did not include visual artists like themselves: "The wall's content evolved throughout its existence until its demolition in 1971, but the original themes included on the wall were portraits of statesmen, rhythm and blues artists, religious leaders, writers, actors, jazz musicians, and athletes."[32] So, in being left out, Burroughs was in good company with her fellow visual artists.

On the day of the Wall's unveiling, Burroughs's presence was surely felt, if not in body, then in spirit: "The *Wall of Respect* gained recognition within the South Side community by the time it was unveiled to the public, and on August 27, 1967, the SNCC and the Forty-Third Street Community Organization held a street rally and inauguration in honor of the mural. Gwendolyn Brooks and Don L. Lee read poems about the wall."[33]

Similarly, in 1971 the Museum of Contemporary Art in Chicago held an exhibition called "Murals for the People" shaped by four guiding principles articulated in the Wall of Respect artists' manifesto, principles that also echo many of Margaret Burroughs's:

1. Artists worked for the people and created for the people.

2. Art was created and displayed in its true context: life.

3. Murals are the necessary form of communication. They are contextualized and unavoidable.

4. The artist is a deliverer of truth.[34]

So perhaps Burroughs did have a point about the next generation's inadequate recognition of their elders' legacies, at least within OBAC and the Black Arts Movement. In 1968 yet another group emerged from OBAC, the African Commune of Bad Relevant Artists, or AfriCOBRA, whose emerging aesthetic philosophy seemed at least superficially to critique artists like Burroughs for drawing upon European aesthetics, rather than a more Afrocentric aesthetic:

> In 1968, the five founding members of AfriCOBRA created
> an aesthetic philosophy to guide their collective work—a shared
> visual language for positive revolutionary ideas. Several mem-
> bers worked together on the "Wall of Respect," a mural at
> Forty-Third Street and Langley in Chicago's Bronzeville neigh-
> borhood. Early exhibitions and meetings were held in nearby
> Woodlawn. The group defined its mission as "an approach to
> image making which would reflect and project the moods, atti-
> tudes, and sensibilities of African Americans independent of the
> technical and aesthetic strictures of Euro-centric modalities.[35]

Perhaps Burroughs's play *But "We Hope Not Tomorrow"* was actually poking fun at some of the absurdities she perceived in aspects of this philosophy when she named her characters' group the "Supreme Revolutionary Council of the Legion of Bad Blacks." While AfriCOBRA may have been playing upon competing meanings of the word "bad" in dominant usage versus African American vernacular, Burroughs may have used "bad" for its original denotation, critiquing the fictional revolutionary group for its "bad" ideas about what constituted African American "moods, attitudes, and sensibilities." She also portrayed awkwardness and confusion around their conversion from "slave" to African names, such as Lillie Mae to Ngozi. And overall, she exposed the shallowness of any revolutionary effort that did not acknowledge or understand its own historical roots. To further extend this critique, some noted that in their efforts to identify a black aesthetic, black artists of this period were "talking black but sleeping white," literally and figuratively, which was perhaps as much a sign of the intense exploration and shifts in African American identity in general as it was a sorting out of relationships between black and white culture.

One artist whose self-acknowledged legacy came straight from Burroughs is the Chicago sculptor Debra Hand. Hand attributed her success as a sculptor to Burroughs, who was a family friend, and whose home Hand, like many young people, had visited over the years to view the Ebony Museum. As one of six children, Hand was sternly warned not to touch anything in the museum, which made the experience "intimidating" to her. To her child's mind, "Dr. Burroughs seemed like a great authoritative figure guarding over these valuable artifacts." Being an artist was not a calling Hand heard early in life. However, Burroughs left an early impact on Hand that survives to this day, namely that of "being a human of consciousness with a spirit of serving the community." Burroughs, along with Hand's mother, Gloria Latimore Peace, modeled for her "how to be in the world—not just for the purpose of absorbing resources, but to try to make myself a vessel for good; to be a conduit for things that will go out into the world and have the same kind of impact as her work did."[36]

Artistic expression nonetheless found a ready audience in the young Hand. She had been mesmerized by older dancers in her ballet class because they had such command and were "very exact in everything they did." As an eight-year-old, she was introduced for the first time to children "who possessed such self-mastery and self-command." Dancers would become a prominent part of her oeuvre, serving as metaphors for individual will and self-empowerment. But visual art itself was not something she came to until many years later. One day, her young son had been assigned a school art project. Hand was in her thirties, had earned a degree in information technology at Northwestern University, and was well established in her career as a data infrastructure technology expert. Although she had no background in art, she recalled once seeing someone paint a picture of a tree by connecting a series of "y's" together to make branches. She began to demonstrate the technique for her son and ended up falling in love with the relaxing process of painting and mixing colors. When her son rose the next morning to go to school, Hand was still at the table. She had been there all night, immersed in her newfound experience of art's appeal. According to Hand, what she produced that night "didn't necessarily look like anything special, but at the same time, it definitely didn't look like something that should be thrown away. Maybe it wasn't 'something,' per se, but it definitely wasn't just 'nothing.' That means it had potential and that alone made it something. All of a sudden, life had given me some additional tool through which to explore my own being. I felt like a monk discovering meditation, or something."[37]

Hand loved the colors and their vibrations so much that she went to an art store the next day and bought paints and canvas. One day her mother saw something that she thought had potential. Hand then asked her mother to ask Burroughs to take a look and share her opinion. She agreed to come the next week.

Before Burroughs came, Hand worked hard to produce as many paintings as possible. The night before she went to pick Burroughs up, she couldn't sleep. She had painted everything she could think of, mostly abstract, and eagerly lined the walls and baseboards of the room with her works. The next day, as she drove to Burroughs's house, Hand was practically shaking, still remembering Burroughs as the iconic museum owner from her childhood, who was now coming to judge her work in what Hand felt to be a make-or-break moment. But on the drive with Burroughs, the latter was disarmingly warm and witty. She wasn't stuck on being an icon, or wearing titles; she was much more focused on planning the next move in her ongoing quest to make a difference in the community and to be a bridge for someone else.

At the time, in her technology job, Hand was a subject matter expert with an advanced data company. As an African American, she was "proud to be one of the top go-to people when it came to complex technical issues." But when she told Burroughs her title, Burroughs replied, "What's that?" She asked as if the title was so far beyond her understanding that she couldn't care less. "I realized something in that moment," said Hand. "No matter how impressive you think your profession is, there is really only one question and answer that is relevant in your life: What are you doing with your time and talent that matters in the lives of the people in the community? Dr. Burroughs couldn't care less about someone's titles, or their fame, or fortune, for that matter." What she did care about, according to Hand, was what you were doing for your community: "Her whole thing was that—how does what you achieve enable you to benefit the larger human community?"[38]

On the way into the house, Burroughs told her to gather some acorns and put them in a bag. Hand did so without question. Once inside, Burroughs carefully looked over Hand's paintings and finally decided that they were a cross between figurative and abstract, as well as "a little bit surreal." Hand associated the surrealism movement with images of "dripping clocks, like Salvador Dalí's work," and felt maybe she had fallen short of impressing Dr. Burroughs. Nevertheless, to Hand's delight, Burroughs offered to help her host a showing of her work. She said she would help Hand set up an exhibition of the paintings in her mother's backyard and that they should serve tea and cookies to formally introduce her as an artist. Hand was surprised that this iconic woman was willing to help her. She had feared she might receive harsh criticism as a beginner, but instead, Burroughs was encouraging. "Plus, she didn't say I was awful," Hand recalled. That alone gave Hand a lift.

After the visit, when they arrived back at Burroughs's home, Hand reached out to give Burroughs the acorns. She waved her hand and said, "Those are for you." Puzzled, Hand asked, "What am I going to do with them?" Burroughs replied, "You'll figure it out." All the way home Hand wondered, "Is this some kind of symbolic gesture, some kind of test I'm apparently not deep enough to pass? Did Picasso pass out acorns? What could those acorns possibly mean? Is she trying to tell me I should give up art and go plant trees?" Years later, after Burroughs had become like family, Hand finally had the courage to ask about the meaning of the acorns. Burroughs laughed and revealed that she was only suggesting "that a true artist can make something out of anything."

As for the backyard show with tea and cookies, Hand felt unworthy to take "this great icon's time" and never bothered her with it, but Burroughs's encouragement led Hand to feverishly teach herself more about art mediums and techniques over the next few years.

During this time, Hand's son received a school assignment to make a brain for a science project. Hand bought some clay and, at the same table where she became a painter, she helped him form the clay. This time, she was struck by an even greater passion: sculpting. She began to teach herself from that day on, and eventually it became the primary focus of her career in the arts: "Painting is physically easier for me, and more meditative, but sculpture is three-dimensional and tangible. Unlike figures in a painting, sculptures exist in the same plane of reality as I do." The allure of that medium was intoxicating.

When Hand thought she had learned enough to warrant an opinion, she invited Burroughs to the house for another showing. At first Burroughs walked around the room quietly, viewing each sculpture with deep consideration. Finally, she smiled broadly and said she wanted Hand to make something for the DuSable Museum collection. Hand was shocked: "Now that was surreal." Hand is still amazed that Burroughs saw her work as something worthy of preserving on such a level and that

she chose to include Hand in her own legacy. Hand treasures a note from
Burroughs where she claims to have seen Hand's talent early on: "That
is why I adopted you and became your other grandmother," the letter
states. Hand noted, "From the first moment that Dr. Burroughs offered
to become involved with showing my work, a door opened within. She
had given me something in myself. It was like being handed a handful of
magic seeds that you are convinced will really work. Your belief in them
causes you to nurture them, and that act is the thing that makes them
magically work. I know I must take the seeds she gave me and pass them
on to young people in some way."[39]

"We talked a lot about serving humanity, but not that often about politics," Hand continued. "However, she did tell me how much she admired
Paul Robeson as a man who stood proudly for the people, and how smitten she was when he visited Chicago in her younger years, and she had
the chance to carry his coat for him. Of course, later she would become
more deeply associated with him and influenced by him and other civil
rights movements."

Hand understood the legacy that these movements had provided to
the Black Panthers and black nationalism while she was growing up.
When Hand was working on the piece Burroughs requested for the
DuSable Museum collection, she was determined to honor Burroughs's
influence by trying to make the piece fit the museum's strong historical
narrative:

> I had created a painting about the day the Emancipation Procla-
> mation was announced. But as I worked on it, it really opened
> up a lot of questions for me about the complexities of not just
> being enslaved, but also regarding the concept of freedom after
> having been stripped of everything: culture, family, deprived
> of your own humanness. Yet, now you are free to go off into
> the world with all your lashes and scars, with nothing. You're
> free to now enter a society that is desperately trying to rebound
> from the sudden loss of all that free labor, a society that has
> quickly restructured its own systems to reclaim that free labor
> by any means, including arresting boys and men and sentencing
> them to hard labor for trumped-up offenses. She'd say, 'There's
> no way for the jails to get hold of that many black people by
> accident.' The painting I was making took on so much dark-

ness and anger that I couldn't stand to turn the canvas to face
me. Just by looking at it, it had the power to create deep anger,
but no real power to propose any solutions for that rage. I just
couldn't be responsible for helping to unleash that kind of rage
in future young people without also creating work with the
power to heal, so I ended up destroying the painting. That
was the moment when I consciously declared who I wanted
and needed to be as an artist. As artists, we are not all meant
to do the same work. Some artists absolutely must keep the
past atrocities of society in the forefront of our collective brains
so we won't forget and repeat them; other artists must focus
their talents on the possibilities of a just world and depict those
ideals in our work; and some of us must help to promote and
reinforce the many aspects of our beauty as a cultural group:
of the strength and dignity that continues to get us through
all that we've had thrust upon us. Just like with music, not all
musicians should make the same genre of music. On that note, I
made a conscious choice to wage a campaign of cultural beauty,
although this does not preclude me from eclipsing any of the
other areas. Even where my work addresses issues such as mass
incarceration, I will use beauty as a subversive element to draw
the viewer closer to the work.

Hand explained her feelings to her mentor, saying, "Dr. Burroughs,
as much as I love you, and as devoted to our history as you have always
been and have done that work very well, I want my focus to be on the
telling of our beauty and of showing our creativity and skill in the arts.
That painting about slavery immersed me in a darkness that said, 'Go
back, this is not the work you're meant to do. Your part of this is to share
the light.'"

While Hand believes that people shouldn't forget about slavery, "different people can show different aspects for how to put, not just slavery,
but also the many other aspects of 'us' into a broader perspective. Remember, we are still trying to rebuild our culture by using vestiges of 'us'
that we retained from Africa. Even through slavery, our unique beauty
and creativity has survived. I want to concern myself with the lineage of
our greatness that persisted throughout our history and that thrives even
today."

Burroughs not only accepted Hand's approach to her artistry, she continued to mentor her and create opportunities to showcase her work. For Burroughs's retrospective at the DuSable Museum, Hand had completed the commission that Burroughs requested, and she set it up in the gift shop so that Burroughs could take a look at it before the event started. When Burroughs saw the piece, she told Hand that she wanted her to present it to the museum onstage during the program that evening. "There's no way I can step on that stage with you during this important occasion in your life," Hand said. Burroughs simply and firmly stated, "You will mind your elders. That's what you will do."

At a certain point in the program in which Burroughs was interviewed on the stage, she introduced Hand, saying "Here's someone you're going to be hearing a lot about." "It was an amazing honor," said Hand. "Besides the interviewer, Haki Madhubuti, and the then president of the DuSable Museum, Antoinette Wright, I was the only person she allowed onstage with her that night. In her own way, she was telling the art world that she saw something in me, and she believed I would live up to it. Not just in terms of art, or talent, but in terms of using my art in some way to serve humanity. I know I owe the Universe a special debt because of her, and I work toward that payment plan every day. I often look at her picture and ask her spirit to guide me in doing my work, or as I create literary content for young people through my writing."

Because of Burroughs's belief in Hand's talent, Hand became "the most determined artist" ever. She told herself, "I can't let her be wrong about me." Burroughs went above and beyond for Hand, personally arranging for Hand's first public exhibit at the South Shore Cultural Center, a gallery which Burroughs also brought into existence as a Chicago Park District commissioner. Coincidentally, it was Burroughs who first proposed to the Park District that there be a sculpture of Paul Laurence Dunbar erected in Dunbar Park. This was long before Hand even became a painter, let alone sculptor. Ultimately it was Hand who would produce a nine-foot-tall bronze statue for this project. As Hand noted, "Artists in Chicago have always, and will continue to be impacted by the legacy of this great icon."

Burroughs's legacy, of course, extended far beyond the next generation of artists. Art was something she believed everyone should own and display in their homes, as her time in Mexico had inspired her. Even if her students at DuSable High School never became artists, they at least could begin to appreciate the purpose and function of art as conveying a powerful message about identity and pride in heritage. Daniel Texidor Parker was one of those individuals who took Burroughs's early influence on him to heart. His mother, Annie Parker, had already initiated him into collecting African and African American art and crafts from thrift stores, flea markets, and yard sales. Then in high school he encountered Margaret Burroughs as his art teacher. The dual influences of his mother and Burroughs set Parker on a lifelong path of collecting, displaying, and sharing art of the African diaspora.[40]

Just as Burroughs began collecting and displaying art in her home, and sharing this resource with others in the community, Parker, over thirty years, amassed a collection of roughly 450 paintings, sculptures, and carvings within his Chicago home. Over time, his collection has overtaken his space so thoroughly that he observed that he now has artwork on the floor. Yet the art is so carefully displayed that it projects a feeling of comfort as opposed to clutter. While he has brought his art history students from Olive Harvey College and later, upon his retirement, students of African art from Chicago State University, into his home and loaned books from his personal library, just as Burroughs did at 3806 S. Michigan, Parker also maintained that living among the art of his heritage and the art that followed was deeply meaningful to him:

> When one enters a room filled with art from one's ancestry,
> it is more than simply a special feeling of pride: the art truly
> becomes an extension of one's cultural memory. In addition, for
> one of African ancestry, it is not only cerebral, but also emo-
> tional, as the art may form a cocoon surround, thereby offering
> a sense of well-being and fulfillment. For some, this experience
> may psychologically complete the circle of life, for the images
> reflected in the art may inform us of the past, unfold the pres-
> ent, and allow us to project into the future![41]

In his book *African Art: The Diaspora and Beyond*, Parker deepens the legacy of Burroughs in his argument to reclaim African and black diaspora art for those whose ancestors produced it:

> It is clear that the world has long recognized the genius of African
> and African American Art. Major museums and private collec-

tors possess a vast amount of this art. Michael Brent, writing in *Plundering Africa's Past* . . . states in part, "[T]ruly fine African objects seem to have become quite rare. Nowadays they are more likely to be found in Europe, at a dealer's or with a collector, than in their place of origin." These institutions and private collectors have long understood the value of African Art. It must now become the mission of African Americans and other Africans of the Diaspora to claim this art so that it is no longer the exclusive property of Europeans and European Americans. And this art should not be housed exclusively in museums; it is imperative that the cultural legacy created by our ancestors be reflected in our homes.[42]

Parker goes on to enumerate other reasons why African-descended people should collect art in their homes. First, exposing children to ancestral art on a daily basis will be what they grow to love as adults, to which Parker himself can attest. In addition, collecting art produced by those enslaved or otherwise not recognized for their knowledge and talents is a way of reclaiming a lost link in history. Parker commented that the African American landscape and portrait traditions came in part out of slave masters requiring their slaves to produce works pleasing to the eye. "They even did portraits of some of their slave masters. And sometimes their slave masters would rent them out to other slave masters so they could do their portraits," claims Parker.[43]

The specific cultural conjunction of art and history in African diaspora art is also "an historical reflection of their political and social struggle." Quoting the poet and author Mari Evans, Parker writes, "[Art] is political since its intent is to speak to the Black community about the quality of life in that community and the ramification of individual responsibility for the community both within and outside the system of the larger society."[44] Finally, Parker observes how financially advantageous it is to collect art, investing in something of enduring meaning and value rather than mere embellishments: "Art may not only enliven and heighten us spiritually, but may also elevate us financially."[45] Parker, like Burroughs, along with the artist Debra Hand, has supported the de-commodification of African diaspora art, seeking to make it accessible to all, while at the same time maintaining a financial security in passing down such legacies from one generation to another.

Parker is proud to claim works by Burroughs among his collection, noting how much she had inspired him throughout the years. Unfortunately, little art history or criticism of her work exists, according to Parker, because she, like Robeson, was more obvious and vocal about her politics, and so paid the price. Parker did not grasp her politics while he was a student at DuSable High School, but only afterward in what he had read. Burroughs did not proselytize but simply shared a pride in heritage. "She was a kind woman . . . a humanitarian. She really was," said Parker. From the writings about her, "you would miss that."[46]

Burroughs's legacy lives on in a South Side group geared toward collecting and appreciating African diaspora art, a group that Parker himself engaged.

> Founded in 2003, Diasporal Rhythms seeks to build a passionate group of collectors engaged in actively acquiring visual art created by contemporary artists of the African diaspora and to expand the appreciation of these artists' work. The organization hosts both public and private (members only) events, including home tours, exhibitions and other opportunities to build knowledge about cultural value. Currently a regional organization, Diasporal Rhythms boasts collections housed in private homes throughout Chicago and even counts a public institution, the Dixon Elementary School, as a member.[47]

Margaret Burroughs's legacy is still alive and vital in the twenty-first century through yet another generation of artist-educator-activists. Skyla Hearn, archivist and special collections librarian at the DuSable Museum, grew up as a "very proud South Sider" in Bronzeville, a few blocks away from Margaret Burroughs's home at Thirty-Eighth Street and Michigan Avenue. While she never actually met Burroughs in person, she was aware of her and her accomplishments. Hearn knew that Burroughs frequented South Side establishments favored by Hearn's family such as Soul Veg ("The Original Soul Vegetarian Restaurant") on East Seventy-Fifth Street and Indiana Avenue, as well as a roller-skating rink in Markham. Her family visited the DuSable Museum while she was growing up, making her aware of how extensive Burroughs's reach into the community was. But it was not until she began a graduate project while studying at the University of Illinois Urbana-Champaign to spread the work of South

Side artists more deeply into the community that she began to truly grasp how immense was Burroughs's influence. She learned about Burroughs not only as the principal founder of the DuSable Museum but also as one of the forces behind the formation of the South Side Community Art Center. She had known about Dr. Burroughs the artist and institution builder, but she had not known about her activism through art.[48]

The more Hearn learned about Burroughs's work and life, the more she saw Burroughs's life inscribing itself into her own narrative. Hearn marveled at how Burroughs, as an important "matriarch," struck a work-life balance that she seeks for herself, between "family first" and "passion projects." She appreciated how Burroughs might have been overwhelmed at times: "This was her shop. Everything fell on her." At the same time, Hearn found a model in Burroughs's adeptness at persuading people to dedicate their time, energies, and resources to her overarching project of "ally-ship" and cultural exchange: "She saw the need to have a symbiotic relationship with other [cultural] groups." As Hearn pursued her graduate degree work, she was encouraged not only to develop a cataloging system with the Art Center, but also to share her experiences in the archives as part of a community outreach program that provided an "intergenerational conversation" about the arts and the cultural continuity of the South Side.[49]

But perhaps the most profound takeaway for Hearn came when, during an outreach moment, she was asked about how Burroughs had been able to recognize "voids" in the community. In other words, the questioner wanted to know, how does one recognize what does not exist? Or, as Hearn put it, how does one "create a template when there is no prototype"? This is the revolutionary legacy for which Burroughs has provided multiple generations a context. She provided concrete models for how to continue with the visionary undertakings of pursuing social justice, equality, and the resources needed to support those endeavors. Hearn hopes that her work at the DuSable Museum will help provide "en masse" access to the existing archives, protect those holdings, and also develop policies and procedures to maintain them into the future. In addition, she foresees her future work as a writer as publishing from Burroughs's archives, providing information about the existence of this massive body of work and why it matters. Burroughs served as a "catalyst" matriarch who set Hearn on her current path to reflect upon the various relationships she has had with cultural groups and organizations in collaborating on arts projects. The more she has learned about Burroughs, the more she understands how Burroughs was not only a mother figure but, as one of Hearn's students pointed out, a critic; she not only produced art but also used it as a means for criticizing injustice and inequality wherever she encountered them.[50]

Hearn also notes others of her generation, such as the artist-educator-community organizer Faheem Majeed, for whom Dr. Burroughs "is at the core of [their] work." He is the originator behind the Floating Museum, a Chicago art space literally floating on the Chicago River to provide a collective space for community institutions to come together.[51] A core goal for Majeed is ultimately to help people understand how relevant Burroughs still is to Chicago culture and the arts. Furthermore, the Prison and Neighborhood Arts Projects (P-NAP) is an example of the continuation of Burroughs's art and history education program at Stateville Penitentiary. Sarah Ross, an educator at the School of the Art Institute, and Damon Locks, an educator and artist, are two principal members who carry on Burroughs's legacy in this area of work.[52]

Hearn believes that the DuSable Museum is "unlike any other institution" in that it was founded by a matriarch, Margaret Burroughs, along with many women and men who gave of their time, energy, and resources to ensure that the community would continue to grow and prosper. She sees Burroughs as having had "a lot of gall" and been "very brave" to have initiated the kinds of programming that she did. Hearn herself is a work in progress, growing into the roles for which Burroughs left "concrete models" to follow, envisioning her path as "activism through archives."[53]

Burroughs continued a steady routine of engagement and service, in addition to producing art, up until her death in 2010. By this time, her reputation had grown within the African American art and curatorial world to prompt many exhibitions as well as awards. Her work with arts education also gained wider recognition outside of Chicago and even the United States. In 1975, President Gerald Ford awarded Burroughs the President's Humanitarian Award. In 1988 the national Women's Caucus for Art gave Burroughs a Lifetime Achievement award. The Paul Robeson Citation Award Committee of the Actors' Equity Association honored her in 1989. She was named to the *Chicago Defender*'s list of most influential women. Many other local and regional groups have honored her as well. Just weeks before her passing, the School of the Art Institute of Chicago feted her as part of their Legends and Legacies award and ball, to which Burroughs responded by saying she was glad to be able to smell the roses before she died.

None of these awards turned the head of a woman who "could not be bought." However, they did cement Burroughs's legacy within the public record, which surely pleased her, concerned as she was that the accomplishments of all African Americans be preserved. And indeed, her legacy still had the power to persuade the Chicago Parks Commission, on which she served faithfully for twenty-five years, to name the Thirty-First Street Beach after her in 2015. That same year she was inducted into the Chicago Literary Hall of Fame.

The artist Debra Hand recalled a story that sheds some light on how Burroughs regarded her own imminent death. When the poet Gwendolyn Brooks died in 2000, Burroughs asked Hand to take her to the funeral. Brooks and Burroughs had been friends since they were seventeen, and despite some tensions between them later in life, Burroughs remained devoted to her friend and her work. Hand was sick and nervous, wondering, "What do I say, what do I do?" in her concern that Burroughs would be distraught about losing her friend. A horrible snowstorm that day only reinforced Hand's anxiety. When Hand told Burroughs of her fears that she would be inconsolable, Burroughs remained peaceful, replying, "No, Gwen earned her right to go be with the ancestors." Hand concluded that this was the way Burroughs saw life, including her own: she had earned the right to be with the ancestors.[54]

In this way, Margaret Taylor Goss Burroughs lives on. She is available to anyone willing to consult the legacy she has left behind and the presence she still radiates, if one is curious enough and dedicated enough to find one's own legacy within hers.

What Will Your Legacy Be?

I ask you, what will your legacy be?
Do you know?
Have you thought about it?
Do you have an answer?
What will you leave as your legacy?
If you have no answer,
If at this point, you cannot say?

Hearken! Listen to me!
This is the moment.
This is the prime moment for you to think
and get to work and identify what you will leave as your
legacy for you to be remembered by.

You are here.
You're still here, alive and
quick and you have time.
You have time on your side.
You have time to begin even
now so get busy and do
something to help
somebody to improve the
condition of life for people now
and for those to come after.

To building institutions to educate and broaden the minds
for people
now and for those who came after and to make your life a
contribution
that will be your legacy.
Do this and your name will be remembered from now on
and into eternity.

What will your legacy be?
Hopefully, it will not be just a gray and decaying
tomb-stone.
Think now! Act now!
To insure that your legacy will be a positive contribution
to humanity
and you will be remembered, yes you will be remembered,
on and on and in eternity as God wills it.

What will your legacy be?[55]

—MARGARET BURROUGHS

NOTES

Prologue

1. "Dr. Margaret Burroughs Is a 91-Year-Old Rollerskater," YouTube, May 19, 2009, http://www.youtube.com/watch?v=W98VO7nG7mw.
2. Clarice Durham in discussion with the author, May 2013.
3. Eric Toller in discussion with the author, March 2012.
4. Moses Jones in discussion with the author, November 2012.

Chapter 1

1. Davarian L. Baldwin, *Chicago's New Negroes: Modernity, the Great Migration, and Black Urban Life* (Chapel Hill: University of North Carolina Press, 2007), 35.
2. Baldwin, *Chicago's New Negroes*, 41.
3. Robert Bone and Richard A. Courage, *The Muse in Bronzeville* (New Jersey: Rutgers University Press, 2011), 218.
4. Bone and Courage, *The Muse in Bronzeville*, 216–24.
5. Anne Meis Knupfer, *The Chicago Black Renaissance and Women's Activism* (Urbana: University of Illinois Press, 2006), 11, 17.
6. Knupfer, *Chicago Black Renaissance*, 11, 17.
7. Knupfer, *Chicago Black Renaissance*, 41.
8. Knupfer, *Chicago Black Renaissance*, 43.
9. Isabel Wilkerson, *The Warmth of Other Suns* (New York: Random House, 2010), 538.
10. St. Clair Drake and Horace Cayton, *Black Metropolis* (Chicago: University of Chicago Press, 1993).
11. Margaret T. G. Burroughs, *Life with Margaret* (Chicago: In Time Publishing and Media Group, 2003), 41–42.
12. Burroughs, *Life with Margaret*, 41–42.
13. Margaret Taylor Burroughs, interviewed November 11–December 5, 1988, by Anna Tyler, Archives of American Art, Smithsonian Institute, 3.
14. Burroughs, interviewed by Tyler, 8.
15. Burroughs, *Life with Margaret*, 33.
16. Burroughs, *Life with Margaret*, 30.
17. Burroughs, *Life with Margaret*, 34–35.

18. Burroughs, interviewed by Tyler, 9.

19. Timuel Black in discussion with the author, November 2012.

20. Burroughs, interviewed by Tyler, 9.

21. Margaret Burroughs, interviewed by Glory Van Scott, June 6, 1975, Hatch Billops Collection, New York, 2005, 41.

22. Burroughs, interviewed by Tyler, 1.

23. Burroughs, interviewed by Tyler, 9.

24. Burroughs, interviewed by Tyler, 11.

25. Burroughs, interviewed by Tyler, 12.

26. Burroughs, interviewed by Van Scott.

27. Burroughs, interviewed by Van Scott.

28. Theresa Christopher in discussion with the author, March 2012.

29. Burroughs, interviewed by Van Scott.

30. Burroughs, interviewed by Tyler, 15.

31. Bone and Courage, *The Muse in Bronzeville*, 145.

32. Burroughs, interviewed by Tyler, 15.

33. Burroughs, interviewed by Tyler, 11–12.

34. Ian Rocksborough-Smith, "Margaret T. G. Burroughs and Black Public History in Cold War Chicago," *The Black Scholar* 41, no. 3 (2011): 28.

35. Rocksborough-Smith, "Margaret T. G. Burroughs," 28.

36. Christopher in discussion with the author, March 2012.

37. Bone and Courage, *The Muse in Bronzeville*.

38. Lawrence Kennon in discussion with the author, May 2013.

39. Black in discussion with the author, November 2012.

40. Burroughs, interviewed by Tyler, 19.

41. Bone and Courage, *The Muse in Bronzeville*, 141.

42. Burroughs, interviewed by Tyler, 22.

43. Sarah Kelly Oehler, *They Seek a City: Chicago and the Art of Migration, 1910–1950* (Chicago: Art Institute of Chicago, 2013), 39.

44. Burroughs, interviewed by Tyler, 20.

45. Burroughs, interviewed by Tyler, 20.

46. Burroughs, interviewed by Tyler, 20.

47. Bone and Courage, *The Muse in Bronzeville*, 140.

48. Bone and Courage, *The Muse in Bronzeville*, 140.

49. Bone and Courage, *The Muse in Bronzeville*, 139.

50. Black in discussion with the author, November 2012.

51. Burroughs, *Life with Margaret*, 67–68.

52. Bone and Courage, *The Muse in Bronzeville*, 146.

53. Burroughs, *Life with Margaret*, 55.

54. Burroughs, interviewed by Tyler, 7.

55. Black in discussion with the author, November 2012.

56. Bone and Courage, *The Muse in Bronzeville*, 142.

57. Bone and Courage, *The Muse in Bronzeville*, 144.

58. Bone and Courage, *The Muse in Bronzeville*, 142.

59. Burroughs, *Life with Margaret*, 36.

60. Burroughs, *Life with Margaret*, 31.

Chapter 2

1. While some references continue to claim this building as the former Comiskey mansion, its actual builder and former owner was Seaverns, according to City of Chicago, 2010–2017, http://webapps.cityofchicago.org/landmarksweb/web/landmarkdetails.htm?lanId=1427.

2. Daniel Parker, whose Chicago home houses a vast repository of African American and African art, displays a Bernard Goss painting on a used wooden door, one example of how many artists drew upon the available means.

3. Burroughs, *Life with Margaret*, 55.

4. Burroughs, *Life with Margaret*, 52.

5. Burroughs, *Life with Margaret*, 51.

6. Knupfer, *Chicago Black Renaissance*, 67.

7. "Federal Art Project," Encyclopedia of Chicago, http://www.encyclopedia.chicagohistory.org/pages/442.html.

8. Bone and Courage, *The Muse in Bronzeville*, 143.

9. Bone and Courage, *The Muse in Bronzeville*, 142–43.

10. Baldwin, *Chicago's New Negroes*, 37; *Chicago Black Renaissance*, 28.

11. Baldwin, *Chicago's New Negroes*, 37.

12. Bone and Courage, *The Muse in Bronzeville*, 141.

13. Bone and Courage, *The Muse in Bronzeville*, 142.

14. Bone and Courage, *The Muse in Bronzeville*, 142.

15. Bill V. Mullen, *Popular Fronts: Chicago and African-American Cultural Politics, 1935–46* (Urbana: University of Illinois Press, 1999), 77.

16. Burroughs, *Life with Margaret*, 165.

17. Burroughs, *Life with Margaret*, 165.

18. Burroughs, *Life with Margaret*, 166.

19. Mullen, *Popular Fronts*, 3.

20. Burroughs, *Life with Margaret*, 68.

21. Burroughs, *Life with Margaret*, 71.

22. "Federal Art Project," Encyclopedia of Chicago.

23. *South Side Community Art Center, 50th Anniversary 1941–1991*, program, Chicago, 1991, 2.

24. *South Side Community Art Center*, 2.

25. *South Side Community Art Center*, 1.

26. Mullen, *Popular Fronts*, 85.

27. Burroughs, *Life with Margaret*, 169.

28. *South Side Community Art Center*, 3.

29. *South Side Community Art Center*, 8.

30. Burroughs, *Life with Margaret*, 168.

31. Oehler, *They Seek a City*, 62–63.

32. *Chicago Defender*, November 1, 1941, 24, qtd. by Mullen, *Popular Fronts*, 93.

33. Mullen, *Popular Fronts*, 93.

34. Erik S. Gellman, "Chicago's Native Son: Charles White and the Laboring of the Black Renaissance," in *The Black Chicago Renaissance*, ed. Darlene Clark Hine et al. (Urbana: University of Illinois Press, 2012), 155.

35. *South Side Community Art Center*, 13.

36. Gellman, "Chicago's Native Son," 154.

37. *South Side Community Art Center*, 13.

38. *South Side Community Art Center*, 13.

39. *South Side Community Art Center*, 14.

40. Mullen, *Popular Fronts*, 92.

41. Knupfer, *Chicago Black Renaissance*.

42. Burroughs, *Life with Margaret*, 167.

43. *South Side Community Art Center*, 14.

44. Gellman, "Chicago's Native Son," 154.

45. Mullen, *Popular Fronts*, 83.

46. Mullen, *Popular Fronts*, 83.

47. Mullen, *Popular Fronts*, 75.

48. Mullen, *Popular Fronts*, 76.

49. Mullen, *Popular Fronts*, 83.

50. Adam Green, *Selling the Race: Culture, Community, and Black Chicago, 1940–1955* (Chicago: University of Chicago Press, 2007), 25.

51. Green, *Selling the Race*, 41.

52. Baldwin, *Chicago's New Negroes*, 29.

53. Baldwin, *Chicago's New Negroes*, 29.

54. *South Side Community Art Center*, 6.

55. *South Side Community Art Center*, 7.

56. *South Side Community Art Center*, 7.

57. *South Side Community Art Center*, 8–9.

58. *South Side Community Art Center*, 10.

59. Mullen, *Popular Fronts*, 91.

Chapter 3

1. "Wendell Phillips Academy High School," Chicago Historic Schools, https://chicagohistoricschools.wordpress.com/2013/09/18/wendell-phillips-academy-high-school.

2. These buildings were torn down shortly thereafter.

3. Maren Strange, *Bronzeville: Black Chicago in Pictures 1941–1943* (New York: New Press, 2003), 68–76.

4. Dempsey J. Travis, *An Autobiography of Black Chicago* (Chicago: Urban Research Institute, 1981), 212–13.

5. Travis, *Autobiography*, 213.

6. Omowale Ketu Oladuwa in discussion with the author, May 2013.

7. John Fleming, "Dr. Margaret T. Burroughs: Artist, Teacher, Administrator, Writer, Political Activist, and Museum Founder," *The Public Historian* 21, no. 1 (Winter 1999): 48.

8. Burroughs, interviewed by Tyler, 44–45.

9. Mullen, *Popular Fronts*, 76.

10. Gellman, "Chicago's Native Son," 160.

11. Sterling Stuckey, *Going through the Storm: The Influence of African-American Art in History* (New York: Oxford University Press, 1994), 223, qtd. by Mullen, *Popular Fronts*, 105.

12. Burroughs, *Life with Margaret*, 61.

13. Burroughs, *Life with Margaret*, 61–62.

14. Gellman, "Chicago's Native Son," 157–61.

15. Gellman, "Chicago's Native Son," 155.

16. Burroughs, interviewed by Tyler, 57–58.

17. Burroughs, *Life with Margaret*, 84.

18. Burroughs, *Life with Margaret*, 84.

19. Burroughs, *Life with Margaret*, 85.

20. Gwendolyn Brooks, *Report from Part One* (Detroit: Broadside, 1972), 68–69.

21. Willard F. Motley, "Negro Art in Chicago," *Opportunity: Journal of Negro Life* 18, no. 1 (January 1940): 20.

22. Martin Duberman, *Paul Robeson: A Biography* (New York: New Press, 1989), 233.

23. Duberman, *Paul Robeson*, 247–49.

24. Duberman, *Paul Robeson*, 248.

25. Gellman, "Chicago's Native Son," 157.

26. Bone and Courage, *The Muse in Bronzeville*, 147.

27. Burroughs, interviewed by Tyler, 33–34.

28. Mullen, *Popular Fronts*, 100.

29. Mullen, *Popular Fronts*, 100.

30. Mullen, *Popular Fronts*, 101.

31. Mullen, *Popular Fronts*, 101.

32. Gellman, "Chicago's Native Son," 157.

33. Mullen, *Popular Fronts*, 193.

34. Burroughs, *Life with Margaret*, 85.

35. Burroughs interviewed by Van Scott, 41.

36. Margaret Burroughs, "My First Husband & His Four Wives (Me, Being the First) by Peggy Gross aka M. T. Burroughs," 5, DuSable Museum, Margaret Burroughs papers, series II, box 46, folder 368.

37. Burroughs, *Life with Margaret*, 90–91.

38. Rocksborough-Smith, "Margaret T. G. Burroughs," 4.

39. Erin P. Cohn, "Art Fronts: Visual Culture and Race Politics in the Mid-Twentieth Century United States" (dissertation, University of Pennsylvania, 2010), 122.

40. Cohn, "Art Fronts," 123.

41. Cohn, "Art Fronts," 123.

42. Cohn, "Art Fronts," 123.

43. Cohn, "Art Fronts," 124.

44. Gellman, "Chicago's Native Son," 157.

45. Rocksborough-Smith, "Margaret T. G. Burroughs," 30.

46. St. Clair Drake, interviewed by Robert Martin, 119–230, qtd. by Rocksborough-Smith, "Margaret T. G. Burroughs," 31.

47. Gellman, "Chicago's Native Son," 157.

48. St. Clair Drake, interviewed by Robert E. Martin, July 28, 1969, number 462, transcript 80, 118–21, Ralph J. Bunche Oral History Collection, Moorland-Spingarn Research Center, Howard University, Washington, D.C., qtd. by Gellman, "Chicago's Native Son," 157.

49. "Negro History Week Mass Meeting at DuSable Sunday," *Chicago Bee*, February 10, 1946, 6, qtd. by Gellman, "Chicago's Native Son," 158.

50. Margaret Taylor Goss, *Chicago Defender*, August 31, 1940, DuSable Museum, Margaret Burroughs papers, series II, box 46, folder 368.

51. Burroughs, *Life with Margaret*, 62.

52. Mullen, *Popular Fronts*, 98.

53. Margaret Goss, "This Is Our War," *N.Y.P.S.* [*Negro Youth Photo-Script*] *Magazine*, 1942 or 1943, DuSable Museum Margaret Burroughs papers, series II, box 46, folder 376.

54. Mullen, *Popular Fronts*, 201.

55. Bone and Courage, *The Muse in Bronzeville*, 141.

56. Margaret Taylor Goss, "Our Changing Race Ideas," 1943, DuSable Museum, Margaret Burroughs papers, series II, box 46, folder 376.

57. Margaret Taylor Goss, "War Letters Wanted," *Sunday Chicago Bee*, 1945, DuSable Museum, Margaret Burroughs papers, series II, box 46, folder 376, 15.

58. Margaret Goss, "GIs Discuss Plans for Post-War Period," 1945, DuSable Museum, Margaret Burroughs papers, series II, box 46, folder 376.

59. Margaret Taylor Goss, "Insidious Propaganda," *Chicago Defender*, 1942, DuSable Museum, Margaret Burroughs papers, series II, box 46, folder 376.

60. Margaret Goss Burroughs, "Woman's Viewpoint," for the Associated Negro Press (ANP), DuSable Museum, Margaret Burroughs papers, series II, box 46, folder 376.

61. Margaret Goss Burroughs, "A Woman's Viewpoint," for the Associated Negro Press (ANP), DuSable Museum, Margaret Burroughs papers, series II, box 46, folder 376.

62. Margaret Taylor Goss, "Improve Race Relations," for the Associated Negro Press (ANP), 194–, DuSable Museum, Margaret Burroughs papers, series II, box 46, folder 376.

63. Robeson eventually understood how such laws did not match practice under Stalin, but the fact that they existed was still important, since the United States lacked any such laws.

64. Margaret Taylor Goss, " 'Race of Mankind' Called Timely," for the Associated Negro Press (ANP), 194–, DuSable Museum, Margaret Burroughs papers, series II, box 46, folder 376.

65. Mullen, *Popular Fronts*, 101, 106.

66. Mullen, *Popular Fronts*, 109.

67. Mullen, *Popular Fronts*, 131.

68. Margaret T. Goss, "Private Jeff Johnson," *Negro Story*, vol. 1 (1944): 28–29.

69. Goss, "Private Jeff Johnson," 28.

70. Taylor Goss, "Improve Race Relations."

Chapter 4

1. "Bronzeville–Victory Monument," Public Art in Chicago, chicago -outdoor-sculptures.blogspot.com.

2. "Supreme Life Building," Wikipedia, https://en.wikipedia.org/wiki /Supreme_Life_Building.

3. "The Historic Olivet Baptist Church," www.olivetbaptistchurchchicago .org/history/index.html.

4. "Olivet Baptist Church (OBC) [Chicago] (1850–)," BlackPast.org, http://www.blackpast.org/aah/olivet-baptist-church-obc-chicago-illinois-1850.

5. "Olivet Baptist Church (OBC) [Chicago] (1850–)."

6. "Olivet Baptist Church (OBC) [Chicago] (1850–)."

7. Black in discussion with the author, November 2012.

8. "The Historic Olivet Baptist Church."

9. A tragic fire in 2006 wiped out the church. It has yet to be rebuilt.

10. Burroughs, *Life with Margaret*, 70–71.

11. Bone and Courage, *The Muse in Bronzeville*.

12. "Burroughs, Charles, 1919–," interview of Charles Burroughs by Camille Billops, October 31, 1976, in *Artist and Influence* 24, Hatch Billops Collection, New York, 2005, 12–13.

13. Billops interview, Charles Burroughs, 13.

14. Cohn, "Art Fronts," 183.

15. Cohn, "Art Fronts," 183.

16. Cohn, "Art Fronts," 183.

17. Cohn, "Art Fronts," 184.

18. Cohn, "Art Fronts," 185.

19. Burroughs, *Life with Margaret*, 87.

20. Eric Toller in discussion with the author, March 2012, November 2014.

21. Burroughs, *Life with Margaret*, 72.

22. Billops interview, Charles Burroughs.

23. Billops interview, Charles Burroughs.

24. Billops interview, Charles Burroughs, 27.

25. Billops interview, Charles Burroughs, 26.

26. Billops interview, Charles Burroughs, 30–32.

27. Toller in discussion with the author, March 2012.

28. Haki Madhubuti in discussion with the author, May 2012.

29. Burroughs, interviewed by Tyler, 35.

30. Diane Dinkins Carr in discussion with the author, November 2013 and May 2014.

31. Clarice Durham in discussion with the author, May 2013.

32. Fleming, "Dr. Margaret T. Burroughs," 37.

33. Fleming, "Dr. Margaret T. Burroughs," 37–38.

34. Fleming, "Dr. Margaret T. Burroughs," 35–36.

35. Fleming, "Dr. Margaret T. Burroughs," 38.

36. Fleming, "Dr. Margaret T. Burroughs," 38.

37. Fleming, "Dr. Margaret T. Burroughs," 38.

38. Fleming, "Dr. Margaret T. Burroughs," 39.

39. Oehler, *They Seek a City*, 52.

40. Oehler, *They Seek a City*, 53.

41. Oehler, *They Seek a City*, 54.

42. Oehler, *They Seek a City*, 54.

43. Margaret G. Burroughs, "Woman's Viewpoint," for the Associated Negro Press (ANP), Summer 1951, DuSable Museum, Margaret Burroughs papers, series II, box 46, folder 376.

44. Burroughs, "Woman's Viewpoint."

45. Burroughs, "Woman's Viewpoint."

46. Burroughs, "Woman's Viewpoint."

47. Margaret Goss Burroughs, "Taxco, Silver Center of Mexico," "A Woman's Viewpoint," for the Associated Negro Press (ANP), Summer 1951, DuSable Museum, Margaret Burroughs papers, series II, box 46, folder 376.

48. The DuSable Museum's collections would echo this emphasis on artifacts, art, and history.

49. Margaret G. Burroughs, "Rivera Murals Overpowering," "A Woman's Viewpoint," for the Associated Negro Press (ANP), Summer 1951, DuSable Museum, Margaret Burroughs papers, series II, box 46, folder 376.

50. Identified as "Mrs. Burroughs," "Largest Market in Mexico," "A Woman's Viewpoint," *Atlanta Daily World*, Friday, October 5, 1951, DuSable Museum, Margaret Burroughs papers, series II, box 46, folder 376.

51. Burroughs, interviewed by Tyler, 59.

52. Burroughs, interviewed by Tyler, 61.

53. I was also amply rewarded with several prints, most of which hang in my home or office.

54. Mullen, *Popular Fronts*, 191.

55. Burroughs, interviewed by Tyler, 59–61.

56. Margaret Burroughs in discussion with the author.

57. Margaret Burroughs in discussion with the author.

58. Moses Jones in discussion with the author, November 2012.

59. Dr. Margaret T. G. Burroughs, *Remembrance of Paul Robeson*, 1987, self-published, 2–3.

60. Burroughs, *Remembrance of Paul Robeson*, 3–4.

61. Burroughs's example helped bolster Madhubuti during a confrontation with university authorities at Chicago State University, the former Chicago Normal School and Burroughs's alma mater, where he took a clear stand against what he perceived to be a corrupt administrative appointment that cost him his job late in his career.

62. Burroughs, *Life with Margaret*, 58.

Chapter 5

1. The business closed in 2016.

2. Rocksborough-Smith, "Margaret T. G. Burroughs," 32.

3. Fleming, "Dr. Margaret T. Burroughs," 39.

4. Rocksborough-Smith, "Margaret T. G. Burroughs," 32.

5. Fleming, "Dr. Margaret T. Burroughs," 39.

6. Rocksborough-Smith, "Margaret T. G. Burroughs," 30.

7. Rocksborough-Smith, "Margaret T. G. Burroughs," 36.

8. Eugene Pieter Feldman, *The Birth and the Building of the DuSable Museum* (Chicago: DuSable Museum, 1981), 20.

9. Rocksborough-Smith, "Margaret T. G. Burroughs," 31–32.

10. Rocksborough-Smith, "Margaret T. G. Burroughs," 36.

11. Rocksborough-Smith, "Margaret T. G. Burroughs," 30.

12. Rocksborough-Smith, "Margaret T. G. Burroughs," 31.

13. Rocksborough-Smith, "Margaret T. G. Burroughs," 30.

14. Rocksborough-Smith, "Margaret T. G. Burroughs," 33.

15. Margaret Burroughs, "Remarks," *South Side Community Art Center, 50th Anniversary 1941–1991*, program, Chicago, 1991, 4.

16. Burroughs, *Life with Margaret*, 74–75.

17. Fleming, "Dr. Margaret T. Burroughs," 37.

18. Doug Williams in discussion with the author, June 2014.

19. Burroughs, *Life with Margaret*, 97.

20. Fleming, "Dr. Margaret T. Burroughs," 41.

21. Feldman, *Birth and Building of the DuSable Museum*, 25–26.

22. Feldman, *Birth and Building of the DuSable Museum*, 29–30.

23. Burroughs, *Life with Margaret*, 97.

24. Burroughs, *Life with Margaret*, 98.

25. Anna Tyler, "Planting and Maintaining a 'Perennial Garden': Chicago's South Side Community Art Center," *The International Review of African American Art*, 11, no. 4 (1994): 25–26.

26. Diane Dinkins Carr in discussion with the author, November 2013.

27. Dinkins Carr in discussion with the author, May 2014.

28. Clarice Durham in discussion with the author, May 2013.

29. Black in discussion with the author, November 2012.

30. Feldman, *Birth and Building of the DuSable Museum*, 31.

31. Feldman, *Birth and Building of the DuSable Museum*, 31–32.

32. Feldman, *Birth and Building of the DuSable Museum*, 12.

33. Eric Toller in discussion with the author, March 2012.

34. Burroughs, *Life with Margaret*, 99.

35. Burroughs, *Life with Margaret*, 100.

36. Fleming, "Dr. Margaret T. Burroughs," 40.

37. Feldman, *Birth and Building of the DuSable Museum*, 14–15.

38. Feldman, *Birth and Building of the DuSable Museum*, 15.

39. Feldman, *Birth and Building of the DuSable Museum*, 15.

40. Feldman, *Birth and Building of the DuSable Museum*, 15.

41. Feldman, *Birth and Building of the DuSable Museum*, 15.

42. Burroughs, interviewed by Van Scott, 3.

43. Fleming, "Dr. Margaret T. Burroughs," 44.

44. Fleming, "Dr. Margaret T. Burroughs," 40.

45. Fleming, "Dr. Margaret T. Burroughs," 40.

46. Fleming, "Dr. Margaret T. Burroughs," 41.

47. Haki Madhubuti in discussion with the author, May 2012.

48. Madhubuti in discussion with the author, May 2012.

49. Madhubuti in discussion with the author, May 2012.

50. Feldman, *Birth and Building of the DuSable Museum*, 62.

51. Fleming, "Dr. Margaret T. Burroughs," 43–44.

52. Feldman, *Birth and Building of the DuSable Museum*, 62.

53. Fleming, "Dr. Margaret T. Burroughs," 44.

54. Fleming, "Dr. Margaret T. Burroughs," 44.

55. Feldman, *Birth and Building of the DuSable Museum*, 72.

56. Fleming, "Dr. Margaret T. Burroughs," 45.

57. Fleming, "Dr. Margaret T. Burroughs," 45.

58. Fleming, "Dr. Margaret T. Burroughs," 45.

59. Fleming, "Dr. Margaret T. Burroughs," 45–46.

60. Fleming, "Dr. Margaret T. Burroughs," 49.

61. Feldman, *Birth and Building of the DuSable Museum*, 62–68.

62. Burroughs, *Life with Margaret*, 155.

63. Fleming, "Dr. Margaret T. Burroughs," 45.

64. Durham in discussion with the author, May 2013.

65. Lawrence Kennon in discussion with the author, May 2013.

66. Fleming, "Dr. Margaret T. Burroughs," 42.

67. Fleming, "Dr. Margaret T. Burroughs," 42.

68. Feldman, *Birth and Building of the DuSable Museum*, 36 (ellipses added).

69. Fleming, "Dr. Margaret T. Burroughs," 42.

70. Fleming, "Dr. Margaret T. Burroughs," 43.

71. Fleming, "Dr. Margaret T. Burroughs," 48.

72. Margaret Burroughs in discussion with the author, August 2003.

73. Burroughs, *Life with Margaret*, 156.

74. Fleming, "Dr. Margaret T. Burroughs," 43–44.

Chapter 6

1. Reverend Helen Sinclair in discussion with the author, May 2014.

2. Margaret Burroughs, "Integration of Learning Material . . . NOW!" *Negro Digest*, March 1966, 31.

3. "Willis Wagons," Encyclopedia of Chicago, http://www.encyclopedia.chicagohistory.org/pages/1357.html.

4. Kennon in discussion with the author, May 2013.

5. Fleming, "Dr. Margaret T. Burroughs," 55.

6. Fleming, "Dr. Margaret T. Burroughs," 53–54.

7. Burroughs, interviewed by Tyler, 74.

8. Burroughs, interviewed by Tyler, 73–77.

9. Omowale Ketu Oladuwa in discussion with the author, May 2013.

10. Oladuwa in discussion with the author, May 2013.

11. Oladuwa in discussion with the author, May 2013.

12. Kennon in discussion with the author, May 2013.

13. Madhubuti in discussion with the author, May 2012.

14. Debra Hand in discussion with the author, June 2017.

15. Sinclair in discussion with the author, May 2014.

16. Sinclair in discussion with the author, May 2014.

17. *Dr. Gloria Peace Presents: Reflections on the Life of an Icon: Dr. Margaret T.G. Burroughs*, Omni-U Presents H³0 Art of Life series, parts 1 and 2, DVD.

18. Burroughs, interviewed by Van Scott, 3.

19. Burroughs, interviewed by Van Scott, 3.

20. Oladuwa in discussion with the author, May 2013.

21. Oladuwa in discussion with the author, May 2013.

22. Dr. Margaret T. G. Burroughs, *But "We Hope Not Tomorrow,"* play; copy gifted to the author.

23. Burroughs, interviewed by Tyler, 53.

24. Burroughs, interviewed by Tyler, 54.

25. Feldman, *Birth and Building of the DuSable Museum*, 13.

26. *Dr. Gloria Peace Presents*, DVD.

27. Durham in discussion with the author, May 2013.

28. *Dr. Gloria Peace Presents*, DVD.

29. Durham in discussion with the author, May 2013.

30. Durham in discussion with the author, May 2013.

31. Ben Campkin, Mariana Mogilevich, and Rebecca Ross, "Chicago's Wall of Respect: How a Mural Elicited a Sense of Collective Ownership," *The Guardian*, Monday, December 8, 2014, https://www.theguardian.com /cities/2014/dec/08/chicago-wall-of-respect-collective-ownership-organisation -black-american-culture.

32. "Mighty Black Wall," The Wall of Respect, The Art Institute of Chicago, www.artic.edu/~ljunki/mightyblackwall.doc.

33. "Mighty Black Wall."

34. Jennifer Roth, "Chicago's Collaborative Community Murals: 1967–2004" (master's thesis, Art Institute of Chicago, 2004), n.p.

35. "AfriCOBRA: Philosophy," UChicagoArts, https://arts.uchicago.edu /logan-center/logan-center-exhibitions/archive/africobra-philosophy.

36. Debra Hand in discussion with the author, November 2013.

37. Hand in discussion with the author.

38. Hand in discussion with the author.

39. Hand in discussion with the author.

40. Daniel Texidor Parker in discussion with the author, May 2014.

41. Daniel Texidor Parker, *African Art: The Diaspora and Beyond* (Chicago: self-published, 2004), vii.

42. Parker, *African Art*, 3.

43. Parker in discussion with the author, May 2014.

44. Parker, *African Art*, 4.

45. Parker, *African Art*, 4.

46. Parker in discussion with the author, May 2014.

47. "Diasporal Rhythms: A Ten-Year Love Affair with Collecting Art of the African Diaspora," UChicagoArts, https://arts.uchicago.edu/logan-center/logan-center-exhibitions/archive/diasporal-rhythms-ten-year-love-affair-collecting-art.

48. Skyla Hearn in discussion with the author, September 2017.

49. Hearn in discussion with the author, September 2017.

50. Hearn in discussion with the author, September 2017.

51. Faheem Majeed, https://www.faheemmajeed.com/floating-museum.

52. Prison + Neighborhood Arts Project, http://p-nap.org/what.html.

53. Hearn in discussion with the author, September 2017.

54. Hand in discussion with the author, November 2013.

55. Margaret Burroughs, "What Will Your Legacy Be?" brochure, DuSable Museum membership form, 2011.

BIBLIOGRAPHY

Art Institute of Chicago. "Mighty Black Wall." The Wall of Respect. www
    .artic.edu/~ljunki/mightyblackwall.doc.

Baldwin, Davarian L. *Chicago's New Negroes: Modernity, the Great Migration, and
    Black Urban Life.* Chapel Hill: University of North Carolina Press, 2007.

Black, Timuel. In discussion with the author. November 2012.

BlackPast.org. "Olivet Baptist Church (OBC) [Chicago] (1850–)." http://www
    .blackpast.org/aah/olivet-baptist-church-obc-chicago-illinois-1850.

Bone, Robert, and Richard A. Courage. *The Muse in Bronzeville.* New Jersey:
    Rutgers University Press, 2011.

Brooks, Gwendolyn. *Report from Part One.* Detroit: Broadside, 1972.

"Burroughs, Charles, 1919–." Interviewed by Camille Billops, October 31,
    1976. *Artist and Influence* 24. Hatch Billops Collection, New York, 2005.

Burroughs, Margaret. In discussion with the author. n.d. and August 2003.

——. "Integration of Learning Material . . . NOW!" *Negro Digest.* March
    1966: 30–34.

——. Interviewed by Glory Van Scott, June 6, 1975. Hatch Billops Collection,
    New York, 2005.

——. "My First Husband & His Four Wives (Me, Being the First) by Peggy
    Gross aka M. T. Burroughs." DuSable Museum, Margaret Burroughs
    papers. Series II, box 46, folder 368.

Burroughs, [Dr.] Margaret. "What Will Your Legacy Be?" Brochure, Du-
    Sable Museum membership form. 2011.

Burroughs, Margaret G. "Rivera Murals Overpowering." "A Woman's View-
    point." For the Associated Negro Press, Summer 1951. DuSable Mu-
    seum, Margaret Burroughs papers. Series II, box 46, folder 376.

——. "Woman's Viewpoint." For the Associated Negro Press. Summer 1951.
    DuSable Museum, Margaret Burroughs papers. Series II, box 46, folder
    376.

——. "Woman's Viewpoint." For the Associated Negro Press. *The Philadelphia
    Tribune,* Summer 1951. DuSable Museum, Margaret Burroughs papers.
    Series II, box 46, folder 376.

Burroughs, Margaret Goss. "Taxco, Silver Center of Mexico." "A Woman's Viewpoint." For the Associated Negro Press, Summer 1951. DuSable Museum, Margaret Burroughs papers. Series II, box 46, folder 376.

——. "Woman's Viewpoint." For the Associated Negro Press. DuSable Museum, Margaret Burroughs papers. Series II, box 46, folder 376.

——. "A Woman's Viewpoint." For the Associated Negro Press. DuSable Museum, Margaret Burroughs papers. Series II, box 46, folder 376.

Burroughs, Margaret Taylor. Interviewed by Anna Tyler. Archives of American Art, Smithsonian Institute, November 11–December 5, 1988.

Burroughs, [Dr.] Margaret T. G. But *"We Hope Not Tomorrow."* Unpublished manuscript. Photocopy gifted to the author.

——. *Life with Margaret.* Chicago: In Time Publishing and Media Group, 2003.

——. *Remembrance of Paul Robeson,* 1987? Self-published.

Burroughs, Mrs. "Largest Market in Mexico." "A Woman's Viewpoint." *Atlanta Daily World,* Friday, October 5, 1951. DuSable Museum, Margaret Burroughs papers. Series II, box 46, folder 376.

[For more works by Margaret Burroughs, see under "Goss."]

Campkin, Ben, Mariana Mogilevich, and Rebecca Ross. "Chicago's Wall of Respect: How a Mural Elicited a Sense of Collective Ownership." *The Guardian.* Monday, December 8, 2014. https://www.theguardian.com/cities/2014/dec/08/chicago-wall-of-respect-collective-ownership-organisation-black-american-culture.

Chicago Historic Schools. "Wendell Phillips Academy High School." https://chicagohistoricschools.wordpress.com/2013/09/18/wendell-phillips-academy-high-school.

Christopher, Theresa. In discussion with the author. March 2012.

Cohn, Erin P. "Art Fronts: Visual Culture and Race Politics in the Mid-Twentieth Century United States." Ph.D. dissertation, University of Pennsylvania, 2010.

Dinkins Carr, Diane. In discussion with the author. November 2013 and May 2014.

Drake, St. Clair, and Horace Cayton. *Black Metropolis.* Chicago: University of Chicago Press, 1993.

Duberman, Martin. *Paul Robeson: A Biography.* New York: New Press, 1989.

Durham, Clarice. In discussion with the author. May 2013.

Encyclopedia of Chicago. "Federal Art Project." http://www.encyclopedia.chicagohistory.org/pages/442.html.

——. "Willis Wagons." http://www.encyclopedia.chicagohistory.org/pages/1357.html.

Feldman, Eugene Pieter. *The Birth and the Building of the DuSable Museum.* Chicago: DuSable Museum, 1981.

Fleming, John. "Dr. Margaret T. Burroughs: Artist, Teacher, Administrator, Writer, Political Activist, and Museum Founder." *The Public Historian* 21, no. 1 (Winter 1999): 31–55.

Gellman, Erik S. "Chicago's Native Son: Charles White and the Laboring of the Black Renaissance." In *The Black Chicago Renaissance*, edited by Darlene Clark Hine and John McCluskey Jr., 147–64. Urbana: University of Illinois Press, 2012.

Goss, Margaret. "GIs Discuss Plans for Post-War Period." 1945. DuSable Museum, Margaret Burroughs papers. Series II, box 46, folder 376.

——. "This Is Our War." *N.Y.P.S.* [*Negro Youth Photo-Script*] *Magazine*, 1942 or 1943. DuSable Museum, Margaret Burroughs papers. Series II, box 46, folder 37, 6.

Goss, Margaret T. "Private Jeff Johnson." *Negro Story*, vol. 1 (1944): 28–30.

Goss, Margaret Taylor. *Chicago Defender*, August 31, 1940. DuSable Museum, Margaret Burroughs papers. Series II, box 46, folder 368.

——. "Improve Race Relations." For the Associated Negro Press. DuSable Museum, Margaret Burroughs papers. Series II, box 46, folder 376.

——. "Insidious Propaganda." *Chicago Defender*, 1942. DuSable Museum, Margaret Burroughs papers. Series II, box 46, folder 376.

——. "Our Changing Race Ideas," 1943, DuSable Museum, Margaret Burroughs papers. Series II, box 46, folder 376.

——. "'Race of Mankind' Called Timely." For the Associated Negro Press. DuSable Museum, Margaret Burroughs papers. Series II, box 46, folder 376.

——. "War Letters Wanted." *Sunday Chicago Bee*, 1945. DuSable Museum, Margaret Burroughs papers. Series II, box 46, folder 376, 15.

Green, Adam. *Selling the Race: Culture, Community, and Black Chicago, 1940–1955*. Chicago: University of Chicago Press, 2007.

Hand, Debra. In discussion with the author. November 2013.

Hearn, Skyla. In discussion with the author. September 2017.

Historic Olivet Baptist Church. www.olivetbaptistchurchchicago.org/history/index.html.

Jones, Moses. In discussion with the author. November 2012.

Kennon, Lawrence. In discussion with the author. May 2013.

Knupfer, Anne Meis. *The Chicago Black Renaissance and Women's Activism*. Urbana: University of Illinois Press, 2006.

Madhubuti, Haki. In discussion with the author. May 2012.

Motley, Willard F. "Negro Art in Chicago." *Opportunity: Journal of Negro Life* 18, no. 1 (January 1940): 19–31.

Mullen, Bill V. *Popular Fronts: Chicago and African-American Cultural Politics, 1935–46*. Urbana: University of Illinois Press, 1999.

Oehler, Sarah Kelly. *They Seek a City: Chicago and the Art of Migration, 1910–1950*. Chicago: Art Institute of Chicago, 2013.

Oladuwa, Omowale Ketu. In discussion with the author. May 2013.

Omni-U. *Dr. Gloria Peace Presents: Reflections on the Life of an Icon: Dr. Margaret T. G. Burroughs*. H³0 Art of Life series, parts 1 and 2. DVD.

Parker, Daniel Texidor. *African Art: The Diaspora and Beyond*. Chicago: self-published, 2004.

——. In discussion with the author. May 2014.

Public Art in Chicago. "Bronzeville–Victory Monument." http://chicago-outdoor-sculptures.blogspot.com.

Rocksborough-Smith, Ian. "Margaret T. G. Burroughs and Black Public History in Cold War Chicago." *The Black Scholar* 41, no. 3 (2011): 26–42.

Roth, Jennifer. "Chicago's Collaborative Community Murals: 1967–2004." Master's thesis, Art Institute of Chicago, 2004.

Sinclair, Reverend Helen. "Queen Mother." In discussion with the author. May 2014.

South Side Community Art Center, 50th Anniversary 1941–1991. Program. Chicago, 1991.

Strange, Maren. *Bronzeville: Black Chicago in Pictures 1941–1943*. New York: New Press, 2003.

Toller, Eric. In discussion with the author. March 2012 and November 2014.

Travis, Dempsey J. *An Autobiography of Black Chicago*. Chicago: Urban Research Institute, 1981.

Tyler, Anna. "Planting and Maintaining a 'Perennial Garden': Chicago's South Side Community Art Center." *The International Review of African American Art* 11, no. 4 (1994): 31–38.

UChicagoArts. "AfriCOBRA: Philosophy." https://arts.uchicago.edu/logan-center/logan-center-exhibitions/archive/africobra-philosophy.

——. "Diasporal Rhythms: A Ten-Year Love Affair with Collecting Art of the African Diaspora." https://arts.uchicago.edu/logan-center/logan-center-exhibitions/archive/diasporal-rhythms-ten-year-love-affair-collecting-art.

Wilkerson, Isabel. *The Warmth of Other Suns*. New York: Random House, 2010.

Williams, Douglas. In discussion with the author. June 2014.

INDEX

193